Booth: Residence, Domicile and UK Taxation

Seventh Edition

D1742833

Booth: Residence, Domicile and UK Taxation

Seventh Edition

Rt Hon Denzil Davies MA (Oxon)
Barrister, Former Minister of State, HM Treasury

Tolley
LexisNexis™

Members of the LexisNexis Group worldwide

United Kingdom	LexisNexis Butterworths Tolley, a Division of Reed Elsevier (UK) Ltd, Halsbury House, 35 Chancery Lane, LONDON, WC2A 1EL, and 4 Hill Street, EDINBURGH EH2 3JZ
Argentina	LexisNexis Argentina, BUENOS AIRES
Australia	LexisNexis Butterworths, CHATSWOOD, New South Wales
Austria	LexisNexis Verlag ARD Orac GmbH & Co KG, VIENNA
Canada	LexisNexis Butterworths, MARKHAM, Ontario
Chile	LexisNexis Chile Ltda, SANTIAGO DE CHILE
Czech Republic	Nakladatelství Orac sro, PRAGUE
France	Editions du Juris-Classeur SA, PARIS
Hong Kong	LexisNexis Butterworths, HONG KONG
Hungary	HVG-Orac, BUDAPEST
India	LexisNexis Butterworths, NEW DELHI
Ireland	Butterworths (Ireland) Ltd, DUBLIN
Italy	Giuffrè Editore, MILAN
Malaysia	Malayan Law Journal Sdn Bhd, KUALA LUMPUR
New Zealand	LexisNexis Butterworths, WELLINGTON
Poland	Wydawnictwo Prawnicze LexisNexis, WARSAW
Singapore	LexisNexis Butterworths, SINGAPORE
South Africa	Butterworths SA, DURBAN
Switzerland	Stämpfli Verlag AG, BERNE
USA	LexisNexis, DAYTON, Ohio

A CIP Catalogue record for this book is available from the British Library.

ISBN 0 754516817

Typeset by M Rules, London
Printed and bound in Great Britain by The Cromwell Press, Trowbridge, Wiltshire

Visit Butterworths LexisNexis *direct* at www.butterworths.com

PREFACE

This, the Seventh Edition of Neil Booth's unique work, reflects the changes in the law which are relevant to the content and character of this work and which have occurred since the Sixth Edition. It also incorporates the Inland Revenue's latest Bulletin IR20 (11 April 2000), which is reproduced in the Appendix, and which deals for the first time with the rules for payment of National Insurance contributions for individuals leaving or coming to the UK.

In his Budget Statement in the House of Commons on 17 April 2002, the Rt. Hon. Gordon Brown M.P., the UK's Chancellor of the Exchequer said 'I am reviewing the complex rules on residence and domicile.' A report will be published before the Budget of 2003. In view of the Chancellor's statement, new paragraphs have been inserted into Chapter 1 of this edition analysing the various options available to the Government and the possible changes that might be introduced.

When Mr Booth published the First Edition in 1986, issues of sovereignty as they related to the European Union and direct taxation lay dormant.

A number of reported cases of the European Court of Justice since then have demonstrated that even in the area of income and corporation tax, the Treaty of Rome can limit national sovereignty. Most of the recent cases heard by the ECJ in the field of income and corporation tax are of direct relevance to the issues covered by this book. They illustrate an increasing tension between two statuses: the status of nationality and the prohibitions under the Treaty against discrimination on the grounds of nationality, and the status of residence and non-residence as enshrined in the tax legislation of member states.

In view of the importance of these cases and the impetus towards the harmonisation of taxes within the EU, Chapter 9 is now wholly devoted to the analysis of the leading and recent ECJ cases on residence and nationality, including *Commerzbank, Bachmann, Schumacher, ICI v Colmer and Hoechst*.

When Mr Booth published his First Edition, the internet and e-commerce were mere specks in cyberspace. Now the growth of e-commerce is not only revolutionising the pattern of international trade but is also challenging the power of national governments to levy and collect taxes. A new chapter, Chapter 10, has been added which seeks to analyse the effect of e-commerce and the new technology on the traditional concepts of residence and permanent establishment.

Denzil Davies
Gray's Inn
August 2002

PREFACE TO THE FIRST EDITION

Open the Income and Corporation Taxes Act at random, glance down the page, or at the page or two before it, and you will find a reference to residence, or ordinary residence, or domicile. They punctuate the text. And why? Because those three concepts are as fundamental to the United Kingdom tax system as the footings are to your house.

But what do they mean? The Inland Revenue publishes a 29 page booklet (IR 20) which *purports* to tell us; but a booklet so short and from such an interested source may hardly be expected to present either a comprehensive or completely unbiased view. The numerous books on revenue law generally allocate even fewer pages to the problem; and such pages as they do allocate they then, disappointingly, use to do little more than reiterate the dubious contents of IR 20 and thus lead us nowhere. Even the major tax encyclopaedias beg as many questions as they answer.

Does it matter? This author thinks it does, and that it matters very much indeed. The world is now a very busy place and taxes are high. In the time it took for Captain Young , master mariner, to travel from Glasgow to New York in 1874 and thus give rise to the first tax case on residence, a thousand planes, today, pick up and set down traders, bankers, representatives, technicians, brokers, directors, and all the other manner of personnel who keep the wheels of international business turning. Many of those passengers have suitcases as well as briefcases. Some will be here – or there – for weeks, or months, or even years; perhaps for the rest of their lives. And the State is ever interested. Profits, earnings, gains and gifts: all are a source of revenue and all, in the final analysis, depend on . . . what else? . . . residence, ordinary residence and domicile.

I have tried to make this a book to read and not one merely to refer to. I have drawn liberally on the tax cases; not only because they are primary source material where these three topics are concerned, but also because they are so very interesting. Mr Brown thumbing his nose at the Colchester inspector of taxes from the safety (so he thought) of his ocean-going yacht; Dave Clark disappearing to Los Angeles on 3 April – just two days before he would have become liable to tax on a $450,000 sale of recording rights; Mr Robson touching his plane down at Heathrow en route from Schipol to North America and being presented with a tax demand; Anderson, the Irishman, being smuggled out of France by his lover Madame Laneuville, under the eyes of the revolutionaries, only to return and make his home with her forty-six years later; Mr Bell, abandoning his Jamaican plantations in disgust at the imminent abolition of slavery and returning home (or was he?) to

Scotland; Colonel Udny, hot-footing it to Boulogne to avoid his bookies – and staying there; and many, many more.

What this book is *not* is an explanation and description of the United Kingdom tax system. For that, the reader must look elsewhere. But having found his other book and encountered its many references to residence, ordinary residence and domicile, he will, it is hoped, having read this book, have a good idea of what they mean!

My thanks go to my partners for the support they have given me as I have worked on this text; and my love, as always, goes to Yvonne, my wife, to whom I dedicate it.

Neil D Booth FCA FTII
Bradford
31 March 1986

CONTENTS

TABLE OF STATUTES

References in this Table to *Statutes* are to Halsbury's Statutes of England (Fourth Edition) showing the volume and page at which the annotated text of the Act may be found.

TABLE OF CASES

CHAPTER 1

United Kingdom taxation

Render therefore unto Caesar the things which are Caesar's.

St Matthew ch 22, v 21

1.01 The nature of taxation

'Residence' and 'domicile' have assumed the high places which they occupy in the United Kingdom tax system not by chance or at the whim of some long-forgotten Chancellor of the Exchequer but because they offer the best practical solution to problems which taxation, by its very nature, has created in our multi-national world. Unless we first reach an understanding of what taxation really *is*, we shall multiply our difficulties in understanding what residence and domicile are and the nature of the role they have been given to play. If we are to consider the nature of taxation, it will help to have a model on which to base our observations, and just such a model has, fortuitously, been provided by William Golding in his novel *Lord of the Flies*.[1]

The story opens with a group of schoolboys – the sole survivors of a plane crash – marooned on a densely-forested tropical island inhabited only by birds and animals. Within a matter of hours, the need to stamp some semblance of order on the chaos which has followed the crash results in the election of Ralph as leader and Jack as his lieutenant. The making of fire becomes the new leaders' first priority, but the only instruments to hand are the lenses in a pair of spectacles belonging to a somewhat overweight, asthmatic child, derisively referred to by the other boys as Piggy. Although, deprived of these, Piggy will be virtually blind, Jack does not hesitate. Ignoring Piggy's screams of protest, he snatches the spectacles off Piggy's face. This, essentially – though in unfamiliar guise – is taxation: the appropriation by the leaders of a body politic (in this case, a newly-emerged and extremely primitive one) of such of the resources of its members as the leaders consider necessary for the well-being of the body politic as a whole.

---

1 Faber and Faber, 1954

Questions of sovereignty

1.02 Consensual limitations

The model should enable us to see that taxation, even at the primitive level described, has an intrinsic limitation in that it may operate only with the consent of the majority of the members of the body politic concerned, for without such consent, Jack could not have taken Piggy's spectacles. This need for consent is in no way related to the manner in which leadership has been obtained. Jack and Ralph were, as it happened, democratically elected but, had they seized or inherited power rather than having it thrust upon them, the need for their subjects' consent to the removal of Piggy's spectacles would have remained. The seizure of the spectacles in the face of majority dissent would have resulted in either the enforced removal of the leaders from their positions of sovereignty or, under the constraint which the threat of such forcible removal would have imposed, their abrogation of the prerogative rights with which sovereignty had endowed them.

In the real world, this process takes time. It was 1199 when King John began to convert the elaborate and well-ordered fiscal system he had inherited from Henry I and Henry II into an instrument of arbitrary and merciless extortion, but it was not until 15 June 1215 that 'in a Thames-side meadow called Runnymede, . . . the taxpayers . . . combined to control the tax-imposer'[1] by forcing the monarch to set his seal to Magna Carta. Clause 12 of the charter provided that 'no scutage or aid shall be imposed in our Kingdom unless by the Common Council of our Realm' but, even then, the control was incomplete. In the fourteenth century, Edward III imposed massive taxation to finance his long war with France and the price of the people's consent to such taxation was that future taxation would be conditional on the 'common consent of prelates, earls, barons and other lords and commons of the realm'.[2]

Although this was 'a major step on the road to parliamentary control of taxation',[3] it was not until 1689 that the prerogative rights of the British monarchy were finally and completely abrogated in that regard. In 1681, Charles II had dissolved the Parliament and begun to rule absolutely. In 1685, he was succeeded by his brother James II and, in 1689, upon the accession to the throne of William and Mary, Parliament secured the passing of the Bill of Rights which vouchsafed for it ultimate supremacy. Ever since then, the British monarch has reigned but not ruled, so that, today just as in 1689, 'levying moneys for or to the use of the Crowne by pretence of prerogative without grant of Parlyament . . . is illegal.'[4]

---

1 Arthur Bryant, *Set in a Silver Sea* (Collins) pp 130–132.
2 Ibid, p 226.
3 Ibid.
4 Bill of Rights 1688.

1.03 Jurisdictional limitations

It is a matter of constitutional law that, because the sovereign power of Parliament is absolute, then unless Parliament chooses voluntarily to abrogate its powers,[1] it may legislate contrary to the requirements of international law, for 'international law . . . yields to statute'[2] and, 'if the language of the statute is clear, it must be followed notwithstanding the conflict between municipal and international law which results'.[3]

If we refer again to our model, what is being said is that Jack and Ralph could, if they so wished, decree that not only should *Piggy's* spectacles be confiscated but that the spectacles of, say, every citizen of China should be confiscated too. Constitutionally, there would be nothing wrong with such a decree and the judiciary (in whatever form it might evolve in that emergent island-state) would be bound to enforce it against any Chinese citizen who could be brought within the jurisdiction of the island's courts. There, however, lies the difficulty and, by making that difficulty so obvious, the model again enables us to identify an intrinsic limitation of any form of taxation: the limitation of jurisdictional competence.

The primary characteristic of law is that it is enforceable by sanction (ie fine, suspension of rights, imprisonment, etc). Before a court may order enforcement, however, it must be competent to hear and determine the alleged non- compliance, and, in the English courts, such competence rests solely on whether a claim has been served on the defendant in person. This – following from the fact that a writ is essentially an assertion of sovereignty and that sovereignty itself is territorial – gives rise to the

> broad general universal proposition that English legislation . . . is applicable only to English subjects or to foreigners who by coming into this country, whether for a long or a short time, have made themselves during that time subject to English jurisdiction.[4]

It may, at this point, be objected that the court has, in fact, power to go beyond the common law principle described and, in certain circumstances, to enlarge its jurisdiction by summoning absent defendants – even foreign ones – under CPR6.17. This is indeed so, but – as the court's discretionary power may be exercised only in cases within the classes specified by CPR6.17, none of which can conceivably be so construed as to embrace the enforcement of a United Kingdom tax liability against foreigners who have no connection with the United Kingdom – the court's jurisdiction remains nonetheless limited by common law principles in relation to the matters with which this book is concerned.

---

1 As, for example, when, on 1 January 1973, Britain acceded to the Treaty of Rome and became bound, as a European Community member state, by certain Community legislation.
2 *Cheney v Conn* (1967) 44 TC 217 at 221, per Ungoed-Thomas J.
3 *Maxwell on the Interpretation of Statutes* (12th edn) p 183.
4 *Re Sawyers, ex p Blain* [1874–80] All ER Rep 708 at 710, per James LJ.

1.04 Enforcement overseas

The alleged limitations of jurisdiction propounded at **1.03** above may, of course, provoke a further objection. Although the requirement of service of process on a defendant personally may prevent an action for the recovery of taxes from a person abroad being brought before an English court, what is to prevent such an action being brought before the court of the foreign state in which that person is present and being heard there in accordance with the principles of international law? The short answer is simply that 'it is the practice of nations not to enforce the fiscal legislation of other nations'.[1]

The principle on which this practice is based emerged over two centuries ago when, in upholding a Frenchman's claim for the purchase monies due in respect of goods which were to be smuggled into England by their purchaser in violation of English revenue laws, Lord Mansfield enunciated the proposition that 'no country ever takes notice of the revenue laws of another'.[2] Stated thus, the proposition is too wide – and may, indeed, no longer even be of application in the circumstances with which Lord Mansfield was concerned.[3] What may be said, however, is that:

> a foreign government cannot come here – nor will the Courts of other countries allow our government to go there – and sue a person found in that jurisdiction for taxes levied and which he is declared to be liable to by the country to which he belongs.[4]

The rationale behind the principle thus stated is that:

> a claim for taxes is but an extension of the sovereign power which imposed the taxes, and . . . an assertion of sovereign authority by one State within the territory of another . . . is (treaty or convention apart) contrary to all concepts of independent sovereignties.[5]

Were the payment of tax a contractual obligation, the situation would, of course, be different and the contract would be not only recognised but enforced if necessary by the courts of a foreign state in accordance with the principles of private international law. Tax collection is, however, 'not a matter of contract, but of authority and administration as between the State and those within its jurisdiction'.[6] Accordingly, foreign courts, while recognising United Kingdom revenue laws, will not entertain a suit for their direct or indirect[7] enforcement and, this being so, the limitation implicitly imposed on the legislature's legislative power by the principle of action *in personam* cannot be circumvented (at least so far as revenue laws are concerned) by recourse to a foreign forum.

---

1 *Clark v Oceanic Contractors Inc* [1983] STC 35 at 41, per Lord Scarman.
2 *Holman v Johnson* (1775) 1 Cowp 341.
3 In *Regazzoni v K C Sethia (1944) Ltd* [1957] 3 All ER 286 at 292, Viscount Simonds said: 'It does not follow from the fact that today the court will not enforce a revenue law at the suit of a foreign state that today it will enforce a contract which requires the doing of an act in a foreign country which violates the Revenue laws of that country.'
4 *King of the Hellenes v Brostrom* (1923) 16 Ll L Rep 167, per Rowlatt J.
5 *Government of India v Taylor* [1955] 1 All ER 292, per Lord Keith of Avonholm.
6 Ibid, per Lord Somervell of Harrow.
7 In *Peter Buchanan Ltd* and *Macharg v McVey* [1954] IR 89, the director of a Scottish company made a deal with the Inland Revenue on which the Revenue authorities subsequently reneged. The director promptly stripped the company of its assets and removed them – along with his private assets and himself – to the Republic of Ireland where he proceeded to 'snap his hands in the face of the disgruntled Scottish Revenue'. The Inland Revenue, realising that a direct attempt to recover taxes through the courts of Eire would fail, attempted to do so indirectly by suing the director on the grounds that he had acted in breach of his duties as a director. The court looked beyond the action, however, and, seeing that it was no more than an indirect attempt to enforce United Kingdom revenue laws in the Republic of Ireland, dismissed it.

1.05 Territorial sovereignty

It is, of course, possible so to frame laws – particularly revenue laws – as to bring within their scope persons who are not amenable to personal action while obviating the need for such personal action ever to rise. TA 1988 s 42A, for example, provides for the collection of income tax on rents under leases of land in the United Kingdom, etc from persons (whether British subjects or not) 'whose usual place of abode is outside the United Kingdom'. They are to be assessed and charged to tax on the *payer* who may then, in making payment to the person whose usual place of abode is outside the United Kingdom, deduct from them the tax with which he (the payer) has been charged. By this device the legislature has circumvented the problem of action *in personam* against a person who may not be present within the legislature's territorial bounds, and has, instead, created a right of action *in personam* against the person (clearly within the jurisdiction) whom it has made responsible for the collection of the tax.[1]

It may be argued that, when carried over into revenue law, the principle encourages a blatant disregard for the rational division of fiscal claims between one state and another and breeds an order of legislation based on nothing more than the power of enforcement. Mr Bridges lives in England and Monsieur Dupont lives in France. The English legislature alone has an intrinsic right to tax Mr Bridges and the French legislature alone has an intrinsic right to tax Monsieur Dupont. Monsieur Dupont, however, has a property in England from which he draws rents, so the English legislature exerts a right to tax Monsieur Dupont too; not because Monsieur Dupont is within its jurisdiction – he is not! – but merely because his property is here and its tenant may legislatively be brought within the English legislature's powers of personal action and made to account for the tax the English legislature has decided to exact from Monsieur Dupont. Certainly (as we shall see) such irrational taxative measures needlessly complicate the taxation system by necessitating bilateral treaties and conventions for the prevention or mitigation of the double taxation they create. This is not to say, however, that no justification can be found for the application of the principle of territorial sovereignty in revenue law. Adverting again to Mr Bridges and Monsieur Dupont:

> The former is taxed because (whether he be a British subject or not) he enjoys the benefit of our laws for the protection of his person and his property. The latter is taxed because in respect of his property in the United Kingdom he enjoys the benefit of our laws for the protection of that property.[2]

Whether or not that is a sufficient rationale for contradicting common law principles and pressing tax legislation to its furthest possible limits is, of course, a question of academic interest only. United Kingdom revenue law has (in common with the revenue laws of many other states) been so pressed from its inception. In interpreting an enactment, however, the courts remain committed to carrying the principle of territorial sovereignty not a fraction further than they strictly need. Almost a century ago, Lord Esher MR expressed his conviction that:

> Parliament ought not to deal in any way, either by regulation or otherwise, directly or indirectly, with any foreign matter or person which is outside the jurisdiction of our Parliament, and . . . the Courts ought always to construe . . . general words to apply only

to the person or thing which will answer the description in them, but which person or thing is also within the jurisdiction of our Parliament.[3]

In more recent times, those same sentiments have been echoed by Lord Asquith, who was adamant that:

an Act of the Imperial Parliament today, unless it provides otherwise, applies . . . to nothing outside the United Kingdom: not even to the Channel Islands or the Isle of Man, let alone a remote overseas colony or possession.[4]

---

1 See **8.10–8.15** below.
2 *Whitney v IRC* (1925) 10 TC 88 at 112, per Lord Wrenbury.
3 *Colquhoun v Heddon* (1890) 2 TC 621 at 626.
4 *A-G for the Province of Alberta v Huggard Assets Ltd* [1953] 2 All ER 951.

1.06   Territorial extension of legislative power

Although Parliament will not, for all the reasons stated thus far, generally legislate beyond the limits of the territory over which it has sovereignty, there is nothing to prevent it so doing if the inhibiting constraints of comity and international law are removed by international consensus. This will, of course, happen only rarely, but one instance of its occurrence may be cited.

In 1958, the Geneva Convention on the Continental Shelf[1] secured agreement at international level concerning exploration or exploitation rights in relation to all resources in the seabed and subsoil of the North Sea continental shelf. Certain of that Convention's provisions were brought within the municipal law of the United Kingdom[2] by the Continental Shelf Act 1964 and that Act provided that areas of the continental shelf outside the United Kingdom's territorial waters[3] might be designated by Order in Council[4] as areas within which the United Kingdom might exercise rights of exploration and exploitation.[5] The Act recognised that any areas so designated would not thereby become part of the United Kingdom[6] and, implicitly, that the sovereignty of Parliament would not extend to them.

Once Orders in Council had been made, however, Parliament decided to extend its revenue legislation so as to bring within the scope of the Taxes Acts any profits or gains from exploration or exploitation activities carried on in the designated areas. This territorial extension of the charge to tax was achieved by the Finance Act 1973.[7]

---

1 29 April 1958.
2 See **1.02** above.
3 See **1.08** below.
4 Orders have been made in relation to the sea around the Orkneys and Shetlands, the sea west and north-west of the Shetlands, the sea off the west coast of Scotland, the Irish Sea, St George's Channel, the Bristol Channel, the sea south of Cornwall, the south-western approaches to the English Channel, the English Channel, the North Sea and the southern North Sea.
5 Continental Shelf Act 1964 s 1(7).
6 Ibid, s 1(1).
7 FA 1973 Sch 15

Questions of territory

1.07 The territory of the United Kingdom

The United Kingdom has three constituent units, each subject to the ultimate sovereignty of the common Parliament at Westminster. The three units are England and Wales, Scotland, and Northern Ireland. Legislation has now been passed which establishes a Parliament for Scotland with powers of primary legislation in some areas including a limited power to vary income tax; a National Assembly for Wales which does not have powers of primary legislation; and an Assembly for Northern Ireland with powers of legislation in certain areas.[1] England, Wales and Scotland are described collectively as Great Britain,[2] and the United Kingdom consists of Great Britain and Northern Ireland.[3] The Isle of Man and the islands of Jersey, Guernsey, Alderney, Sark, Herm and Jethou (ie the Channel Islands) are British Isles outside the United Kingdom[4] and have their own systems of private law.

1 Scotland Act 1998; Government of Wales Act 1998; Northern Ireland Act 1998.
2 Royal and Parliamentary Titles Act 1927.
3 Interpretation Act 1978 s 5 and Sch 1.
4 As to the Channel Islands not being part of the United Kingdom, see *Navigators and General Insurance Co Ltd v Ringrose* [1961] 1 All ER 97.

1.08 The territorial waters

In addition to the land mass described at **1.07** above, the United Kingdom includes territorial waters. These include internal waters such as rivers, lakes and the area of sea which lies upon the landward side of the low-water line along the coast (including the coast of all islands and low-tide elevations comprised in the territory) or, in the case of a bay, the area of sea which lies on the landward side of a straight line (not more than 24 miles in length) joining the low-water lines of the natural entrance points of the bay.[1] They include also the territorial sea which consists of those parts of the sea over which the United Kingdom's sovereignty is subject to the right of innocent passage by foreign ships[2] being any part of the open sea which lies within one marine league[3] on the seaward side of the base-line from which the areas of internal waters are determined.[4]

The relevance of territorial waters in the context of revenue law may not be immediately obvious. As we shall see, however, the precise time at which a person leaves the United Kingdom may be critical in the context of the establishment of non-resident tax status,[5] and that time is the time at which a person moves out of the United Kingdom's territorial waters (or out of the air space above them).

Another possible area of application is suggested by two cases brought by the Post Office under the Wireless Telegraphy Act 1949 s 14(7) against a so-called 'pirate' radio station in the Thames estuary. The defendants, who operated from Red Sands Tower, a structure which rests on the sea-bed more than three nautical miles from the nearest low-water lines of the Kent and Essex coasts, contended that their operations were performed on the high seas outside the United Kingdom's territorial waters and that they did not, therefore, come within the United Kingdom's jurisdiction. It was held, however, that the Red Sands Tower lies within the bay contained by a straight line drawn between the Naze and Foreness Point (the natural entrance points of that coastal indentation which forms part of the Thames estuary) and is accordingly within the internal waters of the United Kingdom.[6] Had Estuary Radio Ltd sought to escape United Kingdom taxation on the grounds advanced in its defence, it would, it seems, have been bound to fail for identical reasons.

It is worth noting that one of the questions raised in the cases described was whether or not the jurisdiction of a magistrates' court could extend over an area of territorial water. As the territorial waters in question adjoined the county of Kent, it was held that the Kent justices did indeed have jurisdiction. On the same premise, therefore, it seems clear that, where matters of revenue law are concerned in relation to persons or sources of income or gains within territorial waters, the General Commissioners (whose function is similar in connection with revenue law to that of the justices in connection with criminal law) appointed for the adjoining tax division will have jurisdiction to the same extent as they would have jurisdiction were the person or source located on the area of land contained within that division.

1 Territorial Waters Order in Council 1964, arts 2–5.
2 Convention on the Territorial Sea and Contiguous Zone, Cmnd 2511, art 11.
3 Ie three nautical miles.
4 Territorial Waters Jurisdiction Act 1878 s 7.
5 See **4.07** below. See also **7.16** below in relation to domicile.
6 *Post Office v Estuary Radio Ltd* [1967] 1 WLR 1396 and *R v Kent Justices, ex p Lye* [1967] 2 WLR 765.

1.09   Commonwealth territories

It is important, for the sake of clarity, to define the position of the British Commonwealth in relation to the United Kingdom and the territorial range of its sovereignty. The British Commonwealth is the free association of such sovereign independent states as choose to recognise the reigning British monarch as Head. Accordingly, the Commonwealth includes not only the United Kingdom, but also the independent states which were once dominions and colonies.[1] It must be understood, however, that because the sovereignty of the monarch is vested in the independent parliament (or the equivalent) of each state, each state is a 'foreign' state within the context of the foregoing discussion and the Parliament of the United Kingdom may no more go to, say, Zimbabwe and sue a person there for taxes levied in the United Kingdom than it may go to, say, Belgium or Sweden for that purpose.

1 In addition to the United Kingdom, members of the Commonwealth are currently Australia, Antigua and Barbuda, the Bahamas, the Republic of Bangladesh, Barbados, Belize, the Republic of Botswana, Brunei Darussalam, Canada, Republic of Cyprus, the Republic of Dominica, the Republic of Gambia, the Republic of Ghana, Grenada, the Cooperative Republic of Guyana, the Republic of India, Jamaica, the Republic of Kenya, the Republic of Kiribati, Lesotho, the Republic of Malawi, the Federation of Malaysia, the Republic of the Maldives, the Republic of Malta, Mauritius, Namibia, the Republic of Nauru (limited membership), New Zealand, the Federal Republic of Nigeria, Pakistan, Papua New Guinea, St Kitts-Nevis, St Lucia, St Vincent and the Grenadines, the Republic of Seychelles, the Republic of Sierra Leone, the Republic of Singapore, Solomon Islands, South Africa, the Republic of Sri Lanka, Swaziland, the United Republic of Tanzania, Tonga, the Republic of Trinidad and Tobago, Tuvalu (limited membership), the Republic of Uganda, the Republic of Vanuatu, Western Samoa, the Republic of Zambia, the Republic of Zimbabwe.

1.10   The European Community

On 1 January 1973, the United Kingdom acceded to the Treaty of Rome which had come into effect on 1 January 1959 and had provided for the establishment of a European Economic Community. While the European Community does not have a specific jurisdiction over direct taxation, EC law may place limitations on the freedom of action of member states in the field of direct taxation as a consequence of the duty of member states to conform to the objectives of the EC.

In view of the increasing number of cases going to the European Court of Justice over recent years, where taxpayers resident within a member state have sought to challenge a member state's residence rules on the ground that they are alleged to infringe the prohibitions in EU law against discrimination on grounds of nationality, Chapter 9 of this book is devoted to analysing the developing jurisprudence of the European Court in this regard.

1.11   Nationality

Every person – unless he has become 'stateless' through the exigencies of war etc – is a member of some body politic from which he may expect protection and to which he owes political allegiance and loyalty. The status endowed by such a relationship is known as nationality and may, dependent on the law of the body politic in question, be obtained by either birth, descent, registration or naturalisation.

Prior to 1 January 1983, the nationality status conferred on those who met the requirements of the British Nationality Acts 1948 to 1965 was that of 'British subject' which was a generic term employed in legislation to include any 'citizen of the United Kingdom and Colonies', any citizen of the Commonwealth countries listed in BNA 1948 s 1(3), any citizen of Eire who had elected under BNA 1948 s 2 to continue to be a British subject, and certain other persons who were given the status of British subject under the Nationality Acts 1948 to 1965 (eg 'alien women' married to British subjects in certain of the other groups).

Under the British Nationality Act 1981 (which came into effect on 1 January 1983 and now amended by the British Overseas Territories Act 2002), the status formerly signified by the term 'British subject' is now reserved for the citizens of Eire and others who have been mentioned above[1] and for some fifty thousand persons in India and Pakistan who had the status of 'British subject without citizenship' under the earlier legislation.

The former status of 'citizen of the United Kingdom and Colonies' no longer exists and anyone who possessed that status immediately before 1 January 1983 acquired on that date the new status of either 'British citizen', 'British Dependent Territories citizen' or 'British Overseas citizen'. Broadly speaking, a 'British citizen' is anyone who was a citizen of the United Kingdom and Colonies and who had the right of abode in the United Kingdom under the Immigration Act 1971 as in force at 1 January 1983,[2] or anyone who by birth or adoption, descent, registration or naturalisation has become a British citizen since that date.[3] A British Dependent Territories citizen is anyone who was a citizen of the United Kingdom and Colonies and who had that citizenship by his birth, naturalisation or registration in a dependent territory,[4] or anyone who by birth or adoption, descent, registration or naturalisation has become a British Dependent Territories citizen since that date.[5] The British Nationality (Hong Kong) Act 1990 enables certain Hong Kong residents to register as British citizens. Persons who are registered cease to be British Dependent Territories citizens and they become subject to the British Nationality Act 1981. A British Overseas citizen is anyone who was a citizen of the United Kingdom and Colonies but who did not become a British citizen or a British Dependent Territories citizen on 1 January 1983,[6] or anyone who by registration has become a British Overseas citizen since that date.[7] The generic term 'Commonwealth citizen' now embraces all British citizens, British Dependent Territories citizens, British Overseas citizens and British subjects as well as citizens of independent members of the British Commonwealth of Nations and certain territories for which the United Kingdom is responsible and which are administered by a department within the Foreign and Commonwealth Office.[8] It does *not* include 'British protected persons'.[9]

Wherever the words 'British subject' occur in any enactment or instrument passed before 1 January 1983, they are to be taken as referring to anyone who, before that date, was a citizen of the United Kingdom and Colonies or a citizen of one of the independent members of the Commonwealth, or who, after that date, is a Commonwealth citizen.[10] Thus, for example, a Scotsman, an Englishman, a Canadian, an Indian, a Tongan and an Australian are all equally 'British subjects' both before and after 1 January 1983 within the meaning of that term as used in the Taxes Acts. Only in enactments and instruments passed after 1 January 1983 will the term carry the restricted meaning given to it by the British Nationality Act 1981.

---

1 BNA 1981 ss 30–35.
2 Ibid, s 11.
3 Ibid, ss 1–10.
4 Ibid, s 23 and Sch 6. British Dependent Territories are Anguilla, Bermuda, British Antarctic Territory, British Indian Ocean Territory, the Cayman Islands, the Falkland Islands and dependencies, Gibraltar, Montserrat, the Pitcairn Islands, St Helena and dependencies, the sovereign base areas of Akrotiri and Dhekelia in Cyprus, the Turks and Caicos Islands and the Virgin Islands. Although the Falkland Islands are, as stated, a British Dependent Territory, British citizenship rather than British Dependent Territories citizenship is extended to Falkland Islanders by the British Nationality (Falkland Islands) Act 1983.
5 BNA 1981 ss 15–22.
6 Ibid, s 26.
7 Ibid, ss 27–28. Registration is available only in the case of certain minors and women who, immediately before 1 January 1983, were married to certain citizens of the United Kingdom and Colonies.
8 Ibid, s 37 and Sch 3. See **1.09** above for a list of Commonwealth nations.
9 Ibid, s 38.
10 Ibid, s 51.

Determinants of chargeability

1.12 Residence

A consideration of the somewhat fanciful model set forth at **1.01** above has shown us that taxation – whenever and wherever anyone seeks to impose it – is inevitably subject to both a consensual and a jurisdictional limitation. We have seen that, in the United Kingdom, the first of these limitations manifests itself in the constitutional requirement that taxation may be imposed only by an Act of Parliament, and that the second limitation manifests itself in the necessity for tax legislation to extend only to persons who either become personally present within the territorial bounds of the Crown's jurisdiction or have possessions or effect transactions within those bounds.

Immediately Parliament seeks to apply this second limitation, however, it is faced with the difficult task of translating 'personal presence' into terms which provide a practical test of chargeability. Madame Dupont's periodic day-trips from Calais to Dover for the purchase of underwear at a certain well-known British store undoubtedly bring her within the territorial limits of Parliament's jurisdiction, but are our tax laws to be so framed as to bring her, on those grounds alone, within their ambit? Surely such legislation would meet with the same problems of unenforceability as have already been considered. Madame Dupont would be back in France before an assessment could be raised and, if a notice of assessment were to be served on her abroad,[1] she would be unlikely to discharge the tax. The court would have no power of service of process on her until her next visit to the United Kingdom[2] and, even if a writ were then served, she would be back in France by the time the action could be brought. A judgment could be obtained against her in her absence but could not be enforced in France[3] and the judgment would, therefore, be a *brutum fulmen* – a mere empty threat – which Madame Dupont would no doubt cheerfully ignore.

It is apparent, therefore, that a more substantive kind of presence than the fleeting, transitory type envisaged in the previous paragraph is needed before it can constitute a rational criterion on which to base tax liability.[4] Permanent presence is, however, also out of the question. The permanent presence in the United Kingdom of many of its inhabitants is frequently broken by overseas visits of varying durations and for varying reasons. It would undoubtedly be more regularly broken – and by many more people – if permanent presence were to become the criterion of chargeability to tax!

What, then, is the answer? So far as the United Kingdom is concerned, it has, from the start, in relation to income, profits or gains,[5] been residence[6] – a concept so vague as to necessitate a work such as this, but a concept which successfully avoids, on the one hand, the Scylla of transitoriness and, on the other, the Charybdis of permanence. The concept of residence is examined in chapter 2.

---

1 See **8.03** below.
2 See **1.03** above.
3 See **1.04** above.
4 Though not, it seems, the obligation to deduct and account for tax under PAYE. In *Clark v Oceanic Contractors Inc* [1983] STC 35, the House of Lords held that, because Oceanic, a non-resident company, had an address for service in the United Kingdom and carried out operations in the designated areas of the North Sea (the profits of which were to be treated under FA 1973 s 38(4) as profits from a trade carried on by it in the United Kingdom and, as such, to be liable to corporation tax under TA 1970 s 246), it had a trading presence in the United Kingdom and that such a trading presence was sufficient to impose an obligation on the company under TA 1970 s 204 to operate a PAYE scheme for the collection of tax in respect of emoluments chargeable to tax under Sch E.
5 See **1.15–1.17** below.
6 But see **8.16** below where the draft EU directive on savings introduces different concepts; and Scotland Act 1998 s 75 which defines 'a Scottish taxpayer'.

1.13 Ordinary residence

If an individual is resident in the United Kingdom year after year he is usually regarded as ordinarily resident. An individual may be resident in the United Kingdom for a given year by being physically present for 183 days or more but still not ordinarily resident for that year. Conversely an individual may be ordinarily resident in a particular year without being resident in that year. As in the case of residence, an individual is ordinarily resident for the whole of a tax year or not at all. The concept of ordinary residence is explained in Chapter 3.

1.14 Domicile

In identifying residence as the criterion of chargeability to tax, the qualification of relatedness to income, profits or gains was introduced. United Kingdom taxation is not, however, confined merely to income, profits or gains, but extends to the value of transfers of capital upon a person's death and, to some extent, during his lifetime.[1] Such taxation creates a special problem for it is linked to the disposition of, or succession to, property or proprietorial interests, and such matters are governed by the 'personal law' which governs the disponer's personal status as a human being

The personal law may be described as the municipal law of the country in which the person has his (to use a neutral term) 'natural home'. It is universally recognised that, though a person may change his shores, the personal law which governs his status remains the same – except in certain extreme circumstances – and is the law to which reference must be made whenever and wherever questions such as the validity of marriage, the legitimacy of children, the effect of marriage on the proprietorial rights of husband and wife, and – of particular relevance to us here – the disposition of property arise. The criterion for the determination of the appropriate personal law is, however, not residence but, in some countries, nationality and, in others, domicile.

As it is by no means uncommon for a person to be resident in a municipal law district other than that in which he has his 'natural home', much confusion and many anomalies will be obviated if the personal law which governs a disposition is allowed to govern also the choice of revenue law under which the disposition is to be taxed. In England, questions of status are determined according to the law of the domicile and domicile has, therefore, been adopted by Parliament as the criterion for determining the chargeability of a person to inheritance tax. Because, however, the disposition of property often lies at the root of a charge to capital gains tax, too, domicile has been given a part to play in determining the extent of a person's chargeability to that tax also. The concept of domicile is examined in Chapter 7.

---

1 See **1.27** below.

Criticisms of the existing system

1.15 Gordon Brown

In his Budget Statement in the House of Commons on 17 April 2002 the Rt. Hon. Gordon Brown M.P., the U.K's Chancellor of the Exchequer, said 'I am reviewing the complex rules on residence and domicile'.[1] A report on the review will be published before the U.K. Budget of 2003.

---

1 *Hassard*, Vol 383; col. 584.

1.16 Complex rules

The present system has over the years become increasingly complex. The three factors of residence, ordinary residence and domicile make the determination of an individual's liability and claim to relief a difficult and time-consuming matter. Domicile in particular can be unsuitable to determine liability to an annual tax such as income tax since it often requires a consideration of a person's life history and future intentions.[1]

The rules are an amalgam of statute law, case law and Inland Revenue guidelines. The guidelines, the latest of which were published in 2000,[2] do not have the force of law but are obviously persuasive when a tribunal, such as the Special Commissioners, has to consider questions of residence. A taxpayer ignores the guidelines at his peril.

The guidelines relating to the liability of those who leave and come to the United Kingdom are detailed and complicated, taking up two chapters of the latest publication.[3] When an individual arrives in or leaves the country the days of arrival and the days of departure are not considered in calculating the length of time which that individual has spent in this country.

---

1 See Ch 7 below.
2 Inland Revenue Booklet IR 20(2000); see Appendix below.
3 Ibid, Chs 2 and 3.

1.17 The remittance basis

Some individuals are charged to income tax and capital gains tax on certain kinds of income and gains on the remittance basis; tax liability is charged only on the income and gains which are received in the United Kingdom. Usually the remittance basis applies where the income or gains arise outside the United Kingdom and where the individuals are not domiciled and in some cases not ordinarily resident in the United Kingdom. These individuals often are able to exercise control over their tax liability by controlling the amount of income or the proceeds of gains which they bring into the United Kingdom.

1.18   Possible future changes

These changes could either be piecemeal changes (that is addressing some of the specific attributes of the existing system such as the remittance basis or the rules of domicile), or they could herald a comprehensive reform by fundamentally changing the basis of liability.

Piecemeal reforms

1.19   Residence sole test

Residence could be made the sole test of the determination of liability to income tax and capital gains tax. Ordinary residence and domicile would then no longer be factors in the determination of liability. It should be appreciated, however, that residence could not be equated solely with merely periods of physical presence and it might still be necessary either to establish a special regime for those who did not have a long-term connection with the United Kingdom (see para 1.24 below) or to define residence to include other factors which had some affinity with ordinary residence and domicile.

1.20   Extend the remittance basis

One approach which has been suggested by the Inland Revenue[1] would be to extend the remittance basis so that all benefits enjoyed in the United Kingdom out of foreign assets were regarded as remittances from overseas and so within the United Kingdom tax charge. United Kingdom tax could thus be levied not only on financial remittances but also on the proceeds of chattels which were brought into the United Kingdom and disposed of while the owner was resident there. In addition the value of benefits in the form, for example, of an interest-free loan or the rent-free use of a property which was provided out of overseas assets would be brought into charge. Relief would be given for any overseas tax.

---

1 See *Residence in the United Kingdom, The Scope of UK Taxation for Individuals, a Consultation Document*, Inland Revenue, July 1988, para 6.28 et seq.

1.21   Deemed domicile

A non-domiciled individual can, for the purposes of inheritance tax,[1] be 'deemed' to be domiciled in the United Kingdom if he was resident in the United Kingdom on or after 10 December 1974 and in not less than seventeen of the twenty years of assessment ending with the relevant year of assessment. The question whether a person was resident in the United Kingdom, in any year of assessment for these purposes is determined according to income tax rules.[2] These rules could be extended and applied to income tax and capital gains tax.

1 See 7.17 below.
2 IHTA 1984 s 2 67(4).

A comprehensive reform

1.22 Inland Revenue – consultation document

In its publication *Residence in the United Kingdom, The Scope of UK Taxation for Individuals, A Consultation Document 1988*, the Inland Revenue appeared to favour a comprehensive reform.[1] The only test would be that of residence which would be determined by physical presence in the United Kingdom. However there would also be an intermediate basis of taxation which would be applied to an individual's world-wide income depending on the length of an individual's residence in the United Kingdom. These two prongs of a possible reform package are considered at paras 1.23 and 1.24 below.

1 See *Residence in the United Kingdom, The Scope of UK Taxation for Individuals, a Consultation Document*, Inland Revenue, July 1988, para 7.2 et seq.

1.23 Residence based on physical presence

An individual who was present in the United Kingdom for 183 days or more would, as now, be resident in that year for income tax and capital gains tax.

An individual who was present for 30 days or less in a year would not be resident in that year.

When an individual was present for between 30 and 183 days in a year, his residence would be determined by including not only the days spent in the United Kingdom during the year in question but also one-third and one-sixth of the days spent in the United Kingdom in the preceding year and the year before that respectively.

Presence for any part of a day would count as presence for the whole day.

1.24 Intermediate basis of taxation

A new intermediate basis of taxation for some residents would be introduced along with the change to a residence system based on physical presence as described at 1.23 above.

Liability to the new intermediate basis would apply to residents of the United Kingdom who have not been resident here for at least seven out of the previous fourteen years. This basis would apply only to those who had not previously been resident in this country for a continuous period of, say, ten or fifteen years.

The intermediate charge would apply to an individual's world-wide income and gains, that is to income and gains arising outside the United Kingdom. Liability would be based not on the remittance basis but on a percentage of the total of world-wide income and gains, the percentage being determined by the number of years during which the individual had been resident in the United Kingdom in the previous, say, fourteen years. The Inland Revenue suggests[1] a percentage of 15 per cent in the case of one year's residence in the fourteen years, going up in steps to 100 per cent where the individual has resided for seven years out of the previous fourteen years. The percentage would be applied to the individual's liability to tax on world-wide income and gains, taking account of any overseas tax paid. If the resultant figure were higher than the amount of tax payable on income and gains arising within the United Kingdom calculated in the normal way, then the individual's total tax charge for that year would be that higher figure. Otherwise total tax liability would be the amount of tax payable on the individual's income and gains arising within the United Kingdom.[1]

---

1 See *Residence in the United Kingdom, The Scope of UK Taxation for Individuals, a Consultation Document*, Inland Revenue, July 1988, Annex F.

United Kingdom revenue law

1.25 Income tax

There are four United Kingdom direct taxes the incidence of which is, to some extent, governed by the residence or domicile status of the person on whom the liability will fall: income tax, corporation tax, capital gains tax and inheritance tax. A detailed consideration of each of those taxes is beyond the scope of this work but, in this and the three subsequent paragraphs, the relevance to each of territoriality and of a person's residence and domicile is noted. Income tax is the first to be considered.

Although income tax is 'one tax, not a collection of taxes essentially distinct',[1] it has, since 1803, been charged under one or other of a number of schedules each of which specifies a chargeable source of income. There are presently four, A, D, E and F, and once income is charged to income tax under one of those schedules, it cannot be charged to income tax under another also.[2]

Two of the schedules – Schedule D and Schedule E – are divided into cases – I to VI so far as Schedule D is concerned and I to III so far as Schedule E is concerned – and the Inland Revenue has the right to decide under which case it chooses to charge to tax income falling within those schedules.[3] It cannot, however, charge annual profits or gains to tax under Schedule D Case VI if those profits or gains fall under some other case of Schedule D,[4] nor can it charge emoluments to tax under Case III of Schedule E if those emoluments fall under Case I or II.[5]

Each of the schedules defines income according to its source and brings within the charge to tax the 'annual' income arising from the source. Income tax is itself an annual tax, being reimposed for each new year of assessment[6] (ie a year which runs from 6 April in one calendar year to 5 April in the next following calendar year)[7] and thus, in principle, if income is to be charged to tax for say, 1997-98, income must arise in the year ended 5 April 1998 and its source must exist in that year. Certain income is to remain chargeable to tax even though its source has ceased.[8]

The assessment process[9] begins with the ascertainment (or estimation) of a person's income from all sources for a year of assessment (by reference to each of the schedules and by application of the computational rules those schedules contain), proceeds to the totalling of all assessable income and the deduction therefrom of any reliefs and allowances to which the person is entitled for that year of assessment, and culminates in the charging of the balance to tax at appropriate rates.

Insofar as any tax shown to be due under the assessment has not already been collected by deduction at source – the process whereby a payer of income is, in certain circumstances, required to deduct tax (usually at basic rate) in making the payment[10] – it is collected directly under a notice of assessment issued by an inspector of taxes.

Schedule A is confined to income from 'land in the United Kingdom'.[11]

Schedule D is the main charging schedule and contains six cases. Case I brings into charge to tax the profits or income gains from trades carried on in the United Kingdom or elsewhere; and Case II charges profits or income gains in respect of any profession or vocation not contained in any other schedule.[12] Case III brings into charge interest, annuities and other annual payments arising from a United Kingdom source,[13] wherever payable,[14] and, accordingly, the residence status of the recipient is irrelevant. Cases IV and V bring into charge income arising from securities and possessions out of the United Kingdom[15] (including trades etc, carried on wholly abroad[16]), and so are confined to such income as arises to persons resident in the United Kingdom[17] or, in the case of persons not domiciled in the United Kingdom or British subjects or citizens of the Republic of Ireland not ordinarily resident here, to such income as is *remitted* to the United Kingdom.[18] Case VI is the residual case of Schedule D which brings into charge income from United Kingdom sources[19] not charged by any other case or schedule and not charged by virtue of Schedules A or E[20] and, accordingly, the residence status of the person to whom the income arises is irrelevant.

Schedule E is concerned with emoluments and has three cases. Case I is limited to the emoluments of persons resident and ordinarily resident in the United Kingdom.[21] Case II is confined to emoluments in respect of duties performed in the United Kingdom by persons who are not resident or, if resident, are not ordinarily resident in the United Kingdom;[22] and Case III is confined to persons resident in the United Kingdom (whether ordinarily resident here or not) insofar as their emoluments do not fall within Cases I or II but are received in the United Kingdom.[23]

Schedule F brings into charge to tax dividends and other distributions from United Kingdom resident companies.[24] As the schedule contains its own territorial limitation as to source, the residence status of the recipient is irrelevant.

1 *A-G v LCC* (1900) 4 TC 265 at 293, per Lord Macnaghten.
2 *Mitchell and Edon v Ross* (1959) 40 TC 11, per Lord Radcliffe at 61.
3 *Liverpool and London and Globe Insurance Co v Bennett* (1913) 6 TC 327. '. . . the alternative lies with the taxing authority', per Lord Shaw at 376.
4 TA 1988 s 18(3).
5 Ibid, s 131(2).
6 The continuing structure is preserved by TA 1988 s 820 but the tax itself requires an annual parliamentary resolution (invested with statutory authority by PCTA 1968) to keep it alive pending the enactment of the annual Finance Act.
7 TA 1988 s 2(2).
8 TA 1988 s 103.
9 For the validity of this process as regards non-residents, see **8.02–8.03** below.

10 See **8.13–8.15** below.
11 TA 1988 s 15.
12 Ibid, s 18(3).
13 *National Bank of Greece SA v Westminster Bank Executor and Trustee Co (Channel Islands) Ltd* (1971) 46 TC 491.
14 TA 1988 s 18(3).
15 Ibid.
16 *Colquhoun v Brooks* (1889) 2 TC 490.
17 TA 1988 s 18(1)(a)(i).
18 Ibid, s 65(4)(5).
19 Residual income from sources outside the United Kingdom is brought into charge to tax under Schedule D, Case V by interpreting 'possessions' as meaning ' all that is possessed in Her Majesty's dominions out of the United Kingdom, or in foreign countries' (*Colquhoun v Brooks* (1889) 2 TC 490 at 502, per Lord Herschell.
20 TA 1988 s 18(3).
21 Ibid, s 19(1), para 1.
22 Ibid.
23 Ibid.
24 Ibid, s 20, para 1.

1.26 Corporation tax

Corporation tax is chargeable on the worldwide profits of any company resident in the United Kingdom.[1] A non-resident company is, however, chargeable to corporation tax only if it carries on a trade in the United Kingdom through a branch or agency in the United Kingdom, and, in that event, the profits brought into charge to corporation tax are those of, or attributable to, the branch.[2]

The profits chargeable to corporation tax are to be arrived at by aggregating with its chargeable gains (if any) its income computed on income tax principles under the schedules and cases described at **1.25** above.[3]

From 6 April 1984, the Board of Inland Revenue has had the power to apportion among persons with an interest in a non-resident company the profits of the company (computed on the basis of it being a company resident in the United Kingdom) if that company is controlled by persons resident in the United Kingdom but is resident in a country where its profits are subject to a level of taxation lower than that to which they would be subject in the United Kingdom.[4]

Residence again is a key factor in determining the tax liability of companies.

1 TA 1988 ss 6(1), (2)(a) and 8(1).
2 Ibid, s 11(1), (2).
3 Ibid, s 9.
4 TA 1988 ss 747–756 and Sch 24, FA 2001 s 82. See **6.13** below.

1.27 Capital gains tax

A charge to capital gains tax arises when a chargeable gain accrues to an individual on the disposal or deemed disposal of a chargeable asset in a year of assessment during any part of which he is resident or during which he is ordinarily resident in the United Kingdom.[1] A chargeable gain accruing to a company is included in its profits for corporation tax purposes.[2]

A disposal occurs whenever the owner of the asset divests himself (or is divested) of his ownership, absolute and beneficial, of the whole or part of the asset; and a chargeable asset is any asset (including incorporeal property) other than an individual's principal private residence,[3] gilt-edged securities and qualifying corporate bonds,[4] savings certificates and non-marketable securities,[5] life policies, and deferred annuities,[6] tangible moveable assets disposed of for £6,000 or less,[7] private motor vehicles,[8] certain interests under settlements,[9] decorations for valour etc,[10] debts other than debts on a security,[11] and foreign currency for personal expenditure.[12]

There is an annual exemption for individuals, for 2002–2003, of £7,700.[13]

The territorial location of an asset disposed of is of no relevance unless the person to whom the chargeable gain accrues is, though resident or ordinarily resident in the United Kingdom, not domiciled in the United Kingdom. Where a person has a foreign domicile, no capital gains tax is to be charged on a gain accruing to him from the disposal of an asset situated outside the United Kingdom except to the extent of any amounts received in the United Kingdom in respect of that gain.[14]

In some instances, the residence status of the disponor determines the location of the asset disposed of. Thus a debt other than a judgment debt, whether secured or unsecured, is situated in the United Kingdom only if the creditor is resident in the United Kingdom, and a ship or aircraft (or an interest or right in or over a ship or aircraft) is situated in the United Kingdom only if the owner (or the person entitled to the interest etc) is resident in the United Kingdom.[15]

Where a person is neither resident nor ordinarily resident in the United Kingdom but carries on a trade in the United Kingdom through a branch or agency, he is to be charged to tax on gains accruing to him from the disposal of assets situated in the United Kingdom and either held by the branch, or used in connection with the trade.[16]

Personal representatives are regarded as possessing the same residence, ordinary residence and domicile status as the deceased person possessed at the date of his death.[17]

---

1   TCGA 1992 ss 1 and 2(1).
2   See **1.27** above.
3   TCGA 1992 s 222.
4   Ibid, s 115.
5   Ibid, s 121.
6   Ibid, s 210.
7   Ibid, s 262.
8   Ibid, s 263.
9   Ibid, s 76.
10 Ibid, s 268.
11 Ibid, s 251.
12 Ibid, s 269.
13 Ibid, s 3; CGT (Annual Exempt Amount) Order, SI 1994/3008.
14 Ibid, s 12.
15 Ibid, s 275(f).
16 Ibid, s 10.
17 Ibid, s 62(3).

1.28 Inheritance tax

Inheritance tax is a direct tax on transfers of value made on, or (at a tapered rate) during the seven years preceding, a person's death;[1] and on transfers by a company or by an individual (during his life) into trusts (other than accumulation and maintenance trusts or trusts for the disabled or interest in possession trusts).[2]

Transfers to a spouse are exempt from tax, provided that the spouse is domiciled in the United Kingdom,[3] as are gifts of £250 or less,[4] certain gifts in consideration of marriage,[5] and gifts to charities etc.[6] Where lifetime transfers by an individual are chargeable to tax, the amount brought into charge is to be reduced by an annual exemption of £3,000.[7]

Domicile is a key concept in relation to inheritance tax. If a person is domiciled in the United Kingdom, the transfer, during the last seven years of his life or upon his death, of any property to which he is beneficially entitled, wherever situated, is within the charge to tax. If, however, a person is domiciled outside the United Kingdom, only transfers of property situated in the United Kingdom will be within the charge.[8] Domicile has, however, an extended meaning for the purpose of inheritance tax as explained in chapter 7 below.

1 IHTA 1984 Pt I as amended by FA 1986.
2 Ibid, ss 3, 71 and 89; F(No 2)A 1987, s 96(2).
3 Ibid, s 18.
4 Ibid, s 20.
5 Ibid, s 22.
6 Ibid, ss 23–29.
7 Ibid, s 19.
8 Ibid, s 6(1).

1.29 Revenue practices and concessions

Almost from its beginnings, the United Kingdom system of taxation has contained concessions and practices which have, from time to time, been introduced by the Inland Revenue to ease the task of administering the statutory provisions made by Parliament. At first, it was thought that the authority for such concessions and practices lay in the Inland Revenue Regulations Act 1890 s 1(2) which provided that the Commissioners of Inland Revenue ('the Board') 'shall have all necessary powers for carrying into execution every Act of Parliament relating to inland revenue', but when, in 1947, three years after the first list of concessions had been published, Sir Stafford Cripps MP, the then Chancellor of the Exchequer, was asked to state their basis in law, he replied that they had been brought into existence 'without any particular legal authority under any Act of Parliament, but by the Inland Revenue under my authority'.[1]

From this clear admission of the fact that Inland Revenue concessions and practices have no statutory foundation but represent merely the will of the Executive, it follows that – whether they work in favour of the Crown or the subject – they have no place in the law for 'the pretended power of suspending laws or the execution of laws by regall authoritie without consent of Parlyament is illegal'.[2]

It is important that this be kept constantly in mind, particularly when questions of residence arise. The Inland Revenue code of practice on the subject of residence has grown exceedingly tall and achieved such importance in Revenue eyes that many textbooks now state the consequences of certain courses of action in terms of that code without even mentioning that, in law, the consequences of following the courses of action described might be quite different. The fact that an appeal to the Commissioners will usually be necessary if the law, as opposed to the Revenue code, is to be brought to bear on a particular situation does not justify the tacit acceptance that the Revenue code is itself some kind of final authority. The judicial attitude towards the code is plain. When, in *Reed v Clark*,[3] Nicholls J was referred to IR 20 (the booklet which then contained the code) he dismissed its authority in a single sentence: 'I do not see', he said, 'how this booklet affects any matter I have to decide.'[4] The latest code is contained in the Revenue booklet IR 20 (11 April 2000) which is reproduced in the Appendix below.

1   446 HC Official Report (5th Series) col 2266.
2   Bill of Rights 1688.
3   [1985] STC 323.
4   Ibid, at 347.

CHAPTER 2

Residence

Come, give us a taste of your quality.

Shakespeare *Hamlet* Act 2 Sc 2

2.01 Introduction

It has been explained in chapter 1 that the jurisdiction of Parliament is confined to the territory over which Parliament exercises its sovereignty and that, accordingly, the legislative ability of Parliament to raise revenue – though theoretically without limit – is effectively restricted to the imposition of taxation only on such persons as are present within, or enter, the territorial bounds of the United Kingdom, or have possessions or effect transactions within those bounds. The Income Tax Act 1806 (which is the foundation on which our present system of direct taxation rests) accorded clear recognition to this limitation by making 'residence' in Great Britain (now the United Kingdom) the chief determinant of chargeability where there would not otherwise be a sufficient connection between the sovereign territory and the source of the profits or gains which Parliament had resolved to tax. Residence is, as we shall see, a concept rooted in, but of greater durability than, the concept of presence[1] and, as a determinant of chargeability to tax, has survived unchanged to the present day.

---

1 As to whether it follows from this that a person cannot be regarded as resident in the United Kingdom for a tax year during which he has at no time been physically present within the territorial bounds of the United Kingdom, see **4.14** below.

The nature of residence

2.02 A qualitative attribute

It has often been observed that, in legislating for the imposition of taxation on the basis of 'residence', Parliament omitted, or declined, to give the term 'residence' any statutory definition. That omission created an immediate difficulty which very soon required judicial resolution for, in the absence of a statutory definition, the word 'residence' has 'no technical or special meaning'[1] and must, therefore, according to accepted principles of construction, be given the meaning it would bear 'in the speech of plain men'.[2] To put it another way: if Parliament uses a word without explaining what it means by that word, it must be assumed to be using that word 'in its common sense'.[3] But what *is* the common sense of 'residence' or any of its variants? As Rowlatt J has said:

> When you speak of a person residing, do you mean that he has attributed to himself a quality which makes him describable in that way with reference to a place, or do you mean that he is really there?[4]

If 'residing' means no more than 'is really there', 'residence' becomes a mere synonym for 'physical presence' and that, as we saw in Chapter 1, is what Parliament sought to avoid. Presence is an attribute which is far too easily acquired or shed for it to serve as an adequate determinant of chargeability to tax, and residence instead of presence was chosen to fill that role because of its ability to provide a more enduring territorial link. Residence can play the part assigned to it, however, only if it carries the *first* of the two senses which Rowlatt J has indicated it may bear and, accordingly, the judiciary has consistently held that, in the context of fiscal legislation, 'residence' is to be regarded only 'as signifying an attribute of the person'.[5] Therefore, one must never, in the context of a fiscal statute, 'think of "residence" in the sense of a house or place of residence';[6] and the same is true of all the variants – 'resident', 'reside', 'resides', 'residing', etc. 'Resident', for example, 'indicates a quality of the person and is not descriptive of . . . property, real or personal'.[7]

Attributes or qualities of the person defy encompassment in a form of words. They have no concrete reality. Their existence may only be inferred or deduced from a person's particular pattern of behaviour in particular circumstances, and rarely, if ever, will the pattern or the circumstances in any two cases be quite the same. 'Residence', taken as a term expressing a quality of the person,

> is not a term of invariable elements, all of which must be satisfied in each instance. It is quite impossible to give it a precise and inclusive definition. It is highly flexible, and its many shades of meaning vary not only in the contexts of different matters, but also in different aspects of the same matter. In one case it is satisfied by certain elements, in another by others, some common, some new.[8]

To bring a person within, or to exclude a person from, the charging sections of a taxing statute solely by reference to a determinant of such inexactitude is, clearly, far from satisfactory and, indeed, brings the Taxes Acts close to defeating the maxim that a taxing statute must impose a charge in clear terms or fail. As Viscount Sumner has pointed out, however, 'the words are plain and it is only their application that is haphazard and beyond all forecast'.[9]

Clearly, Viscount Sumner regretted that such was the case and, over half a century ago was using his bench as a platform from which to press for change. He believed that:

> the subject ought to be told, in statutory and plain terms, when he is chargeable and when he is not. The words 'resident in the United Kingdom' . . ., simple as they look, guide the subject remarkably little as to the limits within which he must pay and beyond which he is free. This is the more likely to be a subject of grievance and to provoke a sense of injustice

when, as now is the case, the facility of communications, character of social habits, and the pressure of taxation have made these intricate and doubtful questions of residence important and urgent in a manner undreamt of by Mr Pitt, Mr Addington or even Sir Robert Peel.[10]

Eight years later, the Committee on Codification of Income Tax Law endorsed those criticisms. The then-present state of affairs was, it said 'intolerable and should not be allowed to continue',[11] and went so far as to imply that the uncertainty was maintained for the advantage and convenience of the Inland Revenue. Certainly, the absence of a precise definition does benefit the Inland Revenue in some ways. It undoubtedly denies a person the guarantee which such a definition would afford him that by ordering his affairs in a particular way he will divest himself of the attribute on which his amenability to the tax legislation rests, and it thus inhibits him from attempting to escape the tax net by artificial means.

The Royal Commission on the Taxation of Profits and Income believed, however, that a precise definition would benefit the Inland Revenue more. 'Fixed rules,' it said, 'would simplify the work of administration even if they worked unreasonably in some instances.'[12] Indeed, the fact that the existing system led to 'the devotion of a great deal of time and skill to considering and adjudicating upon individual cases' was seen by the Commission as one good reason for its abandonment in favour of fixed rules – particularly in the light of their conviction that a person 'would normally prefer certainty to the assurance that there will be the fullest consideration of his personal circumstances'.[13]

The Commission's report concluded by recommending further statutory provisions in this area but, apart from legislation introduced in 1956 in relation to persons working abroad,[14] that recommendation has never been implemented. Instead, the Inland Revenue further developed its own code of practice[15] which, though of no legal standing,[16] is generally applied with a degree of inflexibility normally accorded only to statutory instruments. This has placed the taxpayer in the worst of all possible positions for, though the code is far from being the balanced summary of case law principles which the Inland Revenue hold it out to be, the taxpayer will frequently find that he has no option but to employ the appeal machinery if he wishes to challenge the code on any point.

---

1 *Lysaght v IRC* (1928) 13 TC 511 at 536, per Lord Warrington of Clyffe.
2 Ibid, at 529, per Viscount Sumner.
3 Ibid, at 534, per Lord Buckmaster.
4 *Levene v IRC* (1928) 13 TC 486 at 492.
5 *Pickles v Foulsham* (1923) 9 TC 261 at 274, per Rowlatt J.
6 Ibid
7 *Lysaght v IRC* (1928) 13 TC 511 at 528, per Viscount Sumner.
8 *Thompson v Minster of National Revenue* [1946] SCR 209 at 224, per Rand J, quoted with approval by Wynn-Perry J in *Miesegaes v IRC* (1957) 37 TC 493 at 497.
09 *Levene v IRC* (1928) 13 TC 486 at 502.
10 Ibid.
11 Report, 1936, Cmd 5131, para 59.
12 Final Report, 1955, Cmd 9474, para 292.
13 Ibid.
14 See **4.16–4.20** below.
15 Now contained in Booklet IR 20 (11 April 2000), 'Residents and non-residents: liability to tax in the United Kingdom'. See Appendix below.
16 See **1.28** above.

2.03 A question of fact and degree

The absence of a statutory definition of the term 'residence' is yet more far-reaching in its consequences than even the foregoing paragraphs might suggest. If the Taxes Act contained such a definition, then it would be open to the courts[1] to decide whether or not a person had come within that definition, for 'a proper construction of . . . statutory language is a matter of law'.[2]

As we have seen, however, the Taxes Acts give no definition of the word 'residence' and the judiciary has inclined to the view that 'it is not possible to frame one'.[3] Accordingly, whether a person is resident or not is, within the present state of affairs, a question not of law but of fact.

Because of the way in which the appeal procedure operates, however, it falls not to the courts but to the Commissioners to consider what Rowlatt J called the 'bundle of actual facts'[4] and to form from those facts the 'impression or opinion' in accordance with which a finding of 'resident' or 'non-resident' will be made. As Nicholls J put it in *Reed v Clark*:[5]

> The key word 'residing' is not defined by statute . . . Thus the task of the fact-finding tribunal in the present case was to consider and weigh all the evidence and then, giving the word 'residing' its natural and ordinary meaning, reach a conclusion on the factual question of whether or not the taxpayer was residing in the United Kingdom in the year of assessment.[6]

Once such a conclusion has been reached, the court's powers of intervention become very limited. Its role is restricted by statute[7] to the hearing and determination only of questions of law arising on the case stated by the commissioners for its opinion which means that:

> when commissioners have made findings of fact, their decision is not open to review provided (a) they had before them evidence from which such findings could properly be made and (b) they did not misdirect themselves in law.[8]

Thus a finding by the Commissioners that a person is resident in the United Kingdom in a year of assessment 'only raises a question of law if it can be contended that it is impossible to draw that conclusion of fact as to residence in the United Kingdom from the facts set out in the case'.[9] By reason of the very inexactitude of the term 'resident', such a contention will rarely be upheld, and this places the taxpayer in an unenviable position.

The facts on which the Commissioners make their findings as to residence or non-residence differ from case to case, but have tended to be facts concerning a person's physical presence in the United Kingdom or absence from it, facts concerning his history of residence or non-residence, facts concerning his present habits and manner of life, facts as to his nationality, facts as to the purpose, frequency, regularity and duration of his visits to the United Kingdom or to places overseas, facts as to ties of family and ties of business in the United Kingdom, and facts as to the maintenance or availability of a place of abode in the United Kingdom.

Such facts do not all carry equal weight and, indeed, facts which in one case carry no weight at all may, in another case, be so significant as to completely tip the scales. This is what is meant when residence is referred to (as, from time to time, it has been) as a 'question of degree'. A visit to the United Kingdom this year may signify little, a visit next year may signify not much more, but visits year after year may, in the context of the particular circumstances of a case, push the needle to that point on the Commissioners' scale which reads 'resident'. It is then that the questions of degree resolve themselves into a finding of fact and it is that finding of fact which the courts are powerless to disturb unless 'no person acting judicially and properly instructed as to the relevant law could have come to the determination under appeal'[10] or 'no reasonable person could have arrived at the same conclusion as the Commissioners'.[11]

---

1 Ie on an appeal from a decision of the Commissioners. Anyone wishing to contest an assessment on the grounds that it is based on an incorrect view of his residence, ordinary residence or domicile status is normally free to appeal either to the General Commissioners or to the Special Commissioners (TMA 1970 s 31). If, however, a question as to his ordinary residence or domicile status arises in relation to his assessment under Schedule E or to capital gains tax, the question is to be referred to the Board of Inland Revenue for the Board's decision, against which there is a right of appeal to the Special Commissioners only (TA 1988 s 207, TCGA 1992 s 9(2)). An appeal against an inheritance tax determination may be made only to the Special Commissioners (IHTA 1984 s 222).
2 *IRC v Fraser* (1942) 24 TC 498 at 501, per Lord Normand LP.
3 *Levene v IRC* (1928) 13 TC 486 at 497, per Lord Hanworth MR.
4 *Lowenstein v De Salis* (1926) 10 TC 424 at 437.
5 [1985] STC 323.
6 Ibid, at 338.
7 TMA 1970 s 56(6).
8 *Reed v Clark* [1985] STC 323 at 336–337, per Nicholls J.
9 *Bayard Brown v Burt* (1911) 5 TC 667 at 670, per Hamilton J.
10 *Edwards v Bairstow and Harrison* (1955) 36 TC 207 at 229, per Lord Radcliffe.
11 *Pilkington v Randall* (1966) 42 TC 662 at 674, per Salmon LJ.

2.04 A personal attribute

Because residence is a 'quality of the person'[1] and, therefore, a 'question . . . of degree',[2] it follows that a wife's residence status is not governed by her husband's status but is determined by her own circumstances.

Because corporate bodies such as limited companies are legal entities independent of their members under English law, they too will either possess or lack United Kingdom residence status. 'Resident' is, however, 'a term exceedingly unsuited to describe a statutory "person"'[3] and, accordingly, a corporation's residence status can be determined only 'by analogy from natural persons'.[4] So it is with partnerships. Although a partnership is not a legal entity under English law, it is, for tax purposes, 'treated as an entity distinct from the persons who constitute the firm'[5] and its residence status, too, must be arrived at by analogy. Trusts and settlements present even greater difficulties for, although a trust or a settlement is not even treated as an entity separate from its trustees, it does become necessary in some circumstances to determine its residence status. All these matters are discussed in depth in Chapters 5 and 6.

---

1 *IRC v Lysaght* (1928) 13 TC 511 at 528, per Viscount Sumner.
2 Ibid at 536, per Lord Warrington of Clyffe.
3 *Todd v The Egyptian Delta Land and Investment Co Ltd* (1928) 14 TC 119 at 140, per Viscount Sumner.

4 Ibid.
5 *Watson and Everitt v Blunden* (1933) 18 TC 402.

2.05 An annual attribute

In *Levene v IRC*,[1] Viscount Sumner said that 'the taxpayer's chargeability in each year of charge constitutes a separate issue',[2] and, in so saying, gave recognition to the fact that income tax is an annual tax. It is an annual tax in that the charge must be reimposed by Parliament in the Finance Act each year and it is an annual tax in that the charge is made upon the annual income, ie the income of the year of charge.[3] As was noted in chapter 1, however, residence is a principal determinant of chargeability and it will come as no surprise, therefore, to learn that residence is an annual attribute, ie an attribute which endures for a year.

This was brought out very clearly in the case of *Thomson v Bensted*[4] where it was held that, although during the year 1911–12 Mr Thomson had actually spent only four or so months at his home in Scotland and had spent the remainder of the year in West Africa, he was resident in the United Kingdom 'during the whole year, in the sense of the . . . Acts'.[5]

It is quite possible to argue that what was being recognised in the *Thomson* case was not so much that residence is an annual attribute but simply that Mr Thomson had a quality of residence which, because it had been acquired at some time in the past and because it extended into the foreseeable future, was not disturbed or impaired by the periods of time he spent abroad. That argument did not hold good, however, in the case of *Back v Whitlock*.[6] There, Rowlatt J said that if a person were to become a new permanent resident in the United Kingdom only two days before the end of a year of assessment he would be just as chargeable to tax as would someone who had resided here throughout the year. It could surely not be contended that such a person, *de facto*, had the quality of residence prior to the date on which his period of actual residence began and, indeed, Rowlatt J did not base his statement on that ground. It was rather that:

> there is no question under the Income Tax Acts of any apportionment or adjustment for Income Tax in time, with regard to the date when a person became resident and so became taxable.[7]

This same principle emerged more clearly, but in relation to a person who had permanently left the United Kingdom, in *Neubergh v IRC*[8] when Brightman J had to decide whether a Mr Felix Neubergh, who had lived in the United Kingdom since 1919 but had permanently departed on 26 January 1968, was nevertheless liable to the special charge on investment income imposed by the Finance Act 1968 on persons domiciled in the United Kingdom in the year 1967–68 or resident in the United Kingdom in that fiscal year and throughout the nine preceding years. Having first asked the question: 'Was the taxpayer resident in the United Kingdom in the year 1967–68 and throughout the nine preceding years?',[9] he declared that 'the answer to that question can only be Yes'.[10] His grounds for such a conclusion were that, in accordance with the reasoning in *Mitchell v IRC*[11] 'residence during a part of the year is clearly sufficient'.[12]

It was in the case of *Gubay v Kington*,[13] that the point was finally made clear. The case concerned the chargeability or otherwise of Mr Gubay to capital gains tax on the disposal of shares to his non-resident wife in a tax year during only part of which he was *de facto* resident in the United Kingdom. The argument with which Mr Gubay succeeded before the House of Lords was not the argument on which he had gone to the High Court and then to the Court of Appeal. In the lower courts, he had argued that, as he was actually resident in the United Kingdom for only six and a half months in the tax year 1972–73 he could not be said to be resident 'for the year of assessment' 1972–73 and could not, therefore, be charged with capital gains tax on the notional gain accruing to him on the disposal of shares made to his non-resident wife during that year. This argument was dismissed in both courts. In the High Court, Vinelott J. said:

> The words 'resident in the United Kingdom for a year of assessment' are frequently used by judges and textbook writers to describe the situation of a taxpayer who, because he was resident in the United Kingdom for part of a year of assessment, is assessable to tax from all sources of income arising during that year of assessment. In effect, the words 'resident in the United Kingdom for a year of assessment' are used to predicate of the tax-payer that he had the status or quality of being a resident in the United Kingdom for tax purposes during the year of assessment,[14]

and, in the Court of Appeal, Sir John Donaldson MR, said:

> Being resident in the United Kingdom may be a status or a fact. Where it is a status, it is something which is either enjoyed (if that be the right word) or not enjoyed for a whole tax year.[15]

It has thus been placed beyond doubt that any person who possesses or acquires the attribute of residence for part of a tax year will, unless a statute or an extra-statutory concession or a rule of practice dictates otherwise,[16] be regarded as being resident for the whole of that year; and both residence and its related concept of ordinary residence[17] may, therefore, in general terms, be said to be annual attributes, enduring for the whole of any fiscal year in which they are enjoyed, however briefly.

---

1 *Levene v IRC* (1928) 13 TC 486.
2 Ibid, at 501.
3 Though that income may be quantified by reference to the income of some other period, as in the case of profits assessable to tax under Schedule D, Cases I and II.
4 (1918) 7 TC 137.
5 Ibid at 145, per the Lord President.
6 (1932) 16 TC 723.
7 Ibid, at 726.
8 [1978] STC 181.
9 Ibid, at 184.
10 Ibid, at 185.
11 (1951) 33 TC 53.
12 *Neubergh v IRC* [1978] STC 181 at 185.
13 [1983] STC 443.
14 *Gubay v Kington* [1981] STC 721 at 735.
15 *Gubay v Kington* [1983] STC 443 at 451.
16 No statute other than TCGA 1991 s 2(1) presently so provides, but extra-statutory concessions and Inland Revenue rules of practice do. See **4.21** below.
17 See ch 3.

2.06 The judicial principles

Although, as has been explained, the question of whether or not a person possesses the quality of residence is a question of fact, and although the task of the judiciary is limited to that of examining the facts on which the Commissioners reach their decisions and seeing whether anyone acting judicially and properly instructed as to the relevant law could have arrived at the decisions at which the Commissioners have arrived,[1] judges have, in the course of carrying out their examinations, tended to underline significant facts, formulate principles and outline approaches which would lead them to one conclusion or another – even if, at the end of the day, they are obliged, in the absence of any obvious error of law on the part of the Commissioners, to uphold a decision which they themselves might not have reached. It is these general principles which will now be considered.

---

1 See **2.03** above.

A place of abode

2.07 Occupation of a dwelling-house

In *Levene v IRC*,[1] Lord Cave said:

> The word 'reside' is a familiar English word and is defined in the Oxford English Dictionary as meaning 'to dwell permanently or for a considerable time, to have one's settled or usual abode, to live in or at a particular place'. No doubt this definition must for present purposes be taken subject to any modification which may result from the terms of the Income Tax Act and Schedules; but subject to that observation, it may be accepted as an accurate indication of the meaning of the word 'reside'.[2]

Those words are a useful reminder that, although, as has been pointed out,[3] we must not think of residence in terms of bricks and mortar, we must not overlook the fact that the primary meaning of residence is to do with a person's inhabitation of bricks and mortar – or their equivalent.[4] Thus, in *Lloyd v Sulley*,[5] the President of the Court of the Exchequer said of Mr Lloyd's castle in Scotland and his town house and country villa in Italy:

> They are places to which it is quite easy for [him] to resort as his dwelling place whenever he thinks fit, and to set himself down there with his family and establishment. That is a place of residence, and if he occupies that place of residence for a portion of a year he is then within the meaning of the Clause as I read it, residing there in the course of that year.[6]

The same was true of Sir C. H. Coote. He had a house in Ireland which he occupied for the greater part of each year and a house in Connaught Place, London, in which he stayed from time to time for a few weeks. The Court of the Exchequer held that he was resident in Great Britain and 'clearly within the Act'.[7]

Both these judgments were followed in the case of *Cooper v Cadwalader*.[8] Mr Cadwalader was an American citizen who had a house in New York but spent two months of each year in occupation of Millden Lodge, a furnished house in

Forfar in Scotland, which he leased and kept available for his use throughout each year. Was Mr Cadwalader resident in the United Kingdom? Lord Adam was in doubt as to the answer:

> Can it be said that during . . . these two months in which he is residing continuously in Millden Lodge that he is not residing there? Where is he residing? He is residing . . . in Millden Lodge, and therefore residing in the United Kingdom; and if that be so, then it humbly appears to me that he is a person in the sense of the Act residing in the United Kingdom, and assessable under the Act.[9]

---

1   (1929) 13 TC 486.
2   Ibid, at 505.
3   At **2.02** above.
4   In *Bayard Brown v Burt* (1911) 5 TC 667, it was accepted that an ocean-going yacht anchored in territorial waters was Mr Bayard Brown's place of abode; and in *Hipperson v Electoral Registration Officer for the District of Newbury* [1985] 2 All ER 456, Sir John Donaldson MR (at 462) rejected the submission that ladies living in tents, vehicles and benders (a form of tent) on Greenham Common in furtherance of their protest concerning cruise missiles could not be said to have a home in the camp: 'It may be unusual to make one's home in a tent, bender or vehicle, but we can see no reason in law why it should be impossible.' In *Makins v Elson* [1977] STC 46, it was further held that a wheeled caravan, jacked up and resting on bricks, with water, electricity and telephone services installed, was a dwelling-house, while in *R v Bundy* [1977] 2 All ER 382, even a motor car in which a certain Mr Bundy had been living rough was held to be his place of abode when sited – though not while in transit.
5   (1884) 2 TC 37.
6   Ibid, at 41.
7   *A-G v Coote* (1817) 2 TC 385.
8   (1904) 5 TC 101.
9   Ibid, at 107.

2.08   Multiple residence

The cases cited at **2.07** above not only 'determine that when the individual has a home here in the ordinary sense he is taxable',[1] but also that it is of no consequence that he may also have a home elsewhere.

In *A-G v Coote*,[2] for instance, one of the questions was whether Sir C. H. Coote could possess the quality of United Kingdom residence for a year of assessment during which he undoubtedly possessed the quality of Irish residence. The court found his Irish residence to be no barrier at all. Baron Wood said:

> It is no uncommon thing for a gentleman to have two permanent residences at the same time, in either of which he may establish his abode at any period, and for any length of time. This is just such a case.[3]

The same question arose in *Cooper v Cadwalader*.[4] The fact that Mr Cadwalader was clearly resident in New York did not prevent him being found to be resident in the United Kingdom also.

It must be understood that these cases did not establish that a person may be resident *consecutively* in two or more places during a year, but that a person may *simultaneously* be resident (ie possess the quality of residence) in two or more places for the same year. This both follows from and supports the proposition that residence is an annual quality which endures for the whole of any tax year in which it is enjoyed, however briefly.

This proposition was implicitly confirmed by Viscount Cave LC when, in *Levene v IRC*,[5] he said:

> A man may reside in more than one place . . . he may have a home abroad and a home in the United Kingdom, and in that case he is held to reside in both places and to be chargeable with tax in this country.[6]

In *Lysaght v IRC*,[7] Viscount Sumner admitted that it runs counter to our normal mode of thought to think of such people as Mr Cadwalader[8] as being resident in the United Kingdom:

> Who in New York would have said of Mr Cadwalader: 'His home's in the Highlands; his home is not here?' . . . One thinks of a man's settled and usual place of abode as his residence, but the truth is that in many cases in ordinary speech one residence at a time is the underlying assumption and though a man may be the occupier of two houses, he is thought of as only resident in the one he lives in at the time in question. For Income Tax purposes such meanings are misleading. Residence here may be multiple and manifold.[9]

It is now an established principle, therefore, that the possession of residence status in relation to some foreign place or country is not on its own sufficient to prevent a person becoming attributed with United Kingdom residence status.

Revenue guidance on this matter is true to the decided cases and is that:

> It is possible to be resident . . . in both the UK and some other country (or countries) at the same time. If you are resident . . . in another country, this does not mean that you cannot also be resident . . . in the UK.[10]

In closing this examination of the concept of multiple residence, it should be noted that, as the Inland Revenue booklet points out:

> Where, however, you are resident both in the UK and in a country with which the UK has a double taxation agreement, there may be special provisions in the agreement for treating you as a resident of only one of the countries for the purposes of the agreement.[11]

This aspect of residence is dealt with at **2.21** below.

---

1 *Levene v IRC* (1928) 13 TC 486 at 499, per Sargant LJ.
2 (1817) 2 TC 385.
3 Ibid, at 386.
4 (1904) 5 TC 101.
5 (1928) 13 TC 486.
6 Ibid, at 505.
7 (1928) 13 TC 511.
8 *Cooper v Cadwalader* (1904) 5 TC 101. See **2.07** above.
9 *Lysaght v IRC* (1928) 13 TC 511 at 528 and 529.
10 Appendix IR 20 (11 April 2000) para 1.4.
11 Appendix IR 20 (11 April 2000) para 1.4.

2.09   Ownership irrelevant

The general principle which has been discussed in the foregoing paragraphs is that a person cannot possess a dwelling place in the United Kingdom and occupy it, however briefly, during a tax year without becoming resident in the United Kingdom for that tax year. But is 'possess' the correct word? Sir C. H. Coote owned his house in London,[1] Thomas Lloyd owned his castle in Minard,[2] Robert Thomson owned his house in Hawick,[3] and John Cadwalader leased Millden Lodge from the Earl of Dalhousie.[4] Captain Loewenstein did not possess his accommodation.[5] He was a Belgian subject with a home in Brussels, who visited 'Pinfold', a furnished hunting box at Melton Mowbray in Leicestershire, each year for the purpose of fox hunting. The property was owned by the Belgian Breeding Stock Farm Company Ltd, a company in which he had a controlling interest and of which he was a director. In no year did he spend as many as six months in the United Kingdom and he claimed, therefore, that, on the basis of ITA 1918 Sch 1, Rule 2 of the Miscellaneous Rules of Schedule D (now TA 1988 s 336 (1)), he was exempt from tax under Schedule D. That exemption is discussed in chapter 4 and does not concern us here, but Rowlatt J's view of Captain Loewenstein's central argument is of present concern. On the question of the necessity of a 'proprietorial interest', Rowlatt J said:

> I cannot see what difference that makes . . . this man had this house at his disposal, with everything in it or for his convenience, kept going all the year round, although he only wanted it for a short time. Luckily, he was in relation with a Company who were the owners of it, and he could do that without owning it. It is an accident. It might well have been that he could do that with a relation, or a friend, or a philanthropist, or anybody; but in fact there was this house for him . . . He has got this house to come to when he likes; he does not own it; he has got no proprietary interest in it, but it is just as good as if he had for the purpose of having it for a residence, and there it is.

In the light of this pronouncement, the general principle here may be more accurately stated to be that an individual may be held to be resident here notwithstanding that he does not possess the accommodation, provided that the accommodation is available for the individual throughout the tax year even though he occupies it only briefly during that year.

It should be noted that the precise form which accommodation takes is quite irrelevant. An ocean-going yacht permanently moored in the United Kingdom's territorial waters has been held to be a dwelling house for these purposes[6] and so, too, in other circumstances, has a wheeled but immobilised caravan to which electricity, water and telephone services had been supplied.[7]

The entry of a person's name on an electoral roll may be evidence of the availability of accommodation.[8]

The effect of section 208 of the FA 1993 which provides that the existence or otherwise of available accommodation must be disregarded in determining for the purpose of TA 1988 s 366 whether an individual is in the United Kingdom for some temporary purpose and not with a view to or intent of establishing his residence here will be considered at **4.05** below.[9] While s 208 alters the law in respect of the application of s 336, it is submitted that the presence or otherwise of available accommodation can still be relevant to assist in determining whether an individual is generally resident in the United Kingdom or not.

1 *A-G v Coote* (1817) 2 TC 385. See **2.07** above.
2 *Lloyd v Sulley* (1884) 2 TC 37. See **2.07** above.
3 *Thomson v Bensted* (1918) 7 TC 137.
4 *Cooper v Cadwalader* (1904) 5 TC 101. See **2.07** above.
5 *Loewenstein v De Salis* (1926) 10 TC 424 at 438.
6 *Bayard Brown v Burt* (1911) 5 TC 667.
7 *Makins v Elson* [1977] STC 46.
8 See paras 6 and 5 respectively of the cases stated by the Commissioners in *Lloyd v Sulley* (1884) 2 TC 37 at 38 and *Cooper v Cadwalader* (1904) 5 TC 101 at 103.
9 TA 1988 s 336.

Physical presence

2.10 Duration of presence

There are, of course, many situations in which the principle of occupation of available accommodation is of no application. A person may be in the United Kingdom without ever acquiring a 'settled or usual abode'[1] but that will not necessarily prevent him from being attributed with the status of United Kingdom residence. As Viscount Sumner has said:

> Although setting up an establishment in this country, available for residence at any time throughout the year of charge, even though used but little, may be good ground for finding its master to be 'resident' here, it does not follow that keeping up an establishment abroad and none here is incompatible with being 'resident here' if there is other sufficient evidence of it.[2]

The point is graphically made in *Reid v IRC*[3] by Lord Clyde, the Lord President of the Court of Session. In his frequently quoted words he invited us to:

> take the case of a homeless tramp, who shelters to-night under a bridge, to-morrow in the greenwood and as the unwelcome occupant of a farm outhouse the night after. He wanders in this way all over the United Kingdom. But will anyone say he does not *live* in the United Kingdom? – and will anyone regard it as a misuse of language to say he *resides* in the United Kingdom. In his case there may be no relations with family or friends, no business ties, and none of the ordinary circumstances which create a link between the life of a British subject and the United Kingdom; but, even so, I do not think it could be disputed that he *resides* in the United Kingdom. There are other and very different kinds of tramps, who – being possessed of ample means, and having the ordinary ties of birth, family, and affairs with the United Kingdom or some part of it – yet prefer to enjoy those means without undertaking the domestic responsibility of a home, and who move about from one house of public entertainment to another – in London today, in the provinces to-morrow, and in the Highlands the day after. They too are homeless wanderers in the United Kingdom. But surely it is true to say they *live* in the United Kingdom, and *reside* there? The Section of the Act of Parliament with which we are dealing speaks of persons 'residing', not at a particular locality, but in a region so extensive as the United Kingdom.[4]

Although the person at the centre of the *Reid* case was a lady who possessed many links with the United Kingdom other than mere presence, the principal point which

33

the Lord President was making in that passage was that the duration of a person's presence may alone be sufficient to transform mere presence into residence. Nothing but presence attaches the homeless tramp to the United Kingdom, yet if that presence endures for a significant length of time it alone will be sufficient to imbue the tramp with United Kingdom residence status.[5] If his case falls within TA 1988 s 336(1),[6] 183 days within a tax year will be a significant length of time, but if the case does not fall within that section the question what is a significant length of time will be one for the Commissioners to decide. The Inland Revenue believes that 183 days will, in any case, be significant[7] and with that the Commissioners may or may not agree. In the reported cases, the physical presence which has resulted in the attribution of residence has always been for periods amounting to less than 183 days, but in each case there has been some element other than time to which weight has also had to be given.

1 See **2.07** above for the *Oxford English Dictionary* definition of residence quoted by Lord Cave in *Levene v IRC* (1928) 13 TC 486.
2 *Lysaght v IRC* (1928) 13 TC 511 at 528.
3 (1926) 10 TC 673.
4 Ibid, at 679.
5 As to whether a person can be attributed with residence status without ever setting foot in the United Kingdom during a tax year, see **4.14** below.
6 See **4.07–4.09** below.
7 See Appendix IR 20 (11 April 2000) para 1.2.

2.11 Regularity and frequency of visits

Closely linked to the element of time or duration is the element of regularity and frequency. The duration of a person's physical presence in the United Kingdom during any one tax year may not be sufficiently significant for it to transform the presence into residence, but presence of insignificant duration in a succession of tax years may be sufficient to effect the transformation. This principle is well illustrated by the case of *Kinloch v IRC*.[1] Although Mrs Kinloch spent the greater part of her time abroad, she visited the United Kingdom each year, sometimes for only a few days, other times for weeks or even months. The pattern of her visits from 1921–22 to 1927–28 was as follows: 66 days in 1921–22, 40 days over three visits in 1922–23, 177 days over five visits in 1923–24, five months, twelve days over three visits in 1924–25, 145 days over four visits in 1925–26, 141 days over five visits in 1926–27, and 156 days over four visits in 1927–28. In 1924–25, the Inland Revenue challenged Mrs Kinloch's assertion that she was not resident in the United Kingdom and the question was taken before the Special Commissioners. They decided that Mrs Kinloch was correct: she was not resident in the United Kingdom; and, accordingly, for the following two years the Inland Revenue followed the Commissioners' ruling. In 1927–28, however, the Inland Revenue again challenged Mrs Kinloch's non-resident status, and this time the Inland Revenue's contention was upheld: the Commissioners found that:

> having regard to the continuance through the series of years of the regular and lengthy visits to the United Kingdom the circumstances were different from those under consideration when the appeal for the earlier year was heard.[2]

and that Mrs Kinloch was resident in the United Kingdom. In 1927–28, she 'crossed the line, and . . . now she is resident here'.[3] But what was the line Mrs Kinloch had crossed? Rowlatt J seems to have thought it was the line of duration of presence. He said that in 1927–28 Mrs Kinloch had stayed in the United Kingdom rather longer than previously; but that was not so: her visits in 1927–28 were of shorter duration than her visits in either 1923–24 or 1924–25. The line can only have been the line of frequency and regularity. Although a pattern had begun to emerge by the third year of Mrs Kinloch's visits, that pattern was neither sufficiently clear nor sufficiently well-established for it to have transformed her presence into residence; but, by the fifth year, her continued visits had remedied those defects. In the case of *Levene v IRC*[4] a similar pattern had emerged. Mr Levene, whose circumstances are fully described at **4.15** below, had

elected in each [of the four years from 1920–21 to 1924–25] to adopt a regular system of life in accordance with which he and his wife made their abode and lived in this country for a period of between four and five months in each year, and . . . they were therefore resident in the United Kingdom not merely in the sense of being present here but in the fuller sense of making their home here.[5]

1 (1929) 14 TC 736.
2 Ibid, at 738.
3 Ibid at 738, per Rowlatt J.
4 (1928) 13 TC 486.
5 Ibid, at 499.

2.12 Revenue practice

Perhaps the most extreme case bearing on the principle of regular visits is that of *Lysaght v IRC*.[1] Since 1920, Mr Lysaght had lived in Ireland with his wife and family and had had no definite place of abode in the United Kingdom. Each month, however, he visited England to attend a meeting of the directors of John Lysaght Ltd and remained here on company business for about a week on each occasion. During his visits to the United Kingdom he stayed either at the home of his brother or in hotels. The total number of days spent in the United Kingdom for the three years 1922–23, 1923–24 and 1924–25 were 101, 94 and 84 respectively. The Special Commissioners held that Mr Lysaght was resident in the United Kingdom for each of those years and the House of Lords felt itself bound to uphold their decision on the grounds that the question of residence is a question of degree and fact and not a question of law.[2] Their Lordships' support for the Commissioners was by no means unqualified, however, and Viscount Cave LC went so far as to say:

There appears to me to be no reason whatever for holding that [Mr Lysaght] is resident . . . in this country. It is true that he comes here at regular intervals and for recurrent business purposes; but these facts, while they explain the frequency of his visits, do not make them more than temporary visits or give them the character of residence in this country.[3]

For reasons such as these, Viscount Cave thought the Crown's appeal should have been dismissed; Lord Warrington of Clyffe doubted that he would have come to the Commissioners' conclusion; Viscount Sumner could see several points in

Mr Lysaght's favour but could find no error of law which would enable him to interfere with the Commissioners' decision; and only Lord Atkinson and Lord Buckmaster clearly felt that the Commissioners' decision was the correct one. For all this, however, it is the *Lysaght* case, tainted with uncertainty and stretching the concept of residence almost to its breaking point, on which the Inland Revenue has built its rule concerning the frequency and regularity of visits to the United Kingdom.[4]

As explained at **4.03** below, the Inland Revenue regard three months as equivalent to 92 days, and it may easily be calculated that Mr Lysaght's annual average was that less only one day! Although, as we shall see later,[5] it was Mr Lysaght's strong business link with the United Kingdom which, clearly, combined with the frequency and regularity of his visits so as to give his presence here the quality which transformed it into residence, the Inland Revenue rule betrays no recognition that any such link is a necessary ingredient in the transformational process.

1   (1928) 13 TC 511.
2   See **2.03** above.
3   *Lysaght v IRC* (1928) 13 TC 511 at 532.
4   Appendixt IR 20 (11 April 2000), para 3.3.
5   At **2.17** below.

2.13   Future conduct

Before leaving this discussion of the acquisition of residence status through regular and frequent visits, something must be said about the fact that a determination of residence status on those grounds will necessarily involve the simultaneous consideration of a number of tax years. In the *Levene* case, it was objected that such a global consideration was wrong in law since it involved the taking into account in earlier years of conduct which only occurred subsequently. Viscount Sumner did not accept that this was at all erroneous:

> I agree that the taxpayer's chargeability in each year of charge constitutes a separate issue, even though several years are included in one appeal, but I do not think any error of law is committed if the facts applicable to the whole of the time are found in one continuous story. Light may be thrown on the purpose with which the first departure from the United Kingdom took place, by looking at his proceedings in a series of subsequent years. They go to show method and system and so remove doubt which might be entertained if the years were examined in isolation from one another.[1]

1   *Levene v IRC* (1928) 13 TC 486 at 501.

2.14   Previous history

If it is permissible to look at a person's conduct in years subsequent to the year for which a determination of residence status is being sought,[1] it is certainly permissible to look at a person's conduct in previous years, and this was Viscount Sumner's initial approach in the *Levene* case.[2] Having decided that for the first year in question, 1920–21, Mr Levene was resident in the United Kingdom, Viscount Sumner took Mr Levene's conduct in that year as a reference against which to examine each of the subsequent years in question and concluded that 'no material change occurred in his way of living'.³ It followed, therefore, that Mr Levene was resident in each of the subsequent years also.

This same approach was adopted by the Special Commissioners in the case of *Miesegaes v IRC*.⁴ Stanley Miesegaes was a Dutch national who was at boarding school in Harrow from 1939 until July 1951. The years for which his residence status was in question were 1947–48 to 1951–52. Having found that Mr Miesegaes was resident for the years 1947–48 to 1950–51, the Special Commissioners had still to decide his residence status for the year 1951–52. At the start of that tax year, Mr Miesegaes was in Holland but he was in the United Kingdom from 15 April to 17 August. On 17 August he left the United Kingdom to continue his education in Switzerland. The Commissioners decided the question for 1951–52 by looking back to the previous years. The four months' presence in 1951–52 was, they said, 'in continuation of what we found to be his residence here for the previous four years and we found that he was resident in the United Kingdom for 1951–52 also'.⁵ The Commissioners' decision was upheld by both the High Court and the Court of Appeal, and it is clear, therefore, that the principle applied by the Commissioners will stand: United Kingdom residence status, once acquired, will endure in succeeding years unless there is some change in a person's manner of life of such significance as to throw the question of his residence status into doubt.

---

1 See **2.13** above.
2 *Levene v IRC* (1928) 13 TC 486.
3 Ibid, at 501.
4 (1957) 37 TC 493.
5 Ibid, at 495.

Connecting factors

2.15 The ties of birth

Clearly, the less conclusive are the elements of duration, frequency and regularity of presence where a person's residence status has been called into question, the more important will be the other elements that may, in any particular case, be indicative of that status. One element which obviously carried some weight with the Lord President in the case of *Reid v IRC*¹ was the tie of nationality. Miss Reid, he said 'is a British subject',² and the suggestion would seem to be that the link thus subsisting between Miss Reid and the United Kingdom must necessarily have tinged her periods of presence here with the hue of residence – though the tie of nationality can never alone do more than that. It will be explained later that, because of the operation of TA 1988 s 334, a British subject whose ordinary residence has been in the United Kingdom will find it more difficult than a foreign national to divest himself of United Kingdom residence status³ and, the rationale behind that section – that a British subject may be supposed to wish to cultivate and preserve, rather than sever, his links with the United Kingdom – has a place in the approach to questions of residence even where TA 1988 s 334 is of no direct application. Viscount Cave recognised this in the *Levene* case when he said:

The most difficult case is that of a wanderer who, having no home in any country, spends a part only of his time in hotels in the United Kingdom and the remaining and greater part of his time in hotels abroad . . . If . . . such a man is a foreigner who has never resided in this country, there may be great difficulty in holding that he is resident here. But if he is a British subject the Commissioners are entitled to take into account all the facts of the case.[4]

The link of nationality[5] is, then, of greater importance than it is often acknowledged to be for, if a person is found to be joined to the United Kingdom by that link, the Commissioners have not only the right but also the duty to look much more closely at the circumstances surrounding that person's presence here than would otherwise be the case. A practical example of the difference in approach is given by the *Zorab* case which is described at **4.03** below. Mr Zorab had been born in India and had spent all his life there until his retirement from the Indian civil service. Upon his retirement, however, he began to spend almost half of each year in the United Kingdom, yet, despite the duration and regularity of his visits, the Commissioners found that he was not resident here. His nationality was a decisive factor. 'This gentleman,' said Rowlatt J, 'is a native of India'.[6]

---

1 (1926) 10 TC 673.
2 Ibid, at 679. For the meaning of 'British subject' see **1.11** above.
3 See **4.13** ff below.
4 *Levene v IRC* (1928) 13 TC 486 at 506.
5 See **1.11** above for the meaning of nationality.
6 *IRC v Zorab* (1926) 11 TC 289 at 292.

2.16   The ties of family

As well as being a British subject, Miss Reid[1] had a sister who lived in London. Viewed in isolation, that fact may not seem of particular significance but it was one of the elements listed by Lord Clyde as contributing to the finding that she was resident in the United Kingdom. 'Her family ties', he said, 'are with this country'.[2]

So it was, too, with Mr Levene and his wife:

> They . . . came to visit their relatives in England, and (on one occasion) to make arrangements for the care of a brother of [Mr Levene] who is mentally afflicted [and] to visit the graves of his parents.[3]

> His family ties are in this country, his wife having five sisters and he himself six brothers and sisters residing here.[4]

In the *Levene* case, Lord Hanworth MR had said in the Court of Appeal that an important characteristic factor to look for in determining whether or not a man possesses the quality of residence is 'if he returns to and seeks his own fatherland in order to enjoy a sojourn in proximity to his relations and friends',[5] and this characteristic was very much in evidence in the *Kinloch* case referred to at **2.11** above. Mrs Kinloch was a British subject and a widow who had lived in India from 1909 to 1919. From 1919 onwards she made frequent and regular visits to the United Kingdom in each tax year but her presence here throughout was coloured by the fact that her son was attending boarding schools in England and that:

her various objects in coming to the United Kingdom were to take her son to and from school, to attend to his outfitting, to consult with his doctor, dentist and oculist, to interview those having charge of him, to be with him during illness and to attend his confirmation.[6]

Although, as has been noted,[7] the decisive factor in the Commissioners' decision that Mrs Kinloch was resident in the United Kingdom was the frequency and regularity of Mrs Kinloch's visits here, her family ties with this country were undoubtedly of weight and had a bearing on their determination for here was a lady:

> who spends a good deal of her time in this country but without any settled home, living in hotels here and abroad, but having a reason for coming here, because she has a son who is being educated here and who is sometimes ill, and so on.[8]

---

1 *Reid v IRC* (1926) 10 TC 673.
2 Ibid, at 679.
3 *Levene v IRC* (1928) 13 TC 486 at 504, per Viscount Cave LC.
4 Ibid at 508, per Lord Warrington of Clyffe.
5 Ibid, at 497.
6 *Kinloch v IRC* (1929) 14 TC 736 at 738.
7 At **2.11** above.
8 *Kinloch v IRC* (1929) 14 TC 736 at 739, per Rowlatt J.

2.17 The ties of business

Another factor which, in the *Reid* case,[1] Lord Clyde singled out as being relevant to the finding that the lady in question possessed United Kingdom residence status was that 'her business matters (including her banking) are conducted here'.[2] That tie was of particular importance in the case of Mr Lysaght. It has already been explained[3] that the element of frequency and regularity in Mr Lysaght's visits to the United Kingdom was thought by the House of Lords to be barely sufficient to justify the finding of residence returned by the Commissioners. This feeling was present in each of the lower courts, too, and it seems clear that it was only the strong business link between Mr Lysaght and the United Kingdom which, in the view of Lawrence LJ, added a support which would enable the Commissioners' decision to stand:

> The case is near the line but in my opinion the determining factor is that the post which [Mr Lysaght] holds in John Lysaght Ltd causes him to come regularly to England and to stay in the United Kingdom for a substantial period in each year. The fact that [Mr Lysaght] stays regularly in England for about three months of the year for the discharge of his duties as the servant of an English company in my opinion constitutes him a person who is . . . resident . . . in the United Kingdom.[4]

Mr Levene, too, had ties of business which contributed to the finding that he was resident in the United Kingdom.

> He had gone out of business in England and had broken up his establishment, but he still had in England business interests connected with his Income Tax assessments.[5]

Included in ties of business may be ties of communication. People wishing to get in touch with Miss Reid did so 'c/o Commercial Bank, Glasgow', thus 'the address by which she can be found at any time is in this country'[6] and this factor too was added to the list of those which weighed in favour of Miss Reid's residence in the United Kingdom.

The insertion of a United Kingdom address for Captain Loewenstein[7] in the annual return of The Belgian Breeding Stock Farm Company Ltd weighed against his assertion that he was not resident in the United Kingdom:

> At any rate this gentleman's return to the Registrar of Joint Stock Companies shows him as a Director and having his usual residence at 'Pinfold'. Now it is said that this was only done for convenience . . . The Commissioners say they do not accept that view, and they certainly are entitled to say that, and I am bound by it.[8]

---

1 *Reid v IRC* (1926) 10 TC 673.
2 Ibid, at 679.
3 At **2.12** above.
4 *Lysaght v IRC* (1928) 13 TC 511 at 525.
5 *Levene v IRC* (1928) 13 TC 486 at 500, per Viscount Sumner.
6 *Reid v IRC* (1926) 10 TC 673 at 679, per the Lord President.
7 *Loewenstein v De Salis* (1926) 10 TC 424. See **2.09** above.
8 Ibid, at 436, per Rowlatt J.

2.18 Other ties

In the *Reid* case,[1] the Commissioners noted that, when the house in Glasgow in which Miss Reid had once lived was given up, Miss Reid 'sent three trunks with clothes, jewellery, and a few other personal effects to a store in London and has since, on one or two occasions, been to the store to fetch or put back various articles',[2] and this fact, that 'her personal belongings not required when she is travelling are kept in store in London',[3] duly weighed against her when the question of her residence status was decided.

The ties of religious observance also may weigh against a person's claim to be non-resident. Mr Levene was a member of the English community of Jews and, on occasions, he visited the United Kingdom 'to take part in certain Jewish religious observances'.[4] This, accordingly, became a factor in the determination of his residence status.

Membership of clubs and societies in the United Kingdom will also be a factor of importance.[5] Continued membership will indicate an intention to return and will weigh against any claim that ties with the United Kingdom have been broken.

The list of possible links with the United Kingdom which may so colour a person's presence here as to transform it into residence is inexhaustible. All such links will be of importance, however, should it ever become necessary for the question of a person's residence status to be determined.

---

1 *Reid v IRC* (1926) 10 TC 673.
2 Ibid, at 676.
3 Ibid, at 679, per the Lord President.
4 *Levene v IRC* (1928) 13 TC 486 at 509, per Lord Warrington of Clyffe.

5 See paras 2(6) and 2(m) respectively of the cases stated by the Commissioners in *Lysaght v IRC* (1928) 13 TC 511 at 514 and *Withers v Wynyard* (1938) 21 TC 724 at 727.

Intent and legality

2.19 Involuntary or unintentional presence

While positive intentions may contribute to the transformation of presence into residence, negative intentions will not prevent such a transformation taking place if other indicia would lead to the conclusion that a person is resident in the United Kingdom.

In *Bayard Brown v Burt*,[1] Mr Brown, who had lived on an ocean-going yacht in United Kingdom territorial waters for the last twenty years, contended that 'it was the intention to go to sea at any moment, and the ship could be steamed out of port at an hour's notice',[2] but he was nonetheless held to be resident in the United Kingdom.

In *Lysaght v IRC*[3] it was shown that Mr Lysaght visited the United Kingdom only in fulfilment of his business obligations and not from personal choice. Lord Buckmaster held, however, that this was no bar to residence:

> A man might well be compelled to reside here completely against his will; the exigencies of business often forbid the choice of residence and though a man may make his home elsewhere and stay in this country only because business compels him, yet none the less, if the periods for which and the conditions under which he stays are such that they may be regarded as constituting residence, it is open to the Commissioners to find that in fact he does so reside.[4]

During the years for which his residence status was in question, Stanley Miesegaes was a schoolboy boarding at Harrow. His counsel argued that a stay at a boarding school could not constitute residence because 'it is not voluntary residence; and it is institutional. If one asked a schoolboy . . . where he lived, he would never say that he lived at his public school'.[5] Pearce LJ could not accept that argument, however:

> Lord Buckmaster's remarks [in the *Lysaght* case] as to the exigencies of business seem equally applicable to the exigencies of education. Education is a large, necessary and normal ingredient in the lives of adolescent members of the community, just as work or business is in the lives of its adult members . . . In this case the school terms at Harrow dictated the main residential pattern of the boy's life . . . It would be erroneous to endow educational residence with some esoteric quality that must as a matter of law, remove it from the category of residence.[6]

It was neither business nor education that constrained Lord Inchiquin to stay in the United Kingdom for most of 1940–41 and 1941–42: 'The only reason he was there was because his military duties kept him there.'[7] He had, furthermore, before the outbreak of the Second World War, formed the intention of returning to Dromoland Castle, his ancestral home in Eire, and had carried out that intention as soon as he managed to obtain indefinite release from active service. None of this was, however, of the least effect:

I am quite unable to say that where you find a man has at all times before the war been resident in this country and you find him continuing to serve in this country in His Majesty's Forces during the war, the mere fact that he had, before the outbreak of war, formed the intention of going to live elsewhere makes it impossible to say, as the Commissioners have found, that he was resident in this country during the period of his military service.[8]

In *Re Mackenzie*[9] it was held that an Australian lady who, four months after arriving in England in 1885, was certified to be insane and detained in an asylum for the 54 years ending with her death in 1939, was resident in the United Kingdom for each of those years:

Her residence in England became permanent, no doubt, by reason of her mental condition and the fact that she required care and attention, but I think it may fairly be said that, in the ordinary course of her life as events happened, she resided in England.[10]

The same would, it seems, be true of a person undergoing imprisonment in the United Kingdom. In *Todd v The Egyptian Delta Land and Investment Co Ltd*,[11] Viscount Sumner said:

A man may change his residence at will, except that a certain duration of time or fixity of decision is requisite, and, but for the peculiar cases of a convict in gaol or a lunatic lawfully detained in a madhouse, I do not think that residence is ever determined for a natural person simply by law.[12]

The rationale behind all the decisions referred to above is very simply put. Residence depends upon the fact of residing not (except in the context of TA 1988 s 336)[13] upon the intent or wish to reside. Just as a man is none the less present for not wanting to be where he is, so he cannot be the less resident for not wishing to be where he resides. It must be noted, however, that this does not hold true in questions of ordinary residence. There, as explained in chapter 3, the voluntary adoption of an abode in a particular place or country is essential.

---

1 (1911) 5 TC 667.
2 Ibid, at 672.
3 (1928) 13 TC 511.
4 Ibid, at 534.
5 *Miesegaes v IRC* (1957) 37 TC 493 at 500, per Pearce LJ.
6 Ibid, at 501.
7 *Inchiquin v IRC* (1948) 31 TC 125 at 130, per Singleton J.
8 Ibid, at 134 and 135.
9 (1940) 19 ATC 399.
10 Ibid, at 404, per Morton J.
11 (1928) 14 TC 119.
12 Ibid, at 140.
13 See **4.04** below.

2.20 Unlawful presence

If, as has been demonstrated at **2.19** above, residence is not necessarily a matter of volition, neither is it necessarily a matter of lawful presence. Mr Bayard Brown[1] had no right to anchor his yacht in the tidal waters off Brightlingsea but that did not alter the fact that he was residing there:

> Residence is something which depends upon the fact of residing and not upon the legal right to reside.[2]

Under the Immigration Act 1971 s 33(2) a person is not to be treated as ordinarily resident in the United Kingdom for the purposes of that Act 'at a time when he is there in breach of the immigration laws' but the Taxes Acts contain no such strictures. Thus, in *Re Abdul Manan*,[3] Lord Denning could comment that, although the deserting seaman with whom that case was concerned was not ordinarily resident in the United Kingdom within the context of the Commonwealth Immigration Acts, 'if this were an Income Tax case he would, I expect, be held to be ordinarily resident here'.[4] Although being ordinarily resident is not the same as being resident, the difference is not one which would alter the substance of Lord Denning's remark.

The question of the effect of unlawful or illegal presence on residence status was fully explored by Sir John Donaldson MR in the case of *Hipperson v Electoral Registration Officer for the District of Newbury*.[5] The case concerned the right of ladies living in tents and vehicles on Greenham Common in the furtherance of their protest against the presence of cruise missiles to be placed on the electoral register of the District of Newbury. Under the Representation of the People Act 1983 s 1(1), such a right rests on a person being 'resident' in the relevant district on a specified date, and it was contended that the Greenham ladies could not be resident in the District of Newbury as they were present there in breach of the byelaws and of the Highways Act 1980 s 137. In rejecting this submission, Sir John Donaldson MR pointed out that:

> the consequences of holding that . . . residence must not involve the commission of a criminal offence and, a fortiori, that the residence must be lawful in the sense of not involving a breach of the civil rights of others are startling in the extreme. A whole range of citizens would be disqualified. The county court judge gave, as an example, the occupation as a living room or workroom of a room which is immediately over a cesspool, midden or ashpit contrary to s 49 of the Public Health Act 1936. He could also have referred to breach of conditions relating to the use of caravans under s 269 of the same Act, to the continued occupation of premises to which a closing order has been applied under the Housing Acts, to the use of premises for residential purposes in breach of an enforcement notice under the Town and Country Planning Acts and to adverse possession of residential premises contrary to s 7 of the Criminal Law Act 1977. If the scope of the disqualification is to be extended from the illegal to the unlawful, all those who remain in occupation of residential premises when a possession order has been made would be disqualified.[6]

The Master of the Rolls concluded his rejection of the submission by declaring that 'residence . . . does not depend on law for its existence'.[7]

1 See **4.06** below.
2 *Bayard Brown v Burt* (1911) 5 TC 667 at 672, per Kennedy LJ.
3 [1971] 2 All ER 1016.
4 Ibid, at 1018.
5 [1985] 2 All ER 456.
6 Ibid, at 463.
7 Ibid.

Fiscal residence

2.21 Double tax treaties

Before drawing this chapter to a close, it must be pointed out that there are circumstances in which a person who is found to possess the quality of residence as described in this chapter will, irrespective of his possession of such status, fall to be treated as non-resident for the purpose of determining his liability (if any) to tax on certain of his income, profits or gains. Such circumstances may arise where the United Kingdom has entered into a double taxation treaty with a foreign state and the person concerned has either strong personal ties with that state or his income, profits or gains have their source there, or both.

The United Kingdom has entered into a considerable number of such treaties and each has as its objective the prevention of, or relief from, double taxation, ie the taxation of the same income and gains by both the United Kingdom and the foreign state concerned.[1] A double taxation treaty generally protects a person against double taxation by providing that income arising in one state is not to be charged to tax in the hands of a resident of the other state, or affords him relief by providing that, where he is charged to tax on income accruing to him in the source state, he is to be given a credit for that tax in the state of which he is resident.

Clearly, however, such provisions will be incapable of application if a person is regarded as resident by each of the states concerned, and an article in most treaties does, therefore, provide rules for determining which residence status of the two is to prevail for the purposes of the treaty. That article is, as might be expected, to be of no application if, when a person's status has been determined under the municipal law of each state,[2] he is found to possess residence status[3] in one only of the two states concerned.

Not all treaties contain identical provisions concerning the determination of residence status, but most follow the 1977 Draft Double Taxation Convention on Income and Capital published by the Organisation for Economic Co-operation and Development, Paris as amended by the 1992 Model Convention which was itself amended in March 1994. Article 4(2) of each draft convention states that, where an individual is regarded as a resident of both contracting states, then his status is to be determined by applying in sequence four rules.

The first of these is that:

> he shall be deemed to be a resident of the State in which he has a permanent home available to him.

According to the OECD commentary to the 1977 Draft Convention 'any form of home may be taken into account (house or apartment belonging to or rented by the individual, rented furnished room)' and, if that is to be so, 'home', in the context of article 4(2) (a), may be taken to be synonymous with 'place of abode' as described at **2.07** to **2.09** above.[4] 'Permanent', according to the commentary, means that 'the individual must have arranged and retained [the home] for his permanent use as opposed to staying at a particular place under such conditions that it is evident that the stay is intended to be of short duration'. In other words, 'permanent' is being used as the opposite of 'temporary', rather than in the sense of 'for ever more'. Finally, there are the words 'available to him'. The OECD commentary to the 1977 Draft Convention adds to these words 'at all times continuously', and thus rules out the possibility that a house etc which is let between visits might be a 'permanent home' for fiscal residence purposes.

If a person has a permanent home in both states (but not if he has a permanent home in neither), article 4(1) (a) of both the 1977 Draft Convention and the 1992 Model Convention as amended lays down the second rule, namely:

he shall be deemed to be a resident of the State with which his personal and economic relations are closer (centre of vital interests).

The reason for the addition of the words in parentheses is by no means clear, but they are helpful in that they constitute a criterion identical with that by which the Swiss courts determine the canton of residence for tax purposes. As applied in Swiss domestic law, the rule requires that personal interests prevail over economic interests. Thus, if a person has two permanent homes, one in London where he lives with his family and one in Paris where he works, his centre of vital interests will, on the basis of Swiss jurisprudence, be regarded as his home in London, and the outcome will be the same even if the man is unmarried but has a social life which principally involves around his London home. The OECD commentary to the 1977 Draft Convention confirms this by stating that:

regard will be had to his family and social relations, his occupations, his political, cultural or other activities, his place of business, the place from which he administers his property etc . . . but . . . considerations based on the personal acts of the individual must receive special attention.

If a person's vital interests have no centre but are divided between the two states concerned, or if the person concerned has no permanent home, a third rule is to be applied. Under article 4(2)(b) of both the 1977 Draft Convention and the 1992 Model Convention (as amended), the person is to be regarded as resident in the state 'in which he has an habitual abode'. The OECD commentary to the 1977 Draft Convention does not amplify this expression, but the French version of the text is '*où elle séjourne de façon habituelle*', which indicates that what is being referred to is the state in which a person habitually *stays*. The stay may be, for example, as a guest in someone's home, in hotels, or in a caravan, but, because of the insertion of the word 'habitual', this test will, it is suggested, require the examination of a person's life-style over a substantial period of time; years rather than months.

Where, even after the application of these tests, the question of a person's residence remains unresolved, a fourth rule is to come into effect. Article 4(2)(c) of each convention states that the person's nationality is to be the deciding factor. If the person is a national of both states or of neither of them, however, article 4(2)(d) of both conventions provides that 'the competent authorities of the contracting states shall settle the question by mutual agreement'.

1 Such treaties are made under the authority of TA 1988 s 788.
2 This approach is required by the terms of art 3(2) of both the 1977 Draft Convention and the 1992 Model Convention (as amended).
3 'Resident' for this purpose means 'liable to tax . . . by reason of his domicile, residence, place of management or any other criterion of a similar nature' (OECD 1977 Draft Convention and the 1992 Model Convention (as amended), art 4(1)).
4 It is interesting to note that, in *R v Hammond* (1852) 17 QB 772, Lord Campbell CJ said (at 780 and 781) that 'a man's residence, where he lives with his family and sleeps at night, is always his place of abode in the full sense of that expression'.

Conclusion

2.22 Summary

'Residence' is a term which is undefined in the Taxes Acts but which indicates a quality of the person; a person's possession or otherwise of United Kingdom residence status is a question of fact to be decided, if necessary, by the Commissioners, and, unless the conclusion which the Commissioners reach is one that no reasonable person properly instructed as to the law could have reached on the basis of the evidence offered, the courts are powerless to reject the Commissioners' finding.

Once acquired, United Kingdom residence status endures for the whole of a tax year.

Residence, as a quality of the person, signifies a degree of territorial allegiance. Accordingly, the first test of residence is to ascertain whether or not a person has accommodation available to him in the United Kingdom and, if he has, whether or not he has occupied that accommodation during the tax year. Occupation of any length will be conclusive of residence status.

Where a person has no accommodation available to him in the United Kingdom, the duration of his presence here during the tax year must next be considered. If that presence is sufficiently significant to establish a territorial link, the attribution of residence status will ensue. Inland Revenue practice is to regard presence of 183 days in total as being sufficient to establish that link. The 183-day rule is discussed in Chapter 4.

If neither of these tests establishes a person as being resident in the United Kingdom, a broader consideration of the person's circumstances and life-style is undertaken. The pattern of his visits in years prior to, and subsequent to, the year in question is examined and the duration of such visits is noted. If the person is found to have made visits to the United Kingdom which have averaged 91 days or more a year over a period of four or more consecutive years, it is Inland Revenue practice to regard him as having acquired United Kingdom residence status.

Should none of these tests prove conclusive, the strength of other links which connect a person with the United Kingdom will be examined. These will include ties of birth, ties of family, and ties of business. If such ties are sufficiently strong and the person has made visits to the United Kingdom, a finding that the person is resident in the United Kingdom may ensue. The fact that a person may have had no intention or wish to become resident in the United Kingdom, or that his presence here might have been unlawful, will have no bearing on the determination of his residence status. Fiscal residence is a concept which relates to double taxation and is determined by the tests set out in the OECD draft model Double Taxation Convention.

CHAPTER 3

Ordinary residence

'Sark.'
'Yes, sir,' said the man in the little quayside hut. 'A return fare. Six shillings.'
'A single, my friend,' said Mr Harold Pye.

Mervyn Peake *Mr Pye* ch 1

3.01 Introduction

It has been noted at **1.12** above that residence *simpliciter* was adopted by Parliament as a determinant of chargeability because it is an attribute more difficult to acquire and less easy to shed than the attribute of mere presence. Ordinary residence may be seen as Parliament's attempt to carry that same principle one stage further, for ordinary residence is 'a more elusive concept than simple residence. It can also be more adhesive, in that a person can remain ordinarily resident even though physically absent from the country throughout the year (and, accordingly, not resident)'.[1] Ordinary residence is, in fact,

a point on a scale which ranges from mere presence in this country through 'resident' . . . to 'domicile' which is widely used to specify the nature and quality of the association between person and place which brings the person within the scope of that particular enactment.[2]

In the context of the Taxes Acts, the term 'ordinarily resident', like the term 'resident', has 'no . . . technical or special meaning'[3] and must, therefore, be given its natural and ordinary meaning.[4] The courts have, however, found some difficulty in deciding not only what that natural meaning might be but also how ordinary residence differs from residence *simpliciter* – though the fact that there is a difference between the two terms is evident from the legislation itself.

By virtue of TA 1988 ss 18(1), 18(3) and 65, for example, tax is to be charged under Schedule D, Cases IV and V, in respect of income arising from securities and possessions out of the United Kingdom to 'any person residing in the United Kingdom' unless such a person 'satisfies the Board that he is not domiciled in the United Kingdom, or that, being a Commonwealth citizen or a citizen of the Republic of Ireland, he is not ordinarily resident in the United Kingdom', in which case he is to be charged to tax only on sums received in the United Kingdom. In other words, a person who is resident but not ordinarily resident in the United

Kingdom benefits by being taxed on his income from overseas securities and possessions on a 'remittance' basis rather than on an 'arising' basis.

It is apparent from this example that, in the mind of Parliament, ordinary residence is a more enduring personal attribute than residence *simpliciter*, and TCGA 1992 s 2(1) illustrates the way in which Parliament has sought to exploit its durability in the prevention of tax avoidance:

> Subject to any exceptions provided by this Act, a person shall be chargeable to capital gains tax in respect of chargeable gains accruing to him in a year of assessment during any part of which he is resident in the United Kingdom, or during which he is ordinarily resident in the United Kingdom.

In other words, a person who succeeds in divesting himself of the quality of residence *simpliciter* (by, perhaps, staying out of the United Kingdom for an entire tax year) will, if he remains ordinarily resident here, remain within the charge to capital gains tax on any disposals made during that year.

Because 'ordinary residence' is a term which is undefined by statute, the question whether or not a person possesses the attribute which that term signifies is a question not of law but of fact. The discussion at **2.03** above concerning the determination of questions of fact is, therefore, of equal relevance whether residence *simpliciter* or ordinary residence is the attribute in question.

---

1 Inland Revenue explanatory note relating to a proposed amendment to Finance Bill 1974, cl 18.
2 *R v Barnet London Borough, ex p Shah* [1980] 3 All ER 679 at 681, per Ormrod J.
3 *Levene v IRC* (1928) 13 TC 486 at 507, per Lord Warrington of Clyffe.
4 See **2.02** above.

Concept and application

3.02 The meaning of ordinary residence

Although the question whether a person is 'ordinarily residing in the United Kingdom' is a question of fact, the meaning of those words is a matter of statutory interpretation and thus a matter of law. As such, the words were given careful consideration by the Court of Session in 1926 and by the House of Lords in two leading tax cases decided in 1928. In each case the court made it clear that it was construing the words as bearing their natural and ordinary meaning.

In the case of *Reid v IRC*[1] Lord Clyde LP firmly rejected Miss Reid's argument that, even if she was resident in the United Kingdom by reason of her visits and the various ties which bound her to this country, she could not be ordinarily resident since she had always spent the greater part of each year abroad:

> The argument was that the meaning of the word 'ordinarily' is governed – wholly or mainly – by the test of time or duration. I think it is a test, and an important one; but I think it is only one among many. From the point of view of time, 'ordinarily' would stand in contrast to 'casually'. But [Miss Reid] is not a 'casual' visitor to her home country; on the contrary she regularly returns to it, and 'resides' in it for a part – albeit the smaller part – of every year. I hesitate to give the word 'ordinarily' any more precise interpretation

than 'in the customary course of events', and anyhow I cannot think that the element of time so predominates in its meaning that, unless [Miss Reid] 'resided' in the United Kingdom for at least six months and a day, she could not be said 'ordinarily' to reside there in the year in question.[2]

This point was taken up in the case of *Levene v IRC*[3] by Rowlatt J who said:

'Ordinarily' may mean either preponderatingly in point of time or time plus importance, or it may mean habitually as a matter of course, as one might say: in the ordinary course of a man's life, although in time it might be insignificant . . . I think that 'ordinary' does not mean preponderatingly, I think it means ordinary in the sense that it is habitual in the ordinary course of a man's life, and I think a man is ordinarily resident in the United Kingdom when the ordinary course of his life is such that it discloses a residence in the United Kingdom . . . .[4]

In the House of Lords, Lord Warrington of Clyffe affirmed this view, saying of ordinary residence that it is:

impossible to restrict its connotation to its duration. A member of this House may well be said to be ordinarily resident in London during the Parliamentary session and in the country during the recess. If it has any definite meaning I should say it means according to the way in which a man's life is usually ordered.[5]

In that same case, the Lord Chancellor, Viscount Cave, said:

The expression 'ordinary residence' . . . is contrasted with . . . occasional or temporary residence; and I think it connotes residence in a place with some degree of continuity and apart from accidental or temporary absences. So understood, the expression differs little in meaning from the word 'residence' . . .,[6]

and in *Lysaght v IRC*[7] Viscount Sumner said:

I think the converse to 'ordinarily' is 'extraordinarily', and that part of the regular order of a man's life, adopted voluntarily and for settled purposes, is not 'extraordinary'.[8]

In 1981, the words 'ordinarily resident' again fell to be construed by the courts and, in *R v Barnet London Borough, ex p Shah*,[9] Lord Denning MR said:

The words 'ordinarily resident' mean that the person must be habitually and normally resident here, apart from temporary or occasional absences of long or short duration.[10]

---

1 (1926) 10 TC 673.
2 Ibid, at 680.
3 (1928) 13 TC 486.
4 Ibid, at 493.
5 Ibid, at 509.
6 Ibid, at 507.
7 (1928) 13 TC 511.
8 Ibid, at 528.
9 [1982] 1 All ER 698.
10 Ibid, at 704.

3.03 The relation of residence to ordinary residence

Lord Denning's interpretation of the words 'ordinarily resident'[1] expands Viscount Cave's phrase 'with some degree of continuity' into 'habitually and normally' and takes ordinary residence to be residence *simpliciter* which is customary, usual and confirmed by habit. Thus Miss Reid was ordinarily resident because the residence status she attracted to herself by reason of the regularity of her visits to the United Kingdom[2] and her various links with this country[3] was confirmed by habit as being residence of a customary and usual kind rather than residence which was exceptional, unusual or accidental.

Although Miss Reid undoubtedly had engaged in a great deal of wandering – one month in France, next month in Spain, the month after in Austria, the month after that in Portugal – the Commissioners decided no: Miss Reid every year, without fail (though only for some three and a half months) returned to the United Kingdom and it was this factor which added the quality of ordinariness to her residence *simpliciter*.

It should be noted, however, that had the regularity of Miss Reid's visits to the United Kingdom and her links with this country not, in the opinion of the Commissioners, been sufficient to imbue her with the quality of United Kingdom residence *simpliciter*, she could not, within either Viscount Sumner's, Viscount Cave's or Lord Denning's understanding of the term, have been attributed with the quality of being ordinarily resident during the years in question. In law, ordinary residence springs from residence *simpliciter*, and if residence *simpliciter* is never acquired then ordinary residence cannot be acquired either. Viscount Cave said:

> I find it difficult to imagine a case in which a man while not resident here is yet ordinarily resident here.[4]

As is explained below, such a case *could* have arisen under the law as it stood in Viscount Cave's day, and can certainly arise under the law as it stands today; but this does not invalidate the linking of ordinary residence with residence *simpliciter* in the manner described. In the *Miesegaes* case,[5] the Special Commissioners considered that they had:

> first [to] decide whether [Mr Miesegaes] was resident in the United Kingdom in each of the years in question, and, second, if he was so resident, whether his residence had the quality of ordinary residence,[6]

and Morris LJ commented:

> It seems to me that the Special Commissioners were correct in their approach when they decided that first they should consider whether [Mr Miesegaes] was resident in the United Kingdom in each of the years in question and, in the second place, whether his residence had the quality of ordinary residence.[7]

This approach will still be helpful provided it is borne in mind that, where it leads to the conclusion that a person is not resident *simpliciter*, the additional question, 'But is he not resident *simpliciter* merely by reason of a temporary absence extending over the entire tax year or by reason of the special rules concerning persons working abroad full-time in a trade, profession or vocation?'[8] Except in the case of a person who goes abroad for a period of full-time service under a contract of service,[9] neither of these circumstances will result in the loss of ordinary residence status if that status was possessed immediately prior to the departure which led to the loss of resident *simpliciter* status.

Statutory recognition is given to the fact that a person may be ordinarily resident in the United Kingdom without being resident *simpliciter* here by TCGA 1992 s 2(1) which provides that, subject to certain exceptions:

> a person shall be chargeable to capital gains tax in respect of chargeable gains accruing to him in a year of assessment during any part of which he is resident in the United Kingdom, or during which he is ordinarily resident in the United Kingdom.

It is important to note that, although (subject to what has been said in the preceding paragraphs) a person cannot be ordinarily resident in the United Kingdom unless he is also resident *simpliciter* here, a person may, in certain circumstances (and contrary to all current Revenue guidance)[10], be resident *simpliciter* in the United Kingdom, year after year, without being ordinarily resident here. Those circumstances will subsist where a person's residence *simpliciter* lacks one or more of the elements emphasised by Lord Scarman when he said:

> I unhesitatingly subscribe to the view that 'ordinarily resident' refers to a man's abode in a particular place or country which he has adopted voluntarily and for settled purposes as part of the regular order of his life for the time being, whether of short or long duration.[11]

It is to these three key features of voluntary adoption, settled purpose and the regular order of life – none of which is essential to the acquisition of residence *simpliciter* status but all of which are essential to the acquisition of ordinary residence status – that we must now turn our attention.

---

1 See **3.02** above.
2 See **3.02** above.
3 See **2.15–2.18** above.
4 *Levene v IRC* (1928) 13 TC 486 at 507.
5 *Miesegaes v IRC* (1957) 37 TC 493.
6 Ibid, at 495.
7 Ibid, at 502.
8 See **4.13–4.17** below.
9 See **4.17** below.
10 See **3.07–3.11** below.
11 *Shah v Barnet London Borough Council* [1983] 1 All ER 226 at 235.

Essential elements

3.04 A voluntarily adopted place of abode

It is clear from the facts of the case in which Viscount Sumner gave his interpretation of the words 'ordinarily residing' that he cannot have used the words 'adopted voluntarily' in the sense of 'free of any kind of external constraint' for Mr Lysaght was in Great Britain only because his business commitments compelled him to be here. He would, no doubt, have preferred to be at home in Ireland rather than in the Spa Hotel in Bath, but in choosing to be a director of John Lysaght Ltd he had accepted that he would have to spend one week or so of each month in the United Kingdom. The phrase 'adopted voluntarily' must, therefore, have been understood by Viscount Sumner as being not inconsistent with submission to such constraints as a person's chosen order of life imposed upon him.

On the face of it, however, the first case which came before the courts following the *Lysaght* case and which centred on the phrase 'adopted voluntarily' took the meaning of those words some way beyond that. It concerned Miss Mackenzie, an Australian, who, at the age of 28, came on a visit to England with her mother. There was no evidence as to how long the visit was intended to last but, in the event, Miss Mackenzie, having stayed here four months, remained here until her death at the age of 82 because, after spending those four months here, she was, in 1885, certified as insane and detained, first in Holloway Mental Hospital until 1893, then in the Coppice Lunatic Hospital at Nottingham until her death. The case was an estate duty case which arose because of a disagreement over the meaning of the words 'ordinarily resident' in F(No 2)A 1915 s 47(1), and counsel for the administrator of Miss Mackenzie's estate submitted that:

> Miss Mackenzie could not be said to be ordinarily resident in September, 1885, when she was certified as of unsound mind, and that during the whole of the rest of her life she was under constraint and unable to exercise any will of her own, and that that period, the last 54 years of her life, cannot be taken into account at all as making her ordinarily resident in this country . . . [T]he words of Viscount Sumner 'adopted voluntarily' indicate that no residence can be treated as ordinary residence unless it is the result of a voluntary act on the part of the person residing there.[1]

Morton J could not agree:

> The matter does not wholly depend on choice . . . I do not understand Viscount Sumner . . . as saying that a period of residence in this country which is involuntary must be wholly disregarded for the purpose of ascertaining whether or not a person is ordinarily resident, and it must not be left out of account that Miss Mackenzie came to this country, one presumes, voluntarily at the age of 28, and, as a result of the circumstances . . . described, never left it.[2]

Morton J then went on to comment on some hypothetical case submitted by counsel for the administrator of Miss Mackenzie's estate:

> They put the case of a prisoner of war who has come to this country and been detained here, it might be, for a year. They say that he would not be ordinarily resident, because the

element of constraint is present. They take again the case of a foreigner with a home abroad, who comes to this country on a visit and commits some crime or offence against the laws of this country, and is imprisoned for a considerable time, and ultimately dies in this country. There, they say, he would not be held to be ordinarily resident . . . [S]uch cases must be dealt with on their particular facts, if and when they arise, but I can well imagine, in the case of a prisoner of war, that, if a man had a permanent residence in Germany and came over here in an aeroplane to attack this country, and was captured and kept here for a considerable period, it might well be held that his ordinary residence was his home in Germany.[3]

Comparing Morton J's judgment as regards Miss Mackenzie and his views on the hypothetical case of the German prisoner of war, it is clear that it was in Miss Mackenzie's initial voluntary entry to the United Kingdom for an indefinite period that he found a justification for holding her to have been ordinarily resident here throughout all the years which followed. What he seems to have been saying is that the words are 'voluntarily adopted' not 'voluntarily continued and pursued'. If the beginning is a voluntary matter it is of no consequence that the continuance is enforced. Thus the hypothetical German could not be ordinarily resident in the United Kingdom since his initial entry to this country would not be a matter of free will but of military orders emanating from those in command over him. Indeed, during the 1939–45 war, members of the allied forces who became resident in the United Kingdom were generally treated by the Inland Revenue as not ordinarily resident and so, too, were refugees and displaced persons.

This understanding of Viscount Sumner's words seems perfectly reasonable and the implicit rephrasing of 'adopted voluntarily' as 'adopted (but not necessarily continued) voluntarily' does them no violence.

It has been suggested, however, that in *Shah v Barnet London Borough Council*[4] Lord Scarman rejected this approach and, despite his explicit acceptance of the authority of Viscount Sumner's dictum,[5] so qualified Viscount Sumner's words as to rob them of any meaning. What Lord Scarman said was this:

> The residence must be voluntarily adopted. Enforced presence by reason of kidnapping or imprisonment, or a Robinson Crusoe existence on a desert island with no opportunity of escape, may be so overwhelming a factor as to negative the will to be where one is.[6]

The relation of the second sentence to the first in this quotation is by no means clear, but if, as one writer has suggested,[7] it is to be taken as meaning that:

> to be ordinarily resident an individual must have adopted his residence voluntarily, except for extreme cases such as imprisonment or a desert island existence with no opportunity to escape where the imposed circumstances will override the individual's intention,

then 'adopted (but not necessarily continued) voluntarily' has become 'adopted voluntarily or involuntarily', which is a quite different matter. It must surely be, however, that the writer of those words is misunderstanding the force of Lord Scarman's dictum. His way of reading Lord Scarman's remarks implies the insertion of an additional and somewhat nonsensical clause at the end of the first sentence quoted so that the passage reads as follows:

The residence must be voluntarily adopted [except where it is *in*voluntarily adopted]. Enforced presence by reason of kidnapping or imprisonment, or a Robinson Crusoe existence on a desert island with no opportunity of escape, may be so overwhelming a factor as to negative the will to be where one is.

Only then would the second sentence of the quotation be what the writer of the passage takes it to be: a list of typical circumstances in which voluntary adoption of a place of residence is *not* a prerequisite of ordinary residence. Is it credible, however, that, having been at such pains to impress upon us the continuing relevance and authority of Viscount Sumner's remarks, Lord Scarman should, with his next breath, have set out to render those remarks meaningless? Surely not. It is suggested, therefore, that the correct approach to Lord Scarman's second sentence must be to take it as a list of circumstances in which a place of abode will be involuntarily adopted and in which, accordingly, the attribution of ordinary residence will *not* ensue. This alternative way of reading Lord Scarman's remarks implies the insertion of a perfectly logical additional sentence between the two quoted so that the passage reads as follows:

> The residence must be voluntarily adopted. [Only if a person is where he is because at some point he has chosen to be there can the kind of residence known as ordinary residence ensue; but being where one is is not always a matter of choice.] Enforced presence by reason of kidnapping or imprisonment, or a Robinson Crusoe existence on a desert island with no opportunity of escape, may be so overwhelming a factor as to negative the will to be where one is.

The *Mackenzie* case discussed above is not the only case where, on the face of it, the court appeared to set aside Viscount Sumner's requirement that residence must be voluntarily adopted before it can become ordinary residence. *Miesegaes v IRC*[8] concerned the residence status of Stanley Miesegaes who, during the years 1947–48 to 1951–52, had been a schoolboy boarding at Harrow. Counsel for Mr Miesegaes argued that even if Mr Miesegaes had been resident *simpliciter* in the United Kingdom during those years, such residence could not have constituted ordinary residence because it had not been voluntary residence; it had been institutional. Pearce LJ could not accept that argument. Referring to Viscount Sumner's interpretation of the words 'ordinarily resident' which he later quoted, he said:

> Education is too extensive and universal a phase to justify such descriptions as 'unusual' and 'extraordinary'. . . . The argument based on the institutional or compulsory nature of a boy's life at school is misleading. The compulsion is merely the will of his parents who voluntarily send him to that school. It would be hazardous, and in my opinion irrelevant, to investigate whether adolescents are residing voluntarily where their lot is cast and how far they approve of their parents' choice of a home or school.[9]

Far from constituting a rejection of Viscount Sumner's test, however, those words are a strong affirmation of it. Pearce LJ is saying not that one can set aside Viscount Sumner's words but that, in order to give them due weight in circumstances where the person concerned is not a person of full capacity, one must have regard to the will of the person's parents, trustees or guardians in determining whether or not his place of abode has been adopted voluntarily. That is because, in law, an *incapax* has no will but the will of those who are legally responsible for him.[10] Accordingly, during the years 1947–48 to 1951–52, Stanley Miesegaes was ordinarily resident in Harrow because he was resident *simpliciter* in Harrow for each of those years for the settled purpose of being educated and cared for there and Harrow had been voluntarily adopted *by his father* (who, until his death on 10 July 1948, had custody and control of Stanley at all material times) as Stanley's place of abode.

These two principles concerning the ordinary residence status of a person who, in law, has no will of his own were brought together in the case of *R v Waltham Forest London Borough Council, ex p Vale*.[11] Judith Vale, a severely mentally handicapped child born in London in 1956, was, in 1961, moved by her parents to Dublin where, because of her handicap, she was, until May 1984, boarded at various rural community homes. The last of these was Camp Hill at Wexford. In 1978, her parents returned to England and took up residence in the London Borough of Waltham Forest, visiting Judith two or three times a year. In 1984, Judith became so severely disturbed that, on 6 May, her parents brought her from Ireland to live with them until such time as she could be accommodated at Stoke Place, a residential home in Buckinghamshire. In the event, Judith was placed there just one month later on 6 June 1984. Judith's parents sought the funding of this placement from the London Borough in which they lived but this was refused on the ground that Judith was not ordinarily resident within the borough at the time of her placement in the home in Buckinghamshire and that, under the National Assistance Act 1948 s 24(1), this relieved the borough of responsibility. Judith's parents sought a judicial review of that decision and Taylor J held that:

> Where the propositus . . . is so mentally handicapped as to be totally dependent upon a parent or guardian, the concept of her having an independent ordinary residence of her own which she has adopted voluntarily and for which she has a settled purpose does not arise. She is in the same position as a small child. Her ordinary residence is that of her parents because that is her 'base' . . . It may well be that if the parents delegate their guardianship of her to a school or home for greater or shorter periods she will acquire a second ordinary residence at that establishment . . . It may well be therefore that in the present case Judith, although ordinarily resident with her parents throughout, had a second ordinary residence at Camp Hill for the duration of her stay there, and again acquired a second ordinary residence when she went to Stoke Place. For the period May to June 1984, however, she had only one ordinary residence: at home.[12]

It would seem to be established, therefore, that an infant or incapacitated person will be ordinarily resident wherever his parents, trustees or guardians are ordinarily resident and, if the person resides elsewhere in accordance with the will of those having legal responsibility for him and as part of the settled order of his life, in that other place also. In cases where there is no incapacity, however, a person's residence must be voluntarily adopted by the person himself before it can acquire the character of ordinary residence.

---

1 *Re Mackenzie* (1940) 19 ATC 399 at 402 and 403.
2 Ibid, at 403 and 404.
3 Ibid.
4 [1983] 1 All ER 226.
5 See **3.03** above.
6 *Shah v Barnet London Borough Council* [1983] 1 All ER 226 at 235.
7 J. L. Wosner 'Ordinary Residence, the Law and Practice' [1983] *British Tax Review* 347 at 348.

8 (1957) 37 TC 493.
9 Ibid, at 501.
10 Had this principle been invoked in the Mackenzie case, Miss Mackenzie's ordinary residence status could have been established on grounds far more convincing than those on which it was established.
11 QB, 11 February 1985. Unreported except in (1985) Times, 25 February.
12 Ibid.

3.05 Settled purposes

In *Shah v Barnet London Borough Council*,[1] Lord Scarman said that ordinary residence was dependent not only on a person's voluntary adoption of an abode in some place or country, but also on

> a degree of settled purpose. The purpose may be one or there may be several. It may be specific or general. All the law requires is that there is a settled purpose. This is not to say that the propositus intends to stay where he is indefinitely; indeed his purpose, while settled, may be for a limited period. Education, business or profession, employment, health, family or mere love of the place spring to mind as common reasons for a choice of regular abode. And there may well be many others. All that is necessary is that the purpose of living where one does has a sufficient degree of continuity to be properly described as settled.[2]

In *Reid v IRC*,[3] the settled purpose of Miss Reid in spending some three and a half months in the United Kingdom each year was chiefly, it seems, to visit her homeland and her sister.

In *Lysaght v IRC*,[4] the settled purpose of Mr Lysaght's three months' residence in the United Kingdom each year was business. He came here to attend directors' meetings of John Lysaght Ltd and to deal with business matters arising in connection with that company.

In *Levene v IRC*,[5] the settled purposes of Mr Levene's regular periods of residence in the United Kingdom were to obtain medical advice, to visit relatives, to take part in Jewish religious observances, to visit the graves of his parents and to deal with his tax affairs.

In *Reed v Clark*,[6] the settled purpose of Dave Clark in going to Los Angeles and staying there throughout the tax year 1978–79 was to work there and to avoid a United Kingdom tax liability on income of $450,000. In his judgment of the case, Nicholls J. said:

> Artificial tax avoidance schemes do not find much favour with the courts today. In this case the position, as I see it, is that when deciding issues of residence, ordinary residence and occasional residence all the reasons (including any desire to avoid a liability to United Kingdom income tax) underlying a person's being in a particular place are part of the overall picture. They are part of the material to be looked at and considered when deciding those issues. The presence of a tax avoidance intention may help to show, for instance, why a person went abroad at all, or at the particular time he did, how long he intended to remain away, or where his home in fact was in the year of assessment. But residence abroad for a carefully chosen limited period of work there . . . is no less residence abroad for that period just because the major reason for it was the avoidance of tax. Likewise with ordinary residence.[7]

Although the cases cited above provide examples of settled purposes, they provide no detailed explanation of the term itself. Thus, the question what is meant by 'settled purpose' remained unanswered until it came to the fore in the case of *Shah v Barnet London Borough Council*.[8] That case concerned the eligibility of students for local authority grants in connection with their education. Such eligibility depends on whether or not a student is 'ordinarily resident' in the United Kingdom, but, in the Education Act 1962, as in the Taxes Acts, the term 'ordinarily resident' is undefined. Several of the education authorities involved (Shropshire County Council in particular) tried to suggest that education could not be a settled purpose for the purposes of establishing ordinary residence and that to establish a settled purpose

there must be shown an intention to live here on a permanent basis as part of the general community; if a person's presence here was for a 'specific or limited purpose only', eg to pursue a course of study, he would not be ordinarily resident.[9]

Lord Scarman, however, firmly rebutted that suggestion:

A man's settled purpose will be different at different ages. Education in adolescence or early adulthood can be as settled a purpose as a profession or business in later years . . . study can be as settled a purpose as business or pleasure. And the notion of permanent or indefinitely enduring purpose as an element in ordinary residence derives not from the natural and ordinary meaning of the words 'ordinarily resident' but from a confusion of it with domicile.[10]

Earlier,[11] Lord Scarman had said, 'all that is necessary is that the purpose of living where one does has a sufficient degree of continuity to be properly described as settled'. A settled purpose is, therefore, a purpose which, though it need not provide a person with a motivation for becoming permanently or indefinitely present in a particular place, will provide him with the motivation to be more than transitorily or fleetingly present there. The purpose must, in other words, have a certain intrinsic durability. The difference between the two kinds of purpose may be illustrated by contrasting the motivation of the man who takes a holiday in the Cotswolds with that of the man who makes being in the Cotswolds part of his life; or the motivation of the woman who pays a visit to her invalid mother with that of the woman who makes caring for her invalid mother part of her life. In the first of both cases, the purpose is essentially transitory and results in a deviation from the person's normal mode of life; but in the second of both cases the purpose has an inbuilt element of continuity which results in the normal mode of life itself being modified so as to accommodate the presence of the person in the place in question. In either case the purpose which possesses an intrinsic element of continuity may, of course, be terminated very shortly after the mode of life has been altered to accommodate that purpose: the man may discover a preferred alternative to the Cotswolds and may further modify his mode of life so as to exclude presence in the Cotswolds and allow for presence in Tenerife, and the woman's mother may die. But in neither case can the early termination of the purpose change the settled nature it once possessed or retrospectively divest the person of the ordinary residence status to which it will have given rise.

How small a degree of continuity of purpose is needed for a purpose to be settled is well illustrated in *University College London v Newman*.[12] Edward Newman was a New Zealand citizen who, in 1977, left New Zealand and, after travelling extensively, arrived in the European Community in August 1978 whereupon, using France as his base, he became

> a rather aimless drifter who has spent his time in what is inelegantly but descriptively called colloquially 'bumming' around Europe.[13]

In October 1983, however, he embarked upon a degree course at University College London and claimed to be eligible for lower rate fees on the grounds of having been ordinarily resident within the European Community during the course of the three years ended 1 September 1983 within the terms of the Education (Fees and Awards) Regulations 1983 Sch 2(2). In the Westminster County Court, McDonnell J held that he had not been ordinarily resident as claimed, but, in the Court of Appeal, his judgment was reversed. Croom-Johnson LJ said that Mr Newman

> had been living in the EC for the necessary three years. But was he 'ordinarily resident'? He has put down roots nowhere. He used France 'as my base for travelling'. He went from country to country, in short spells, returning again and again. His work record is spasmodic, and was described by the judge as 'the token effort required to ensure that he receives social security payments'.[14]

Nevertheless, Croom-Johnson LJ concluded that if McDonnell J had asked himself 'Has Mr Newman been shown to have been ordinarily resident in the EEC for the three qualifying years?' and had he applied Lord Scarman's test [ie, Had Mr Newman's purpose of living where he did a sufficient degree of continuity to be properly described as settled?], the answer would have to be 'yes' . . . 'Mr Newman was ordinarily resident, after his casual fashion, somewhere in the EC for the whole of the qualifying three years'.[15]

It was accepted in the Court of Appeal that Mr Newman had not been ordinarily resident in any particular European Community member state during the three year period, but that is not relevant to the point being made. On the basis of the court's judgment, Mr Newman would have been ordinarily resident in the United Kingdom had he confined himself to merely 'bumming around' England, Scotland, Wales and Northern Ireland. 'Bumming around' may be a settled purpose.

---

1 [1983] 1 All ER 226.
2 Ibid, at 235.
3 (1926) 10 TC 673.
4 (1928) 13 TC 511.
5 (1928) 13 TC 486.
6 [1985] STC 323.
7 Ibid, at 346.
8 [1983] 1 All ER 226.
9 Ibid, at 237.
10 Ibid, at 236, 238 and 239.
11 Ibid, at 235.
12 CA, 19 December 1985. Unreported except in (1986) Times, 8 January.
13 Ibid.
14 Ibid.
15 Ibid.

3.06 Regular order of life

Given that a person voluntarily adopts the United Kingdom as a place of abode and comes here in pursuit of one or more settled purposes, over what period must he be present here in pursuit of those purposes before his presence becomes part of the 'regular order' of his life and before he can thus be attributed with ordinary residence status? The body of case law preceding the *Shah* case[1] had suggested that the answer is three or more years – not because any of the judges hearing the cases concerned had declared that that was the required period but because, in every instance, the appellants had, in fact, visited the United Kingdom in three or more consecutive years before the Inland Revenue chose to assert that the status of ordinary residence had been acquired and before the Commissioners (subsequently supported by the courts) upheld its assertion that that was so. Where the settled purpose involves but a single visit to the United Kingdom in each tax year, that answer will no doubt be correct: common sense would dictate that three such visits are the minimum required to give those visits regularity and habituality; but – by the same logic – where the settled purpose involves monthly or weekly visits, will surely have become regular and habitual once the third or fourth such monthly or weekly visit has been made.

Where the settled purpose involves not merely visits to the United Kingdom but continuous presence here, a person's presence in the United Kingdom will necessarily have become part of the regular order of his life after only a few days have elapsed; and – just as early termination or fulfilment of the purpose will not retrospectively rob that purpose of any settled nature it possessed[2] – early termination or fulfilment of the purpose will not prevent the person's presence here from being presence as part of the regular order of his life. In the *Shah* case, Lord Scarman had said:

> If there be proved a regular, habitual mode of life in a particular place, the continuity of which has persisted despite temporary absences, ordinary residence is established provided only it is adopted voluntarily and for a settled purpose.[3]

Likewise, in *Reed v Clark*,[4] Nicholls J was satisfied that a period of just over a year abroad was not too short a period for a person to have established an ordinary residence overseas.

The test which Nicholls J would (following Lord Scarman) seem to have been applying, however, was: Did the period of residence in question, however long or short, represent an intrusion into or a deviation from the person's regular and habitual mode of life, or was it, in fact, a component part of the person's regular and habitual mode of life for the time being? If it was intrusive or deviatory it could not be ordinary residence, but if it was a component part of the normal pattern it could not be other than ordinary residence.

This would seem to bring the matter round full circle. In the *Levene* case, Lord Hanworth had said:

> I find it difficult to attach any distinction of meaning to the word 'ordinarily' as affecting the term 'resident', unless it be to prevent facts which would amount to residence being so estimated on the ground that they arose from some fortuitous cause, such as illness of the so-called resident or of some other person, which demanded his continuance at a place for a special purpose otherwise than in accordance with his own usual arrangements and shaping of his movements[5]

In other words, residence always will be ordinary residence unless it either lacks settled purpose or is enforced. That was the stance of the courts in 1928 and that, despite Revenue insistence (not always to the taxpayer's detriment) during the intervening years that ordinary residence necessitates the establishment of an annually recurrent pattern of residence *simpliciter*, has now been affirmed by the courts as being their stance today.

One further point must be made. Viscount Cave,[6] Lord Denning[7] and Lord Scarman[8] all made reference to the irrelevance of temporary absences in the context of the 'regular order of life' which is under discussion here. What each was saying is that once a person has, by reason of his voluntary presence in the United Kingdom in pursuit of one or more settled purposes, made his presence here part of the regular order of his life for the time being and thus attracted to himself the status of ordinary residence, his absence from the United Kingdom will not affect that status provided that the absences are temporary, occasional or accidental. This will be so even where an absence extends over an entire tax year – though in such an instance residence *simpliciter* status may be lost.

It is worth observing that this principle of disregarding temporary absences provides additional support for the proposition that a person who makes voluntary regular visits to the United Kingdom in pursuit of settled purposes is ordinarily resident here. If the periods between visits are treated as temporary absences from the United Kingdom and are disregarded, the visitor's periodic presence in the United Kingdom is, effectively, transformed into a continuous presence.

---

1 *Shah v Barnet London Borough Council* [1983] 1 All ER 226 at 236.
2 See **3.05** above.
3 *Shah v Barnet London Borough Council* [1983] 1 All ER 226 at 236.
4 [1985] STC 323.
5 *Levene v IRC* (1928) 13 TC 486 at 496.
6 *Levene v IRC* (1928) 13 TC 486 at 507.
7 *R v Barnet London Borough, ex p Shah* [1982] 1 All ER 698 at 704.
8 *Shah v Barnet London Borough Council* [1983] 1 All ER 226 at 236.

3.07 Unlawful residence

It has already been explained that residence is a question of fact not of law[1] so that, unless an Act contains specific provision to the contrary, residence does not need to be lawful for it to be residence which is voluntarily adopted and for a settled purpose as part of the regular order of a person's life. Thus although a deserting seaman who is living in the United Kingdom in breach of the immigration laws cannot be ordinarily resident here for the purposes of the Commonwealth Immigration Acts since those Acts make specific provision to that effect,[2] he may be ordinarily resident here for tax purposes since the Taxes Acts contain no such prohibiting provision. The principle underlying these rules is that a person who would appear to be ordinarily resident to anyone observing the way in which he is living but who is not entitled lawfully so to live cannot be allowed to benefit from his apparent status but 'for the purposes of taxation he will not be allowed to deny his apparent status'.[3] This, according to Oliver LJ in *R v Secretary of State for Home Department, ex p Margueritte*[4] made 'good common sense'.

1 See **2.20** above
2 *Re Abdul Manan* [1971] 2 All ER 1016.
3 *R v Barnet London Borough Council, ex p Shah* [1982] 1 All ER 698 at 706, per Eveleigh LJ.
4 [1982] 3 All ER 909.

3.08 The impropriety of the 'real home' test

In *Shah v Barnet London Borough Council*,[1] Lord Scarman emphasised that:

> there are two, and no more than two, respects in which the mind of the propositus is important in determining ordinary residence. The residence must be voluntarily adopted . . . And there must be a degree of settled purpose.[2]

These two *animus* factors have been discussed at **3.04** and **3.05** above. In their place, it has sometimes been sought to substitute *animus manendi* as a test of ordinary residence: the test of whether a person has formed the 'intention to remain' in a particular place. This test – which is sometimes referred to as the 'real home' test – is, however, the subjective test of domicile[3] and has no part whatsoever to play in the determination of ordinary residence. Both its attraction and its danger lie in its very simplicity – But where is X's real home? – and the fact that that question can only admit of one answer; whereas the proper question – where is the place or country in which X has an abode, adopted voluntarily and for a settled purpose as part of the regular order of his life? – may admit of two answers, or more, or none!

That a person may be ordinarily resident nowhere was affirmed in *University College London v Newman*.[4] Croom-Johnston LJ said:

> I agree that it is possible for someone to be ordinarily resident nowhere. People who spend their lives sailing about the world are such. So are the well-known class of tax-evaders who move on from country to country, always one move ahead of the tax man.[5]

And that a man may be ordinarily resident in two places at one and the same time was established in bankruptcy law in *Re Norris, ex p Reynolds*[6] and has been admitted in tax law also:

> I am not sure there is anything impossible in a person 'ordinarily residing' in two places.[7]

> I think . . . that a man can have two ordinary residences not because he commonly is to be found at those places, but because the ordinary course of his life is such that he acquires the attribute of residence at those two places.[8]

The Inland Revenue agrees that this is so and states this in its guidance notes.[9]

1 [1983] 1 All ER 226.
2 Ibid, at 235.
3 See **7.13** below.
4 CA, 19 December 1985. Unreported except in (1986) Times, 8 January.
5 Ibid.
6 (1888) 4 TLR 452.
7 *Reid v IRC* (1926) 10 TC 673 at 680, per Lord Clyde LP.
8 *Levene v IRC* (1928) 13 TC 486 at 494, per Rowlatt J.
9 Appendix IR 20 (11 April 2000), para 1.4.

Revenue practice

3.09 Year by year residence

In its guidance notes, the Inland Revenue states that:

> If you are resident in the UK year after year, you are treated as ordinarily resident here.[1]

As will become increasingly clear, that sentence is the maxim upon which the Inland Revenue has based its entire code of practice concerning the attribution or otherwise of ordinary residence status; and it is, therefore, unfortunate, to say the least, that that maxim does not accurately reflect the principle which the courts have established as being applicable in the determination of a person's ordinary residence status. It may be faulted on two counts.

First, it disregards the fact that before the year-by-year residence to which it refers can acquire the character of ordinary residence it must have resulted from the voluntary adoption of the United Kingdom as a place of abode[2] and must relate to one or more settled (as opposed to casual or temporary) purposes.[3] By its silence on these points, the Revenue statement implies that the possession of residence *simpliciter* in each of a number of successive years will alone be sufficient to transform residence *simpliciter* into ordinary residence and that the 'year after year' element will override the need to have regard to any other factors; but such is not the case.

Secondly, the statement betrays no recognition of the fact that, although a person's possession of residence *simpliciter* year after year will (subject to the conditions described above being met) result in his being attributed with ordinary residence status, residence which is of only short duration and which results in the attribution of residence *simpliciter* in only a single tax year will also, in law, take on the character of ordinary residence if the three judicially prescribed conditions referred to earlier[4] are met. This assertion runs counter to the Revenue statement that:

> You may be resident but not ordinarily resident in the UK for a tax year if, for example, you normally live outside the UK but are in this country for 183 days or more in the year,[5]

yet the *Vale* case[6] provides a striking affirmation of its truth.

Because this second defect in the principle adopted by the Inland Revenue will invariably work in the taxpayer's favour by resulting in the non-attribution of ordinary residence status in certain instances where such attribution is due, it is tempting to regard those Revenue rules which rest on this defect as concessions of which the taxpayer may take advantage. This would be a dangerous attitude. Almost all the Revenue rules are qualified by the insertion of the word 'normally' or by the use of 'may' rather than 'will' and, as the *Clark* case[7] demonstrates, the Inland Revenue will have no hesitation in relying on those qualifications and setting aside a rule if it is thus enabled to pursue a taxpayer for a significant amount of tax which, under the rule, would be avoided.

Thus the Revenue statement at paras 3.4–3.5 of IR 20 (11 April 2000)[8] and the Revenue statement quoted above must both be viewed with a certain amount of scepticism. Any voluntary visitor to the United Kingdom who comes here with more than a casual or temporary purpose and whose presence here becomes for the time being part of the regular order of his life will, in law, be liable to be regarded as ordinarily resident here from the outset irrespective of the number of weeks, months or years spanned by his visit.

Contrariwise, no visitor to the United Kingdom whose presence here is enforced or who is here in pursuit of a purpose which is merely temporary or casual can, in law, be regarded as ordinarily resident, even in the unlikely event of his visit extending beyond the third anniversary of his arrival.

It was said earlier that the Inland Revenue has based its entire code of practice concerning the attribution or otherwise of ordinary residence status on the maxim under discussion here, namely that if a person is resident in the United Kingdom year after year, he is ordinarily resident here. That is not immediately apparent when one reads the Inland Revenue guide for, on the face of it, the guide appears to be asserting that the attribution of ordinary residence status is dependent on factors such as periodic visits here of a certain average length,[9] and a person's future intentions.[10] A closer examination will reveal, however, that the guide is relating these factors to ordinary residence only in so far as it is relating them to the establishment, on a year-by-year basis, of the status of residence *simpliciter*. Again, in the mind of the Revenue, it is the year after year attribution of residence *simpliciter* status which is critical and which will inevitably result in the attribution of ordinary residence status.

---

1 Appendix IR 20 (11 April 2000), para 1.3.
2 See **3.04** above.
3 See **3.05** above.
4 See **3.04**, **3.05** and **3.06** above.
5 Appendix IR 20 (11 April 2000), para 1.3.
6 *R v Waltham Forest London Borough Council, ex p Vale* QB, 11 February 1985. Unreported except in (1985) Times, 25 February. See **3.04** above.
7 *Reed v Clark* [1985] STC 323. Despite the Inland Revenue's assertion in para 8 of its booklet IR 20 that 'If a person is to be regarded as resident in the United Kingdom for a given tax year he must normally be present in the country for at least part of that year', the Revenue assessed Clark to tax on £275,700 for 1978–79 although he had been absent from the United Kingdom throughout the whole of that year. The Revenue case was that, notwithstanding his absence, Clark was resident in the United Kingdom.
8 See Appendix below.
9 See **3.11** below.
10 See **3.12** below.

3.10 Available accommodation

It has been explained at **2.07** to **2.09** above that a person who has accommodation available to him in the United Kingdom and who occupies that accommodation, however briefly, during the course of a tax year, will (unless he is working full-time overseas)[1] fall to be attributed with residence *simpliciter* for the whole of that tax year. It follows from this that, if the Inland Revenue maxim discussed at **3.09** above (namely, that 'if a person is resident in the United Kingdom year after year, he is ordinarily resident here') is taken as a valid principle of law, anyone who has accommodation available to him in the United Kingdom and who occupies that accommodation, however briefly, in each of a number of successive tax years will be not only resident *simpliciter* for each of those years but ordinarily resident here also. The effect of section 208 of the FA 1993 which provides that for the purposes of the TA 1988 s 336 the existence or otherwise of available accommodation must be disregarded in determining whether an individual is in the United Kingdom for some temporary purpose and not with a view to or intent of establishing his residence here will be considered at **4.05** below.[2] While section 208 alters the law in respect of the application of s 336, it is submitted that the presence or otherwise of available accommodation can still be relevant in assisting in determining whether an individual is generally ordinarily resident in the United Kingdom or not.

1 See **4.16**ff below.
2 TA 1988 s 336.

3.11 Annual visits

Persons who come to the United Kingdom regularly on annual visits, and where those visits average 91 days or more in a tax year, will be treated as short-term visitors for the purpose of determining whether they are ordinarily resident in the United Kingdom according to the latest Statement of Practice from the Inland Revenue.[1]

Short-term visitors are treated as ordinarily resident where visits average 91 days or more in a tax year – days which are spent in the United Kingdom for exceptional circumstances beyond the visitor's control, for example through the illness of the visitor or a member of the visitor's immediate family, are not normally counted for the purpose of arriving at the 91 days.

For all tax years before 1993–94, a short-term visitor who came regularly to the United Kingdom and had accommodation available in the United Kingdom for the visitor's use is treated as ordinarily resident even if the visitor averaged less than 91 days in a tax year.

In the latest Statement of Practice the Inland Revenue couples physical presence with intention.[2] A short-term visitor who fulfils the criteria for physical presence as explained above is treated as being ordinarily resident from a date which is determined by the visitor's intentions.

The visitor will be treated as ordinarily resident from 6 April of the tax year of his first arrival if it is clear at that period that the visitor intended visiting the United Kingdom regularly for at least four tax years. If the visitor came originally with no definite plans about the number of years for which the visitor would visit, he is treated as ordinarily resident from 6 April of the fifth tax year after he has visited the United Kingdom for four years. If the decision to visit the United Kingdom regularly is made before the start of the fifth tax year, then the visitor is treated as being ordinarily resident from 6 April of the tax year in which that decision is taken.[3]

1 Appendix IR 20 (11 April 2000), para 3.4.
2 Ibid, para 3.5.
3 Ibid, para 3.5.

3.12 Intention

It will have been noted that the first of the Revenue rules described at **3.11** above involves the use of a continuous base period of four years in assessing whether the length of an overseas visitor's visits to the United Kingdom have been of sufficient average length to trigger the attribution to him of residence and ordinary residence status. The first rule is expressed as an intention to visit the United Kingdom regularly. In formulating a rule based on intention the Inland Revenue has ventured onto shaky ground. In the *Vale* case,[1] for instance, Taylor J said that, in considering the question of a person's ordinary residence,

> future intention is to be left out of account.[2]

and in taking that line he was quite properly following Lord Scarman who, in the *Shah* case,[3] had said that:

> ordinary residence ... lays emphasis not on intention or expectation for the future ... but on immediately past events, namely the usual order of the [person's] way of life ....[4]

In law, therefore, a person who comes to the United Kingdom from overseas may be attributed with ordinary residence status only if he has come here voluntarily and with one or more settled (as opposed to temporary or casual) purposes and only when his presence here has, despite any temporary absences of long or short duration, acquired a degree of continuity and become a part of (rather than a deviation from) his regular and habitual mode of life. As the *Vale* case[5] demonstrates, this need not take long if the person has no ordinary residence elsewhere – a month may be sufficient; but if the person has an ordinary residence elsewhere and merely makes short intermittent visits here it may take several years before the characteristics of continuity, regularity and habituality are sufficiently pronounced for attribution of ordinary residence status validly to take place. The fact that the establishment of ordinary residence status may take several years does not, however, justify the Inland Revenue in setting aside established judicial principles in favour of its own; and it is submitted that the Inland Revenue will find no support in law should it, by applying the rules under discussion here, anticipate a person's acquisition of ordinary residence status by having regard to his future intent rather than to his immediate past mode of life.

The factor of intent or expectation is irrelevant and four years is an arbitrary length of time which has no special significance in law.

Reliance on a person's future intent lies behind two other rules in the Inland Revenue's code of practice concerning ordinary residence. The first states that:

> You are treated as resident and ordinarily resident from the date you arrive if your home has been abroad and you intend –
> – to come to the UK to live here permanently, or
> – to come and remain here for three years or more,[6]

and the second states that:

> You will be treated as ordinarily resident in the UK from the date you arrive, whether to work here or not, if it is clear that you intend to stay for at least three years.[7]

It will be clear from the foregoing discussion that mere intent to settle permanently in the United Kingdom is not in itself sufficient to imbue with ordinary residence status either the new arrival to these shores or the hitherto undecided visitor. Although both will possess a settled purpose and will have voluntarily adopted the United Kingdom as their place of residence, it will still remain for each to establish a regular and habitual mode of life here which displays a certain degree of continuity. Until that has taken place, any judgment as to their residence status will be premature. This, as pointed out above, may not take long – particularly if their arrival here or decision to stay here coincides with their severing of ties with elsewhere – but until it has taken place, attribution of ordinary residence status will have no foundation in law. Having made the point that these rules are wrong in principle, however, it is conceded that, in almost every case in which the Inland Revenue, by application of these rules, attributes a person with ordinary residence status, the qualities of life which a person's presence here must display for him validly to be regarded as ordinarily resident will have emerged by the time the attribution of ordinary residence status is made.

1 *R v Waltham Forest London Borough Council, ex p Vale*, QB, 11 February 1985. Unreported except in (1985) Times, 25 February.
2 Ibid.
3 *Shah v Barnet London Borough Council* [1983] 1 All ER 226.
4 Ibid at 236.
5 *R v Waltham Forest London Borough Council, ex p Vale*, QB, 11 February 1985. Unreported except in (1985) Times, 25 February.
6 Appendix IR 20 (11 April 2000), para 3.1.
7 Ibid, para 3.8.

3.13 Summary

Ordinary residence, like residence *simpliciter*, is a quality of the person,[1] but it is a quality which is less easily acquired and less easily shed than residence *simpliciter*. Like residence *simpliciter* it is undefined by statute[2] and its possession or otherwise is, therefore, a question of degree and fact.[3] It has been held by the highest judicial authorities, however, that before a person may – in the eyes of the law – be attributed with United Kingdom ordinary residence status he must be proved to have established here a regular, habitual mode of life which has been voluntarily adopted,[4] which serves one or more settled purposes[5] and which possesses a continuity that has persisted despite any temporary absences of whatever duration.[6]

Unfortunately, the Inland Revenue has substituted for this judicially approved test the test of year-by-year possession of residence *simpliciter* status and has thus linked ordinary residence with such factors as availability of accommodation in the United Kingdom, the length and frequency of visits here, and explicit or implicit intentions as to length of stay.[7] While it is conceded that application of the Revenue test will frequently result in ordinary residence status being attributed to persons who would fail to be attributed with that status were only the judicially approved test to be applied, it is submitted that the Revenue test will, on occasions, result not only in the attribution of ordinary residence status to persons who would not be attributed with that status were the matter to be decided by the courts but also in the failure to attribute ordinary residence status where it properly ought to be attributed. Despite its ease of application, therefore, the Inland Revenue's code of practice concerning the attribution or otherwise of ordinary residence status cannot be regarded as an acceptable substitute for the principles established by the courts as governing the attribution or otherwise of that status.

---

1 See **2.02** above.
2 See **3.01** above.
3 See **2.03** above.
4 See **3.04** above.
5 See **3.05** above.
6 *Shah v Barnet London Borough Council* [1983] 1 All ER 226 at 236, per Lord Scarman. See **3.06** above.
7 See **3.09–3.12** above.

CHAPTER 4

Arrivals and departures

They sailed away for a year and a day,
To the land where the Bong-tree grows.

Edward Lear *The Owl and the Pussy-Cat*

4.01 Introduction

It might be supposed that, in the light of the discussion in Chapters 2 and 3, the question of the residence and ordinary residence status of a person who arrives on the shores of the United Kingdom or leaves them for other shores across the sea will be determined merely by reference to the various factors discussed in those chapters. This is not the case, however. Although none of those factors cease to be relevant, Parliament has enacted various provisions which deal specifically with the determination of residence status in circumstances of arrival in and departure from the United Kingdom, and those provisions impose certain overriding tests and rules. Furthermore – because the consequences of the attribution of residence and ordinary residence status in accordance with the statutory provisions may be some-what severe – the Inland Revenue has introduced certain extra-statutory concessions and practice rules to soften the impact in the years of arrival or, as the case might be, in the year of departure.

Persons arriving in the United Kingdom

4.02 Conditional exemption

In 1889, Sir E. Clarke who was at that time the Solicitor General, had the task of replying to a clearly astonished and disbelieving Lord Chancellor (Halsbury, no less) who had asked him:

> Do you contend that a subject of a foreign state residing here, carrying on a business abroad from which profits are derived, but not one farthing of which is earned in this country or ever comes here, is liable to pay Income Tax thereon in consequence of simply residing here?

His answer was,

> Yes, subject to this limitation: he must be residing here; he must not be here merely for a temporary purpose. If he is residing here there is no hardship. Persons residing here and enjoying the protection of the laws of this country ought to bear its burdens.[1]

It was just such sentiment that guided Parliament when it included in the taxing statutes the predecessor of TA 1988 s 336. That section has the twofold objective of bringing within the tax net anyone who, although ostensibly merely visiting the United Kingdom, is, in any tax year, here for a period sufficiently long to justify his being treated as resident whether he is truly resident here or not, and of keeping out of the net any genuine short-term visitor who might otherwise find himself attributed with the quality of residence in the United Kingdom by reason of his visits here or other factors. TCGA 1992 s 9(3) which, on the face of it, has the same objectives with regard to capital gains tax as TA 1988 s 336 has with regard to income tax, does, in fact, present special difficulties and is discussed at **4.10** to **4.12** below, both on its own account and in relation to TA 1988 s 336.

Taxes Act 1988 s 336(1) provides:

> A person shall not be charged to income tax under Schedule D as a person residing in the United Kingdom, in respect of profits or gains received in respect of possessions or securities out of the United Kingdom, if – (a) he is in the United Kingdom for some temporary purpose only and not with any view or intent of establishing his residence there, and (b) he has not actually resided in the United Kingdom at one time or several times for a period equal in the whole to six months in any year of assessment, but if any such person resides in the United Kingdom for such a period he shall be so chargeable for that year.

while TA 1988 s 336(2) provides:

> For the purposes of Cases I, II and III of Schedule E, a person who is in the United Kingdom for some temporary purpose only and not with the intention of establishing his residence there shall not be treated as resident in the United Kingdom if he has not in the aggregate spent at least six months in the United Kingdom in the year of assessment, but shall be treated as resident there if he has.

Each provision is concerned with only a single class of persons who are described in identical terms. They are persons who have both the positive quality of being present in the United Kingdom 'for some temporary purpose only' *and* the negative quality of being in the United Kingdom 'not with the intention of establishing . . . residence there'. It is not sufficient that a person seeking the exemption contained in TA 1988 s 336 is able to demonstrate possession of only one of the qualities (eg having no intention of establishing residence in the United Kingdom); he must demonstrate possession of both.

---

1 Colquhoun v Brooks (1889) 2 TC 490 at 492.

4.03   Temporary purpose

The expression 'temporary purpose' in TA 1988 s 336(1) and (2) is not without difficulty as is illustrated by the case of Mr Cadwalader, an American citizen, who was ordinarily resident in New York but who rented a house and shooting rights in Scotland and there spent some two months of each year. Was visiting Scotland each year for the shooting season a temporary purpose? The Commissioners seem to have been of the opinion that it was for they found against the Crown. The Court of Exchequer, however, reversed their decision. Lord McLaren said:

> I don't think that Mr Cadwalader is in a position to affirm, when he comes year after year during the currency of his lease to spend the shooting season in Scotland, that he is here for a temporary purpose only. I don't mean that you might not frame a definition which would bring this within the scope of temporary purposes, but taking the ordinary meaning of the word, I should say that temporary purposes means casual purposes as distinguished from the case of a person who is here in the pursuance of his regular habits of life . . .. [The word] 'temporary' . . . means that it is casual or transitory residence, as distinguished from a residence, of which there may be more than one, but which may be habitual or permanent.[1]

In the previous chapter, we saw that a purpose which results in a person becoming present in the United Kingdom as part of the regular order of his life is properly describable as a 'settled purpose'.[2] What Lord McLaren is saying, therefore (in the current vocabulary of the law of residence), is that the terms 'settled purpose' and 'temporary purpose' are mutually exclusive and that for a purpose to be a temporary purpose within the context of what is now TA 1988 s 336(1) it must be a non-settled purpose, ie a purpose which, if it brings a person to the United Kingdom, does so only in deviation from the regular order of his life.

The Inland Revenue was quick to take up Lord McLaren's definition and, over the years following the *Cadwalader* case, the Crown's rejection of many an individual's claim to exemption within the terms of what is now TA 1988 s 336(1) was based on a contention that the person 'was in this country in pursuance of his regular habits of life and therefore not "for some temporary purpose only"'. Thus it was in the case of Mr Zorab.[3]

Mr Zorab was a native of India who had lived there all his life and held office in the Indian Civil Service. In May 1920, however, he left India on two years' furlough at the end of which he intended to (and did) retire from the Indian Civil Service. In 1920–21 he spent a little over five months in the United Kingdom, just short of six months in 1921–22, 1922–23 and 1923–24, and a little short of five months in 1924–25. The remainder of each year he spent in Paris or Belgium. He had no business interests in the United Kingdom and his visits here were made solely with the object of seeing his friends. The Crown contended that Mr Zorab's visits were not 'for some temporary purpose only' within the meaning of rule 2 of the Miscellaneous Rules of Schedule D but that he was 'in this country in pursuance of his regular habits of life'. The Commissioners found against the Crown, however, and Rowlatt J upheld their decision. Contrasting the case of Mr Zorab with that of someone who, when absent from the United Kingdom, has links here which perpetuate and particularise his attachment to the United Kingdom (a house, a bank account, stored furniture and the like),[4] he said of Mr Zorab:

This gentleman seems to be a mere traveller . . . . He is a native of India, he has retired from his work there and he really travels in Europe. All that can be said about it is that in the course of his habitual travels he spends a considerable period every year in England.[5]

This judgment reinforces what has been said earlier,[6] namely, that mere recurrence of visits is by no means conclusive proof of the existence of a settled purpose. A person may visit the United Kingdom in each of a succession of years and yet each visit may (to use Lord McLaren's words in the *Cadwalader* case) be only 'casual or transitory' and possess a temporary character. Indeed, Viscount Cave LC argued in *Lysaght v IRC*[7] that although Mr Lysaght made monthly visits from Ireland to England for the purpose of attending directors' meetings and stayed for about one week on each occasion, that did not make his visits 'more than temporary visits or give them the character of residence in this country'.[8] Again, presumably, in Viscount Cave's view, the visits were merely 'casual or transitory' despite their regularity and frequency.

In its latest booklet, the Inland Revenue stipulates '91 days or more'. Any days spent in the United Kingdom for exceptional circumstances such as the illness of the individual or a member of his family will not normally be counted.[9]

Section 208(1)–(4) of the FA 1993 inserted a new sub-s (3) into TA 1988 s 336 with effect from 1993–94 and subsequent years of assessment. The new s 336(3) provides that for the purposes of whether a person is in the UK for a temporary purpose and not with any view or intent of establishing residence here the question whether the person has available accommodation here must be disregarded. See **4.05** below. The old rules still apply for years prior to 1993–94.

---

1 *Cooper v Cadwalader* (1904) 5 TC 101 at 109.
2 See **3.05** and **3.06** above.
3 *IRC v Zorab* (1926) 11 TC 289.
4 See Ch 2.
5 *IRC v Zorab* (1926) 11 TC 289 at 292.
6 See **3.10** above.
7 (1928) 13 TC 511. Viscount Sumner, on the other hand, saw Mr Lysaght's commitment to monthly attendance at directors' meetings in the United Kingdom as a settled purpose (a term which Viscount Sumner coined in the *Lysaght* case) and, accordingly, he held that Mr Lysaght's visits to the United Kingdom were precluded from possessing the temporary character which might have brought them within the scope of what is now TA 1988 s 336(1).
8 (1928) 13 TC 511 at 532.
9 Appendix IR 20 (11 April 2000) paras 3.4, 3.5.

4.04 View or intent of establishing residence

The earliest recorded commentary on what is now TA 1988 s 336(1) is found in *A-G v Coote*.[1] In that case the court had to decide whether Sir C. H. Coote, who was domiciled in Ireland and spent most of his time there but visited a furnished house which he owned in Connaught Place, London, for a few weeks each year, fell within the excepting provisions of ITA 1806 s 51. It was held that:

The fact of the defendant's domicile has nothing to do with the question, nor has the time of his residence any effect on the construction of the words of the Act; for if the defendant came here for the purpose of establishing a residence it were enough, although he should reside here only two weeks.[2]

As Baron Graham made clear, the availability of the accommodation was the all-important fact, not the actual duration of Sir C. H. Coote's stay in it:

> At any period of the year he might have come to Connaught Place, where he would have found his house ready for him,[3]

and this point was taken up almost a century later by Lord McLaren who said of the phrase 'not with any view or intent of establishing his residence':

> The words are somewhat vague, but they seem to me to recognise what may be called a constructive residence as distinguished from actual residence.[4]

In the case of Mr Cadwalader, this meant leasing a furnished house which, though he actually occupied it for only two months in each year, was maintained for him and placed at his disposal so that he was able to occupy it whenever he chose. As in the *Coote* case, the essence of constructive residence was held to be that a person 'has a residence always ready for him if he should choose to come to it',[5] not that when in the United Kingdom he necessarily ever does set foot there. As Lord McLaren has said:

> If you are looking forward to it . . . that makes you liable to taxation, because in order to get the benefit of the exemption you must say that you have no view and no intention of acquiring a residence there.[6]

Lord McLaren was there using the term 'looking forward' not in its modern sense of 'anticipating with pleasure' but in its plain sense of seeing oneself in occupation of the dwelling place in question at some future time. In TA 1988 s 336 and its predecessors, the 'view or intent of establishing . . . residence' is not necessarily a view or intent in relation to the particular visit in question. So long as a person has a dwelling place maintained and available for his use in the United Kingdom, he cannot be free of a view or intent of establishing his residence here. If a man has no such view, he will not acquire or have made available to him a dwelling place in the United Kingdom. If he once had such a view but has now abandoned it, he will dispose of the accommodation[7] or in some way negate its availability – by, for example, renting it out to another – and if he does not do so the presumption must be that a view or intent to reside there, at some time in the future, remains.

---

1 (1817) 2 TC 385.
2 Ibid at 385, per Richards CB.
3 Ibid, at 385.
4 *Cooper v Cadwalader* (1904) 5 TC 101 at 109.
5 Ibid at 106, per the Lord President.
6 Ibid at 109, per Lord McLaren.
7 Or attempt to dispose of it. See *Withers v Wynyard* (1938) 21 TC 724.

4.05 A place of abode

The principle that no one who has a place of residence in the United Kingdom, maintained and available for his use, can be free of a view or intent of establishing his residence in the United Kingdom, was, in 1926, challenged by a certain Captain

Loewenstein.[1] He noted that in both the *Coote* case and the *Cadwalader* case the persons attributed with a view or intent of establishing residence had proprietary interests in the dwelling houses concerned and he contended that unless there was such a proprietary interest the principle was of no application.

As has been noted at **2.09** above, Captain Loewenstein was a Belgian subject, resident in Brussels, who visited a property at Melton Mowbray in Leicestershire each year for the purpose of fox hunting. The property was a furnished hunting box called 'Pinfold' which was owned by The Belgian Breeding Stock Farm Company Ltd, a company in which Captain Loewenstein had a controlling interest and of which he was a director. In no year did he spend as many as six months in the United Kingdom and he claimed, therefore, that, on the basis of ITA 1918 1 Sch, rule 2 of the Miscellaneous Rules of Schedule D (now TA 1988 s 336(1)), he was exempt from tax under Schedule D. Rowlatt J did not agree. Taking up the question of the application of rule 2, he said:

> It really comes to this, – whether it is of the essence of the case that a man should be treated under the Rule . . . as coming here with a view to establishing his residence, and not for a temporary purpose only, that he should have at any rate a proprietary interest, such as a lease or something of that sort, in the house. I cannot see what difference that makes . . . this man had this house at his disposal, with everything in it or for his convenience, kept going all the year round, although he only wanted it for a short time. Luckily, he was in relation with a Company who were the owners of it, and he could do that without owning it. It is an accident. It might well have been that he could do that with a relation, or a friend, or a philanthropist, or anybody; but in fact there was this house for him . . . He has got this house to come to when he likes; he does not own it; he has got no proprietary interest in it, but it is just as good as if he had for the purpose of having it for a residence, and there is is.[2]

The *Loewenstein* case therefore established that to have a place of abode in the United Kingdom at one's disposal *de facto* was sufficient, if a person set foot in the United Kingdom, to attribute that person with a view or intent of establishing residence here, whether the place of abode was *actually* occupied or not. The 'place of abode' test was pressed to its fullest extent by the Inland Revenue until the law was changed by FA 1993 s 208(1)(4) which inserted a new subsection into TA 1988 s 336. Subsection 336(3) reads:

> The question whether –
> (a) a person falls within subsection (1)(a) above, or
> (b) for the purposes of subsection (2) above a person is in the United Kingdom for some temporary purpose only and not with the intention of establishing his residence there, shall be decided without regard to any living accommodation available in the United Kingdom for his use.

The new subsection 336(3) applies with effect from the year 1993–94 and subsequent years of assessment.

From 1993–94 *Loewenstein* ceases to be applicable law for the purposes of section 336. It should be realised that the availability of accommodation in the United Kingdom may still be one of the relevant conditions that may have to be taken into account, along with other conditions, in determining the general question whether a person is resident or ordinarily resident in the United Kingdom. See **2.09** and **3.10** above.

The old law still applies for years of assessment prior to 1993–94. See **2.07** to **2.09** above.

---

1 *Loewenstein v De Salis* (1926) 10 TC 424.
2 Ibid, at 437 and 438.

4.06 Actual residence

As emphasised at **4.02** above, anyone who is in the United Kingdom for a settled (ie non-temporary) purpose or who is here with a view or intent of establishing his residence is beyond the scope of TA 1988 s 336 and his residence and ordinary residence status will fall to be determined in accordance with the general principles discussed in Chapters 2 and 3. Anyone who establishes that his purpose in being here was temporary and that he had no view or intent of establishing his residence here is, however, then to be subjected to a 'six month' test in order that it may be determined whether he is to be treated as resident or non-resident for the purposes of Schedule D, Cases IV and V, and Schedule E, Cases I to III. The statutory terms in which the six-month test is framed are, however, not without their difficulties of construction.

In relation to the question of chargeability to tax in respect of profits or gains received in respect of possessions or securities out of the United Kingdom (ie under Cases IV and V of Schedule D), the test asks whether a person who is in the United Kingdom for some temporary purpose only has 'actually resided in the United Kingdom at one time or several times for a period equal in the whole to six months in any year of assessment',[1] whereas for the purposes of Cases I to III of Schedule E, the test is whether a person who is in the United Kingdom for some temporary purpose only has 'in the aggregate spent at least six months in the United Kingdom in the year of assessment'.[2]

The ambiguity lies in the terms 'actually resided' in respect of Cases IV and V and 'spent' in respect of Cases I to III. Are the two terms synonymous and do both, or does only the second, refer to physical presence?

Whereas the provisions of TA 1988 s 336(2) first appeared comparatively recently, originating as FA 1956 Sch 2, para 3, the provisions of TA 1988 s 336(1) are, as has already been noted, of great antiquity, first appearing as ITA 1799 s 8 and then being re-enacted, first as ITA 1806 s 51, then as ITA 1812 s 39 and then as ITA 1918 Sch 1, rule 2 of the Miscellaneous Rules applicable to Schedule D. It was in that guise that they became the subject of comment by Lawrence LJ who considered them to mean that 'a person actually staying in the United Kingdom for 6 months is resident therein for the purposes of the charge to tax under Schedule D'.[3] 'Actually residing' has, it will be noted, been paraphrased as 'actually staying' and, clearly, in the view of Lawrence LJ, refers to nothing more than physical presence. Rowlatt J was more direct. He considered the force of rule 2 to be that 'if the person is in the United Kingdom for six months, then that is enough, if you have no other ground to make him chargeable as a person residing'[4] and with this Sargant LJ agreed:

> The language of this Rule draws a marked distinction between mere physical presence, called 'actual residence', which by the final words of the Rule makes a person chargeable

75

if he is actually resident for six months, and that presence which is in the course of being at home and therefore amounts to residence in the ordinary sense.[5]

On the basis of such pronouncements, Donovan J held, in the case of *Wilkie v IRC*[6] that '"actual" means "truly" and "in fact", and is the reverse of notional',[7] and paraphrased 'actually resided in the United Kingdom' as 'was here'. He concerned himself with the time Mr Wilkie 'spent' in the United Kingdom,[8] and declared that the point at issue in rule 2 was the length of a person's 'stay' in the United Kingdom. It would seem, therefore, that Lawrence LJ, Rowlatt J, Sargant LJ and Donovan J have, between them, satisfactorily eliminated any distinction that might otherwise be drawn between the terms 'actually resided' and 'spent', and that for either term we may safely read 'was physically present'.

Before turning to another and more important aspect of the *Wilkie* case, it is worth noting that the 'physical presence' of six months duration which will result in a visitor to the United Kingdom becoming attributed with residence status for the prescribed purposes of TA 1988 s 336 need not be on-shore physical presence. The United Kingdom consists of territorial land and territorial waters, and the territorial waters include both inland waters and the territorial sea. It was this fact which Mr Bayard Brown, an American citizen living on a yacht anchored in the tidal waters off Brightlingsea within the Port of Colchester, appears to have overlooked when he sought to avoid United Kingdom taxation. The yacht had, under the harbour-master's sufferance, been anchored off the Essex coast for some twenty years and though it had no lawful right to be there, the Court of Appeal recognised that, in point of fact, it *was* there and that Mr Bayard Brown was upon it 'for more than six months' in the year 1908–09. Accordingly, as the yacht was within the United Kingdom's territorial waters, 'in the body of the County of Essex', Mr Bayard was chargeable to income tax 'as a person residing in the United Kingdom'.[9]

1 TA 1988 s 336(1).
2 Ibid, s 336(2).
3 *Lysaght v IRC* (1925) 13 TC 511 at 524.
4 *Levene v IRC* (1928) 13 TC 486 at 492.
5 Ibid, at 498.
6 (1951) 32 TC 495.
7 Ibid, at 511.
8 Thus anticipating the precise terminology which, in 1956, took, in section 336(2), the place which 'actually resided' occupies in what is now section 336(1) but was then rule 2.
9 *Bayard Brown v Burt* (1911) 5 TC 667.

4.07 Six months

The *Wilkie* case has already been referred to at **4.06** above in connection with the meaning of the words 'actually resides'. The case's real importance lies, however, in the fact that it provides a judicial answer to the question of what is meant by 'six months'.

Mr Wilkie, a Scotsman, had spent his working life in India but visited the United Kingdom when on leave every few years. At 2 p.m. on 2 June 1947, he and his wife arrived in England by air for one such visit, intending to return to India not later than the end of November, but, unfortunately, Mr Wilkie had to undergo a medical operation in October and was not discharged from hospital until 10 November. Thereupon he booked a flight from Poole for 30 November – the earliest date on which a flight to India was available – but, on 14 November, those flight arrangements were cancelled by the airline and, in consequence, he was unable to actually leave the United Kingdom until 10 a.m. on 2 December 1947.

The Crown contended (a) that a fraction of a day falls to be treated as a full day, and (b) that 'six months' means six lunar months of 28 days each. By Inland Revenue reckoning, therefore, Mr Wilkie had actually resided in the United Kingdom for 184 days and had fallen to be treated as resident (by reason of his actual residence for a period equal in the whole to six months in 1947–48) after 168 days.

Mr Wilkie, on the other hand, contended (a) that fractions of a day fall to be taken account of as fractions, and (b) that 'six months' means six calendar months. By his reckoning, therefore, he had actually resided in the United Kingdom for 182 days and 20 hours and would not have fallen to be treated as resident (on the grounds of actual residence equal in the whole to six months in 1947–48) unless he had stayed in the United Kingdom for 183 days, ie until 2 p.m. on 2 December, four hours after his actual time of departure.

Donovan J allowed Mr Wilkie's appeal, holding that, because under the Interpretation Act 1889 s 3, 'month' in all Acts passed since 1850 means calendar month unless a contrary intention appears, '"six months" . . . means six calendar months'[1] and that when computing the length of a person's stay in the United Kingdom

> there is nothing in the language of the Rule to prevent hours being taken into the computation; but that, on the other hand, since what has to be determined is the period of actual residence it is legitimate to do so.[2]

Accordingly, in order to determine whether or not a person falls to be treated as resident under the six-month rule, one has simply to

> look at complete days of actual residence . . . and at the hours in the case of days when the Appellant was here for a part of the day and elsewhere for the rest; and then see whether or not it all adds up to the amount of time that there is in six months.[3]

On the face of it, this construction would appear to have provided a complete answer to the 'six months' question, but some have suggested that this is not so, arguing that it leaves open the question of which six calendar months are to provide the norm.

Revenue guidance on the six-month rule is that:

> To be regarded as resident in the UK you must normally be physically present in the country at some time in the tax year. You will always be resident if you are here for 183 days or more in the tax year. There are no exceptions to this. A count is made of the total number of days you spend in the UK – it does not matter if you come and go several times during the year or if you are here for one stay of 183 days or more. If you are here for less than 183 days you may still be treated as resident for the year under other tests.[4]

In a letter to the Consultative Committee of Accountancy Bodies dated 4 March 1983, the Inland Revenue commented that:

The treatment for residence purposes, as outlined in paragraph 8 of Booklet IR 20, was adopted in 1972 following a review of our practice in the light of the decision in *Wilkie v IRC* (1951) 32 TC 495. That case established the principle that, in deciding whether a temporary visitor had actually resided in the United Kingdom for a period equal to six months, periods of time in terms of hours were relevant for days of less than total residence. In view of the difficulties which would arise in following the strict rule it was decided to regard 183 days as equal to six months and to disregard days of arrival and departure in making the count.[5]

1 *Wilkie v IRC* (1951) 32 TC 495 at 508.
2 Ibid, at 511.
3 Ibid.
4 IR 20 (11 April 2000) para 1.2 and Ch 3 and in particular para 3.3.
5 CCAB Notes (TR 508) on Taxation Anomalies and Practical Difficulties, Appendix.

4.08 The limitations of the six-month test

The Revenue's chosen method of applying the six-month test is quite unobjectionable (working as it does to the taxpayer's advantage in every instance), but the statement which has been emphasised above is open to challenge. It will have been observed that, within the precise terms of TA 1988 s 336, the six-month test is of application, statutorily, only for the purposes of Cases IV and V of Schedule D and Cases I to III of Schedule E – not for the purposes of taxation in general. As has been noted at **1.15** above, however, it frequently becomes necessary to decide the question of a person's residence status for purposes under the Taxes Acts quite unconnected with those cases of Schedule D and Schedule E. For example, personal reliefs under TA 1988 s 278(1) are not, subject to certain exceptions, to be given in the case of any individual who is 'not resident in the United Kingdom'.[1] Credit against United Kingdom taxes is not to be allowed under any double taxation arrangements unless the person in respect of whose income the United Kingdom taxation is chargeable is 'resident in the United Kingdom'.[2]

When deciding the question of a person's residence in the context of these and other matters, TA 1988 s 336 is of no application and actual residence of six months duration during a tax year will not, therefore, in such circumstances, endow a person with residential status by operation of statute. The six-month test is, as was pointed out in the *Wilkie* case, an arbitrary test. Its statutory application is limited to prescribed purposes and, where its results are positive, it does not thereby establish the possession of the intrinsic quality of residence but merely imposes a notional or deemed residence status in order to bring the charging sections of Schedule D, Cases IV and V, and Schedule E, Cases I to III, into operation as regards certain persons otherwise beyond their reach.

It is, of course, open to anyone deciding a question of residence status outside of the context of TA 1988 s 336 to attach significance and weight to actual residence of six months or more and to regard it as strong evidence of the possession of such status, but it alone ought not to be regarded as conclusive. In the *Lysaght*[3] case, which related to the determination of residence for the purposes of Schedule C, Rowlatt J said:

Rule 2 of the Miscellaneous Rules applicable to Schedule D does not apply to this case at all, because it only deals with foreign possessions and securities. It has reference to the case of a taxpayer who has foreign possessions and securities.[4]

but he conceded that the language of what was then rule 2 had 'an illustrative value'. This is, however, not the same as saying – as paragraph 1.2 of Inland Revenue Booklet IR 20 (11 April 2000) implicitly says – that the six-month provisions of TA 1988 s 336 are binding in relation to the determination of residence for *all* purposes and not only for those to which the section specifically relates. The Inland Revenue, it seems, have derived this general rule from Sargant LJ's dictum in the *Levene* case:

> The residence which makes a person chargeable depends not on mere presence in the United Kingdom (unless that is for six months in all), but on the quality of the presence in relation to the objects and intentions of the person sought to be made chargeable.[5]

That statement, however, far from being of general application, is in fact part of Sargant LJ's commentary on ITA 1918 Sch 1, rule 2 of the Miscellaneous Rules applicable to Schedule D – now TA 1988 s 336. There is no suggestion in his commentary that six months' actual presence will, or should, endow a person with the status of residence for any purposes other than those laid down in TA 1988 s 336, and, indeed, the whole tenor of his commentary, including the part quoted above, runs against any such wider application.

1 TMA 1970 s 78.
2 TA 1988 s 794(1).
3 *Lysaght v IRC* (1928) 13 TC 511 at 515.
4 Ibid.
5 *Levene v IRC* (1928) 13 TC 486 at 498.

4.09 The significance of 'in the year of assessment'

Taxes Act 1988 s 336 refers to actual residence of six months 'in the year of assessment'. It is perfectly possible, therefore, for a person to arrive in the United Kingdom on 5 October in one year and to leave on 5 October in the following year (4 October if that year is a leap year) and thus spend a full twelve months in the United Kingdom without becoming attributed with the status of residence under the provisions of that section. Although 364 days will have been spent in the United Kingdom, only 182 days will have been spent in each of two consecutive but separate tax years. In the *Zorab* case,[1] Mr Zorab arrived in the United Kingdom on 1 November 1920 and departed on 3 October 1921 thus spending 337 consecutive days in the United Kingdom. Of those 337 days, only 156 were spent here in 1920–21 and only 181 were spent here in 1921–22 in consequence of which no challenge on 'six-month rule' grounds was raised against his non-resident status.

Any temporary visitor who so arranges the dates of his visit as to take advantage of this opportunity of law may, of course, find himself attributed with the status of residence on one or more of the circumstantial grounds described in Chapter 2. Although presence for six months of the tax year will ensure that he is attributed with the quality of residence for the purposes prescribed in TA 1988 s 336, presence for less than six months will not ensure that he is *not* attributed with the quality of residence for those or any other purposes under the Taxes Acts.

---

1 *IRC v Zorab* (1926) 11 TC 289. See **4.03** above.

4.10 The capital gains tax six-month test

At **4.02** above it was stated that the six-month test for capital gains tax purposes posed special difficulties and that it would, therefore, be discussed in isolation from TA 1988 s 336.

TCGA 1992 s 2(1) provides that, subject to certain exceptions:

> a person shall be chargeable to capital gains tax in respect of chargeable gains accruing to him in a year of assessment during any part of which he is resident in the United Kingdom, or during which he is ordinarily resident in the United Kingdom,

and goes on to provide in s 9(3) that subject to s 10 (non-residents with UK branch or agency) and subject to s 10A (temporary non-residents):

> an individual who is in the United Kingdom for some temporary purpose only and not with any view or intent to establish his residence in the United Kingdom shall be charged to capital gains tax on chargeable gains accruing in any year of assessment if and only if the period (or the sum of the periods) for which he is resident in the United Kingdom in the year of assessment exceeds six months.

It seems beyond doubt that the terms 'temporary purpose', 'view or intent to establish his residence' and 'six months' fall to be construed in the manner indicated at **4.03**, **4.04** and **4.07** above; but what of the term 'is resident' which here takes the place occupied by the term 'has . . . actually resided' in TA 1988 s 336(1)?

TCGA 1992 s 9(3) is a precise re-enactment of FA 1965 s 43(2) and Simon's commentary on that section states (albeit somewhat hesitantly) that '"is resident" means "is present"'.[1] But does it? Only two subsections earlier TCGA 1992 s 9(1) states that '"resident" and "ordinarily resident" have the same meanings as in the Income Tax Acts', and it has already been demonstrated at **2.02** above that 'resident', although not defined in the Income Tax Acts, means in those Acts 'possessed of the quality or status of residence' as opposed to 'being really there'. It is surely in accordance with that understanding of the meaning of the term that TCGA 1992 s 2(1) is to be construed (that section will certainly not sustain a reading in which 'resident' is taken to mean 'physically present') but, if that is so, what justification can there be – other than the similarity between parts of the text of TCGA 1992 s 9(3) and parts of TA 1988 s 336(1) and (2) – for construing TCGA 1992 s 9(3) with some other understanding of the term 'resident' in mind?

As has already been observed, physical presence is not in itself a determinant of residence status (except in relation to the two areas of chargeability to tax described at **4.06** above). On the contrary, a person may, dependent on his other circumstances, find himself attributed with that status after little or no physical presence in the United Kingdom and, if a person is so attributed with residence status in a tax year for however brief a period, then, within the terms of TCGA 1992 s 2(1), a charge to capital gains tax will normally arise in respect of any chargeable gains accruing during that tax year.

That being so, is not TCGA 1992 s 9(3) simply stating that, in order to alleviate such a burden in the case of individuals who have come to the United Kingdom for some temporary purpose but have become attributed with residence status, no charge to capital gains tax is to be made unless the total period for which residence status is possessed exceeds six months? The fact that residence is an annual attribute for taxation purposes is no bar to such a construction. As has been explained at **2.05** above (and as is, indeed, implied in the wording of TCGA 1992 s 2(1) itself), a person may acquire or lose the quality of residence at any time; its predication to him throughout the year is merely an expedient to which the annual nature of income tax gives rise.

This interpretation of TCGA 1992 s 9(3) necessitates rejection of the idea that it and TA 1988 s 336 are parallel provisions – though the Inland Revenue treats them as such.[2] It sees TCGA 1992 s 9(3) not as a charging provision but as a relieving provision; and the words 'and only if' within the section affirm that that is so. The only charge intended by TCGA 1992 or referred to in s 9(3) is the charge imposed by s 2(1). TCGA 1992 s 9(3) is not extending that charge to anyone not already within the reach of s 2(1). On the contrary, it has been enacted to extricate from the charge under s 2(1) anyone who, though in the United Kingdom for a short visit only, is trapped by that section. It is for that reason that s 9(3) (the relieving section) does not use the terminology of 'presence' but uses instead the same terminology of 'residence' as is used in s 2(1) (the charging section). That, surely, is as it should be, for, had Parliament couched the exempting provisions of s 9(3) in terms of physical presence, it would have made the exemption wider than the charge and would be setting free certain individuals who were not even caught!

When construed in the way it is here being suggested it ought to be construed, TCGA 1992 s 9(3) implicitly contains the words 'in accordance with section 2(1)' as follows:

> . . . an individual who is in the United Kingdom for some temporary purpose only and not with any view or intent to establish his residence in the United Kingdom shall be charged to capital gains tax [in accordance with section 2(1)] on capital gains accruing in any year of assessment if and only if the period (or the sum of the periods) for which he is resident in the United Kingdom [in accordance with section 2(1)] in that year of assessment exceeds six months.

---

1 *Simon's Income Tax Service*, Finance Act 1965, p. 81.
2 See **4.12** below

4.11 TCGA 1992 s 9(3) and TA 1988 s 336 compared

TCGA 1992 s 9(3) and TA 1988 s 336 serve different purposes. The object of TA 1988 s 336 is not only to remove from the charge imposed under certain cases of Schedule D and Schedule E certain persons who would otherwise unjustifiably be trapped there, but also to draw into the charge certain persons who would otherwise unjustifiably (in Parliament's view) be beyond its reach. Although TA 1988 s 336 is, in part, a relieving section, it is, therefore, also, in part (and unlike TCGA 1992 s 9(3)),[1] a charging section. No charge is imposed by Schedule D, Case IV or V or Schedule E, Cases I or III on a person who does not possess residence status, and an occasional visitor to the United Kingdom might, in the light of all his personal circumstances, succeed in satisfying the court (if not the Inland Revenue) that he does not possess such status. Parliament has ensured, however, that he will then have to contend with TA 1988 s 336. That section fills the gap which the longer-term casual visitor might walk through unscathed and, provided the period for which the visitor is physically present in the United Kingdom during the year of assessment is, in aggregate, six months or more, permits the Inland Revenue to *treat* him as possessing residence status and to impose on him the charge which would be imposed were he *actually* in possession of such status. As Lord Shand said in *Lloyd v Sulley*:[2]

> Although the provision . . . is in the language of exemption . . . it rather appears to me to be a section which is intended to impose liability,[3]

and, as Sir R. Webster A-G put it even more positively in *Colquhoun v Brooks*,[4] the section is

> not an exempting section in the proper sense of the word; it is a special charging section under limited circumstances.[5]

In short, TA 1988 s 336 is saying (in this author's view) that, once a temporary visitor has been here six months, he must, if he is found not to possess residence status on general grounds, be attributed with quasi-residence status and charged to tax under Schedule D, Cases IV and V and Schedule E accordingly; while TCGA 1992 s 9(3) is saying (again, in this author's view) that if a temporary visitor has acquired residence status on general grounds and would therefore fall to be charged to capital gains tax, he must be excused from the charge provided he possesses that status for six months or less in the year.

Section 208(2)(4) of the FA 1993 inserted a new subjection (4) into section 9 of TCGA 1992. This new subsection is identical to the new subsection (3) inserted into section 336 of TA 1988, see **4.05** above, and provides that in determining whether for capital gains tax, as for income tax, a person is in the United Kingdom for some temporary purpose only and not with any view or intent to establish residence no regard shall be taken of any living accommodation available in the United Kingdom for that person's use. The new subsection 9(4) applies with effect for the year 1993–94 and subsequent years of assessment.

---

1 See **4.12** below.
2 (1884) 2 TC 37.
3 Ibid, at 44.
4 (1889) 2 TC 490.
5 Ibid, at 493.

4.12 The Inland Revenue view of TCGA 1992 s 9(3)

The construction of TCGA 1992 s 9(3) propounded at **4.10** and **4.11** above is not (as one might expect) the construction placed on it by the Inland Revenue. The Inland Revenue would like to believe that the effect of TCGA 1992 s 9(3) is that *actual* residence of six months' duration in a tax year will automatically bring a temporary visitor into charge to capital gains tax, and it is Inland Revenue practice to treat such actual residence as doing so. It must be questioned, however, whether that practice is within the law.

Were the practice ever to be challenged in the courts, the Inland Revenue might be expected to attempt to justify it by referring to the use of the word 'resides' in the final charging part of TA 1988 s 336(1). That section begins by saying that a temporary visitor is not to be charged to tax if he has not 'actually resided' in the United Kingdom for six months, but then goes on to say that if such a visitor 'resides' in the United Kingdom for six months or more he is to be charged to tax. The Inland Revenue would no doubt argue (correctly) that 'resides' in TA 1988 s 336(1) takes its meaning from the term 'actually resides' earlier in the same section and thus also means 'actually resides'. That being so (the argument might proceed), the term 'resident' may, in certain contexts in the Income Tax Acts, mean 'actually resident' and, by virtue of TCGA 1992 s 9(1), the same must be true of the word when it is employed in TCGA 1992. Section 9 (it might be said) is one such context and, although 'resident' in TCGA 1992 s 2(1) clearly means 'qualitatively resident', 'resident' in TCGA 1992 s 9(3) clearly means 'actually resident'. In short (the Inland Revenue would probably say), TCGA 1992 s 9(3) is intended to do for capital gains tax what TA 1988 s 336(1) does for income tax and, that being so, TCGA 1992 s 9(3) implicitly contains the words 'to which he would not be chargeable by virtue of section 2(1)' and 'actually', as follows:

> . . . an individual who is in the United Kingdom for some temporary purpose only and not with any view or intent to establish his residence in the United Kingdom shall be charged to capital gains tax [to which he would not be chargeable by virtue of section 2(1) on capital gains accruing in any year of assessment if and only if the period (or the sum of the periods) for which he is [actually] resident in the United Kingdom in that year of assessment exceeds six months'.

If the Inland Revenue view of TCGA 1992 s 9(3) is ever to receive judicial blessing, the court will need to be convinced that Parliament did indeed intend 'residence' to be read as 'actual residence', and that such a construction is not favoured by the Inland Revenue merely because it is both administratively easier to apply and more rewarding in terms of taxation than the alternative construction propounded at **4.10** and **4.11** above. So far as TCGA 1992 s 9(3) is concerned, the court would no doubt ask itself why a parliamentary draftsman, knowing he was entering a legislative minefield when he came to a provision concerning residence and having before him TA 1988 s 336(1) to serve him as a model (part of the wording of which he proceeded to adopt), should have omitted from TCGA 1992 s 9(3) the very word in that model section which the Inland Revenue says we should read into it and should have chosen to leave 'resides' without the only qualifying adverb that would have imbued it with the meaning the Inland Revenue seeks.

Although the consequences of adopting one view rather than the other may not affect large numbers of visitors to the United Kingdom, the choice of view could be of material effect in certain circumstances.

A new section 10A of the TCGA 1992 has been added which affects certain individuals who arrive in the United Kingdom following a period when they have left the United Kingdom for a temporary purpose, such as to dispose of assets which otherwise would be chargable to capital gains tax.[1]

---

1 See **4.22** below.

Persons leaving the United Kingdom

4.13 British subjects temporarily abroad

Taxes Act 1988 s 334 provides that:

> Every Commonwealth citizen or citizen of the Republic of Ireland –
> (a) shall if his ordinary residence has been in the United Kingdom be assessed and charged to income tax notwithstanding that at the time the assessment or charge is made he may have left the United Kingdom, if he has so left the United Kingdom for the purpose only of occasional residence abroad, and
> (b) shall be charged as a person actually residing in the United Kingdom upon the whole amount of his profits or gains, whether they arise from property in the United Kingdom or elsewhere or from any allowance, annuity or stipend, or from any trade, profession, employment or vocation in the United Kingdom or elsewhere.

The first point to note about this provision is that it contains an overall limitation by reference to nationality,[1] for the section is of no application to any individual who is neither a British subject nor a citizen of the Irish Republic. The first of these terms, under British Nationality Act 1981 s 51, includes anyone who, after 1 January 1983,[2] is a British citizen, a British Dependent Territories citizen, a Commonwealth citizen or a citizen of any of the independent nations of the Commonwealth,[3] or who, before that date, had the status of citizen of the United Kingdom and Colonies or citizen of any of the independent nations of the Commonwealth.[4] The provision may, therefore, apply to a Canadian as well as to an Englishman and to an Australian as well as to a Scotsman.

Citizens of the Republic of Ireland are brought within the provision because, although the Republic of Ireland ceased to be a member of the Commonwealth in 1949, it is not regarded as a foreign state, nor are her citizens regarded as aliens, either by Great Britain or other Commonwealth nations.

The second point to note is that section 334 contains a further limitation in that it concerns itself only with individuals whose 'ordinary residence' has been in the United Kingdom. The concept of ordinary residence has been fully explored in Chapter 3 and may here be defined as residence in a particular country, adopted voluntarily and for a settled purpose as part of the regular order of an individual's life. Although, as has been said, TA 1988 s 334 may apply equally to a Canadian and an Englishman, it may, therefore, only so apply if, in either case, the individual has, as part of the regular order of his life, voluntarily adopted the United Kingdom as his place of abode for one or more settled purposes.

---

1 See **1.11** above.
2 The date the Act came into effect.
3 See **1.09** above.
4 Ibid.

4.14 Occasional residence

Having thus narrowed the area of concern to one of persons with strong attachments to the United Kingdom, the section comes to its point. If any such person leaves the United Kingdom for the purpose 'only of occasional residence abroad' he is, despite his absence, to be treated as resident here. The words in quotation marks are of very great importance for, despite the limitations built into TA 1988 s 334, most United Kingdom taxpayers remain within its ambit and, whenever one of them claims to have become non-resident by reason of taking up residence abroad, the Crown, if it wishes to resist that claim, will attempt to do so by contending that the residence abroad is occasional residence only.

Although the term 'occasional residence abroad' may suggest only short periods of absence, it was, in one of the earliest cases on the subject of residence,[1] held to include a temporary absence which extended over an entire tax year. This should immediately alert us to the fact that the words have been construed as possessing a far wider meaning than we might otherwise suppose. The case concerned the validity of a charge to tax within the context of the first part of ITA 1842 s 39 – one of the predecessors of TA 1988 s 334 – which provided (somewhat more picturesquely than its 1988 successor) that:

> any subject of Her Majesty whose ordinary residence shall have been in Great Britain, and who shall have departed from Great Britain and gone into any parts beyond the seas, for the purpose only of occasional residence . . . shall be deemed, notwithstanding such temporary absence, a person chargeable to the duties granted by this Act as a person actually residing in Great Britain.

The case concerned a master mariner who, because he was absent from the United Kingdom throughout the whole of 1878–79, contended that his residence abroad was not merely 'occasional' and that he was, therefore, beyond the scope of s 39 and thus not liable to tax for that year. The Lord President Inglis did not agree:

> The circumstance that Captain Rogers has been absent from the country during the whole year to which the assessment applies does not seem to me to be a speciality of the least consequence. That is a mere accident. He is not a bit the less a resident of Great Britain because the exigencies of his business have happened to carry him away for a somewhat longer time than usual during this particular voyage.[2]

Captain Rogers was a British subject, commanded a British ship, owned a house at Innerleven in the county of Fife in which his wife and children dwelt throughout the year in question, owned no house elsewhere, and was absent merely by reason of following his vocation of master mariner. Despite the fact that he was not physically present for even a single day in the tax year 1878–79, he was, therefore, qualitatively resident in the United Kingdom throughout that tax year.[3]

The principle – that occasional residence abroad may extend to absences in excess of an entire tax year – remained unchanged and, indeed, was reiterated a quarter of a century later in the Irish case of *Iveagh v Revenue Comrs*[4] when, in the course of expressing his opinion on the application of what had then become rule 3 of the General Rules applicable to Schedules A, B, C, D and E under ITA 1918, Hanna J declared:

It may well be that under this rule a citizen absent through illness for a lengthy period, even two years, may be liable to tax[5]

and when, in that same case, it was held that the Special Commissioners had not misdirected themselves in point of law in holding that

> there must be personal presence . . . at some time during the year of assessment, except in a case coming within the terms of Rule 3 of the General Rules.[6]

Anyone who is 'resident in the United Kingdom for a year of assessment, but . . . absent from the United Kingdom throughout that year' can clearly only be someone who has been attributed with the quality of residence in the United Kingdom for a particular tax year without ever having been physically present in the United Kingdom during any part of that year. This was noted by Nicholls J in *Reed v Clark*[7] who later confirmed that:

> There is nothing in the language or in my view the context of s 49 to show that regardless of the circumstances a person can never be said to have left for the purpose of occasional residence abroad if his residence abroad extends throughout an entire tax year. A man ordinarily resident here may go to live abroad in March intending to return some months later but through serious illness of himself or others or other unforeseen change of circumstances not return until the end of the following March. I can see no reason why, depending on all the facts, such a man may not fall within s 49. If that is right, it would be absurd that such a man should fall outside s 49 if the emergency which kept him abroad should chance to last for a week or two longer and not permit his return until after 5 April.[8]

In the eyes of the Inland Revenue, however, 'residence is essentially related to physical presence'[9] so that 'to be regarded as resident in the United Kingdom you must normally be physically present in the country at some time in the tax year'[10] and even if he usually lives in the United Kingdom but has gone abroad for a long holiday and does not set foot in the United Kingdom during the year,[11] he will be regarded as non-resident for that year. The Inland Revenue shows consistency, therefore, when it equates 'occasional residence abroad' with absence of 'short periods'[12] only, but it must be emphasised that this view of the meaning of occasional residence is unsupported by case law and that the strict position of any British subject or citizen of the Irish Republic falling within the provisions of TA 1988 s 334 (previously TA 1970 s 49) is as it was in Captain Rogers' day. Furthermore, the rule of practice does, it should be noted, include the qualification 'normally' which leaves it open to the Inland Revenue to decide in any particular case that a person is resident in the United Kingdom for a tax year throughout the whole of which he has been physically absent. This was the Revenue stance in *Reed v Clark*[13] where Dave Clark's absence was admittedly motivated by tax avoidance considerations. In *IRC v Combe*,[14] Lord Clyde LP said that:

> 'occasional residence' is residence taken up or happening as passing opportunity requires, in one case, or admits in another, and contrasts with the residence, or ordinary residence, of a person who . . . is 'resident' or 'ordinarily resident' in some place or country,[15]

and in *Reed v Clark*[16] Nicholls J, commenting on s 49, said:

> In this section occasional residence is the converse of ordinary residence.[17]

The duration of the physical absence from the United Kingdom of a person falling within TA 1988 s 334 is of relevance, therefore, only to the extent to which it bears on whether or not that person has, in fact, become resident or ordinarily resident elsewhere. If he has, then his residence in that other place or country cannot be 'occasional residence' abroad, for one cannot be resident and occasionally resident in one and the same place at one and the same time.[18] If a person has *not* become resident or ordinarily resident elsewhere, however, but, having been ordinarily resident in the United Kingdom, has left these shores, his residence overseas *is* 'occasional residence'. In short, a person within the category prescribed by TA 1988 s 334 *will* be attributed with the status of residence in accordance with that section unless there is evidence of 'a distinct break'[19] with the United Kingdom. Although general Revenue practice is to treat physical absence which extends over a whole tax year as creating such a break, such absence alone is, as the earlier cases show, not conclusive evidence in law of such a break, and although even the courts have conceded that the attribution of residential status to a person who 'during a whole year, the year of assessment . . . has never been in this country . . . would require a pretty strong case indeed',[20] that is not to say that there are no circumstances in which such a case could be made by the Revenue – as *Reed v Clark*[21] plainly shows.

1 *Rogers v IRC* (1879) 1 TC 225.
2 Ibid, at 227.
3 It is unlikely that any present-day Captain Rogers would be regarded as resident in the circumstances described, but this would be because of the application of TA 1988 s 335 – see **4.16** below – not because of any change in the judicial view of the meaning of 'occasional residence abroad'.
4 (1930) 1 ITC 316.
5 Ibid, at 349.
6 Ibid, at 356–357.
7 [1985] STC 323.
8 Ibid, at 344.
9 Inland Revenue explanatory note relating to a proposed amendment to Finance Bill 1974, cl 18.
10 Appendix IR 20, (11 April 2000), para 1.2.
11 Ibid, para 1.3.
12 Ibid, para 2.1.
13 [1985] STC 323.
14 (1932) 17 TC 405.
15 Ibid, at 410.
16 [1985] STC 323.
17 Ibid, at 345.
18 One can, however, be resident in two or more places at the same time – see **2.08** above – and the fact that a person may escape the provisions of TA 1988 s 334 by proving that his residence overseas is not merely occasional, does not mean, therefore, that he cannot be found to be nonetheless resident in the United Kingdom as well as resident elsewhere and thus to be liable for United Kingdom taxes.
19 *IRC v Combe* (1932) 17 TC 405 at 411, per Lord Sands.
20 *Turnbull v Foster* (1904) 6 TC 206 at 209, per Clerk LJ.
21 [1985] STC 323.

4.15 A distinct break

The foregoing discussion should have served to illustrate how adhesive the quality of residence is in the case of a Commonwealth citizen or citizen of the Irish Republic whose ordinary residence has been in the United Kingdom. Indeed, nothing less than a distinct break with the United Kingdom will suffice to divest a person of that quality, as the leading case[1] concerning the application of ITA 1918 Sch 1, rule 3 of the General Rules applicable to Schedules A, B, C, D and E (the predecessor of TA 1988 s 334) makes very plain.

Until March 1918, Mr Louis Levene, a British subject, leased a house in Curzon Street, London. On that date he surrendered the lease, sold his furniture and, until January 1925, was of no fixed abode but stayed at hotels either in the United Kingdom or abroad. Until December 1919, he stayed in England and was, on his own admission, resident and ordinarily resident in the United Kingdom until that date. In December 1919, however, he went abroad but returned to the United Kingdom in July 1920 and, from then until January 1925, spent between four and five months here in each tax year. The purpose of his annual visits to the United Kingdom was to obtain medical advice for himself and his wife, to visit relatives and the graves of his parents, to take part in certain Jewish religious observances and to deal with his tax affairs. In January 1925 he took a nine-year lease on a flat in Monaco.

Mr Levene contended that for the years 1920–21 to 1924–25 he was neither resident nor ordinarily resident in the United Kingdom and that, in consequence, he was entitled to exemption from tax on certain interest and dividends from securities. The Special Commissioners did not agree and the High Court, the Court of Appeal and finally the House of Lords upheld the Commissioners' decision. Key passages from Viscount Sumner's lucid judgment are given below.

> My Lords, early in 1918 Mr Levene, a British subject, formed the intention to 'live abroad'. He sold his house in Mayfair, sold such furniture as was not in settlement, and then lived in hotels in England for the best part of two years. I will assume that, but for passport difficulties and the condition of his wife's health, he would have gone abroad sooner. He left England in December, 1919.
>
> Accordingly on 6 April 1920, at the beginning of the five years of charge now in question, he was, in the words of Rule 3 of the General Rules, 'a British subject, whose ordinary residence has been in the United Kingdom' and so he remained chargeable to tax notwithstanding, if he had left the United Kingdom for the purpose only of occasional residence abroad. Was that the only purpose of his leaving so far as residence is concerned?
>
> The Special Commissioners found that it was, and I think it is clear that they had evidence before them on which they could so find. His only declaration was that he meant to live abroad, not saying whether it was to be an occasional or a constant, a part time or a whole time sojourn. He was advised by his doctor to seek a better climate, which is consistent with returning to England when English weather mends. He had gone out of business in England and broken up his establishment, but he still had in England business interests connected with his Income Tax assessments, and ties of filial piety and religious observance, for his father was buried at Southampton and he was himself a member of the English community of Jews. What he actually did was to come back to England after an absence of about seven months, and he remained for nearly five. In the meantime he had not set up an establishment abroad but had lived in hotels. This, however, was only what he had done in England from March, 1918, to December, 1919. I think there was

ample evidence before the Commissioners to show that a man, who left England to live abroad as he had been living here, and when warm weather came returned to his native country and to his permanent associations, had in 1919 'left the United Kingdom for the purposes of occasional residence only'. If so, he remained chargeable.

So much for the year of charge 1920–21. In the following years he was a bird of passage of almost mechanical regularity. No material change occurred in his way of living, for his enquiries for a permanent flat came to nothing until so late as not to affect his life and residence for the period in question . . . The evidence as a whole disclosed that Mr Levene continued to go to and fro during the years in question, leaving at the beginning of winter and coming back in summer, his home thus remaining as before. He changed his sky but not his home.[2] On this I see no error in law in saying of each year that his purpose in leaving the United Kingdom was occasional residence abroad only. The occasion was the approach of an English winter and when with the promise of summer here that occasion passed away, back came Mr Levene to attend the calls of interest, of friendship and of piety.[3]

Not until January 1925 was there evidence of a distinct break with Mr Levene's former residence in the United Kingdom and, accordingly, not until 1925 could his periods of residence abroad be anything other than occasional residence within the context of what is now TA 1988 s 334 despite the fact that for a period of five years Mr Levene had no fixed abode in this country and consistently spent the greater part of each year overseas.

The case of Mr Levene may usefully be compared and contrasted with that of Mr F. L. Brown.[4] Mr Brown was a British subject whose ordinary residence had been in the United Kingdom from 1893 until February 1918. On that date he, like Mr Levene, gave up his house in Folkestone, stored his furniture and, until October 1919, lived at hotels in various places in the United Kingdom. In October 1919, however he departed for a hotel in Menton on the French Riviera where he had habitually stayed for two or three months every winter since 1906, and from October 1919 his ordinary and usual habit of life was to spend seven months of each year in the same suite of rooms in that hotel (ie practically the whole of the hotel's open season), two months in Switzerland or at the Italian lakes, and three months in the United Kingdom. Mr Brown had four sons living in the United Kingdom and his visits to the United Kingdom were to see them, other relations and friends, and for a change. Sometimes he stayed with friends or relatives, other times he stayed at hotels or boarding houses. He had no business ties in the United Kingdom but he had a banking account here into which dividends were paid. The Inland Revenue contended that Mr Brown, being a British subject whose ordinary residence had been in the United Kingdom, had gone abroad for the purpose of occasional residence only within the meaning of rule 3 of the General Rules, but the Special Commissioners did not agree. They held that 'there had been a definite break in his habit of life in February 1918, when the house in the United Kingdom was given up'.[5] In a remarkably brief judgment, Rowlatt J dismissed the Crown's appeal on the grounds that he could see no error of law in the Commissioners' finding and could not, therefore, interfere with it. Nevertheless, he made his reservations plain: Mr Brown 'had some furniture and a banking account and he had connections with England, and if the Commissioners had found the other way I should not have disturbed them'.[6] There was a break, but one which, clearly, was not as clean as Rowlatt J would have liked to find it. Because of that break, however, Mr Brown became non-resident from 6 April 1918 and his residence status for

1924–25, the tax year in question, was determined by the Commissioners under the statutory provisions now contained in TA 1988 s 336 which relate to visitors in the United Kingdom.[7] Because the Commissioners considered that Mr Levene had made no such break prior to January 1925, however, his residence status for the years 1920-21 to 1924-25 could not be determined under those provisions. Hence the difference in outcome of what, on the face of them, were very similar cases.

The principle that once there is a 'distinct break' in a person's residence in the United Kingdom, the overseas residence that ensues will necessarily be more than 'occasional' residence, was emphasised some six years later by Lord Sands in *IRC v Combe*.[8] Captain Combe, a British subject, left the United Kingdom for America and there served an apprenticeship under a New York employer with a view to becoming that employer's European representative. During each of the three years following his departure, he made visits here on his employer's business but, having no place of abode in the United Kingdom, stayed in hotels. The Crown claimed that Captain Combe had remained resident in the United Kingdom throughout the three years in question as, within the terms of what is now TA 1988 s 334, he had left the United Kingdom for the purpose only of occasional residence abroad. This claim was, however, rejected by the Commissioners and, on appeal, by the Court of Session. Lord Sands, referring to the fact that Captain Combe had left the United Kingdom on 24 April 1926 and had not returned for a visit until 4 March 1927, said:

> There was a distinct break. Any residence in the first year in this country was what might have been accounted for by simply not very prolonged holidays.[9]

It was that opinion on which, in part, Nicholls J based his judgment in *Reed v Clark*.[10] Dave Clark was a British subject whose ordinary residence had been in England until, on 3 April 1978, he left England to live and work in Los Angeles for thirteen months. The thirteen months intentionally spanned the tax year 1978–79 because Dave Clark had been advised that, by staying abroad throughout that year, he would avoid tax on $450,000 received in the previous year from the sale of Polydor Ltd – a German recording company – of the right to make and sell certain recordings of the 'Dave Clark Five' – a band which he had formed and which had enjoyed considerable success in the 1960s.

Mr Clark was unmarried and, before leaving for America, he lived with his mother in a house he had bought for her in North London. Upon returning to the United Kingdom on 2 May 1979 he resumed residence there. Throughout the period, Dave Clark (London) Ltd – a company of which Mr Clark was sole director – owned the lease of a flat in Mayfair and, until leaving for America, Mr Clark had an office and bedroom there. A firm of estate agents were instructed to sub-let the flat during the period of his absence but they were unable to do so. Mr Clark had, however, packed away his files and other belongings and the flat was in a state of readiness for a sub-tenant had one been found.

In contending that Mr Clark's residence in America was merely occasional residence abroad, the Crown stressed the fact that it was, from the outset, Mr Clark's intention to return to the United Kingdom after thirteen months; the fact that during his absence his established domestic and business arrangements in this country were maintained to such a degree that, immediately upon his return, his ordinary pattern of life could be resumed without any significant disruption; and the fact that his absence was contrived for tax avoidance purposes.

Nicholls J was of the opinion that none of those facts brought Mr Clark's residence within the term 'occasional residence' as used in TA 1970s 49. He said:

> In this case there was a distinct break in the pattern of the taxpayer's life which lasted (as from the outset he intended) for just over a year. He ceased living in London and for that year he lived in or near Los Angeles, mostly in one fixed place of abode, and he worked from there. For that year Los Angeles was his headquarters. He did not visit this country at all. On the whole I do not think he can be said to have left the United Kingdom for the purpose only of occasional residence abroad. In my judgment the conclusion of the commissioners on this was correct.[11]

1 *Levene v IRC* (1928) 13 TC 486.
2 Although Viscount Sumner is generally credited with the coining of this striking phrase, it seems clear that he was, in fact, either consciously or unconsciously, misquoting the Latin poet Horace who centuries earlier had written 'caelum non animum mutant qui trans mare currunt' (Epist I.xi.27) – 'they change their sky but not their soul who speed across the sea'.
3 *Levene v IRC* (1928) 13 TC 486 at 501.
4 *IRC v Brown* (1926) 11 TC 292.
5 Ibid, at 295.
6 Ibid, at 296.
7 See **4.02–4.09** above.
8 (1932) 17 TC 405.
9 Ibid, at 411.
10 [1985] STC 323.
11 Ibid, at 346.

4.16 Persons working abroad

The statutory provision concerning residence which next falls to be discussed is that contained in TA 1988 s 335:

(1) Where –
(a) a person works full time in one or more of the following, that is to say, a trade, profession, vocation, office or employment; and
(b) no part of the trade, profession or vocation is carried on in the United Kingdom and all the duties of the office or employment are performed outside the United Kingdom;
the question whether he is resident in the United Kingdom shall be decided without regard to any place of abode maintained within the United Kingdom for his use.
(2) Where an office or employment is in substance one of which the duties fall in the year of assessment to be performed outside the United Kingdom there shall be treated for the purposes of this section as so performed any duties performed in the United Kingdom the performance of which is merely incidental to the performance of the other duties outside the United Kingdom.

This section originated as FA 1956 s 11 and was enacted in response to one of the recommendations of the Royal Commission on the Taxation of Profits and Income. The Royal Commission found that, following the decisions of the courts in *Lloyd v Sulley*,[1] *Cooper v Cadwalader*[2] and *Loewenstein v De Salis*,[3] the practice of the Inland Revenue was to treat the possession of available accommodation in the United Kingdom as conclusive evidence of 'a view or intent to establish residence' in the case of any person who visited the United Kingdom and whose residence was in question for the purposes of Case IV or V of Schedule D[4] and as conclusive evidence of residential status itself in the case of any person who set foot in the United Kingdom and whose residence was in question for other purposes under the Taxes Acts. The Commission felt that, in the case of persons working full-time abroad and making visits to the United Kingdom, this practice bore

> with obvious harshness upon the man who keeps up a home here for his family while he is abroad, and distinguishes him absolutely from the man who comes back and stays in a hotel or in furnished rooms, or the batchelor who comes back to spend his time in his parents' home[5]

and recommended that the situation be remedied by statutory provision. The result was FA 1956 s 11 which is now TA 1988 s 335.

---

1 (1884) 2 TC 37.
2 (1904) 5 TC 101.
3 (1926) 10 TC 424.
4 See **4.04** above.
5 Final Report, 1955, Cmd 9474, para 294(1).

4.17 Full-time work

Taxes Act 1988 s 335 is of no application to anyone who does not work full-time in one, or more than one, trade, profession, vocation, office or employment. 'Full-time' is, however, a term which is undefined in the statute and which must, therefore, be given its ordinary, accepted meaning. This, according to *Chambers Twentieth Century Dictionary*[1] is: 'extending over the whole working day, week etc'; but the Inland Revenue may, in practice, be expected to interpret it more liberally than that dictionary definition would suggest. The words 'works full- time' appear in only one other place in the Taxes Acts and that is in relation to loans to participators by close companies.[2] In that context, it is Inland Revenue practice to treat a director or employee as working full-time if his hours of work are equivalent to at least three-quarters of the company's normal working hours; and this would accord with the statutory definition of a 'full-time working director' as 'a director who is required to devote *substantially* the whole of his time to the service of the company in a managerial and technical capacity'.[3] Furthermore, it was disclosed by the Financial Secretary to the Treasury during the debate on what is now FA 1984 s 38 and Sch 10[4] that an employee must, in the Inland Revenue's view, work for at least 25 hours a week before he can be treated as carrying out full-time duties.[5]

Even if we take TA 1988 s 335 as being directed, therefore, only at those who, apart from periods of holiday, leave, sickness etc, are occupied in their work throughout substantially the whole (ie at least 25 hours) of each working week, the term 'full-time' has not, however, been cleared of all its difficulties of construction. Although the term is clearly intended to contrast full-time work with part-time work, the words 'in one or more of the following, that is to say, a trade, profession, vocation, office or employment' do not, on a strict construction, exclude a person who, although working only part-time in relation to any one trade, profession, employment or the like, does so in relation to more than one trade, profession, employment or the like so that his various part-time occupations extend over the whole of each working week. The Inland Revenue now appears to accept this view.[6] Taxes Act 1988 s 335 is silent as to whether the full-time occupation to which it refers must extend over an entire tax year in order that its provisions might be effective for that tax year but there would seem to be no strong argument in favour of such a construction. The section is not granting a full-time overseas worker non-resident status; it is merely saying that his residence status is to be decided without regard to any place of abode he maintains in the United Kingdom. Disregard of a person's maintained place of abode in the United Kingdom will, however, in the majority of cases, not prevent the attribution of residence status to a person whose period of full-time work abroad does not span an entire tax year. The various connecting factors described at **2.15** to **2.18** above will alone be sufficient, in most cases, to imbue the person with residence status upon his return to the United Kingdom and, as explained at **2.05** above, that status will, in law, be attributed to him for the whole of the tax year in which the return takes place. It is Inland Revenue practice to refuse non-resident status to a person working overseas unless

your absence from the UK and your employment abroad both last for at least a whole tax year; during your absence any visits you make to the UK (i) total less than 183 days in any tax year, and (ii) average less than 91 days a tax year (the average is taken over a period of absence up to a maximum of four years;[7] any days spent in the UK because of exceptional circumstances beyond your control, for example the illness of yourself or a member of your immediate family are not normally counted for this purpose).[8]

Clearly, the timing of relatively short overseas assignments can assume great importance in the light of these considerations.

---

1 1983 edn.
2 TA 1988 s 420(2)(b).
3 TA 1988 s 168(10), author's italics.
4 Which concern eligibility for participation in an approved share option scheme.
5 Official Report, Standing Committee A, 24 May 1984, col 683.
6 Revenue Interpretation 40 (February) 1993.
7 Appendix IR 20 (11 April 2000), para 2.10.
8 Ibid, para 2.2.

4.18 Trades and professions

It has been stressed[1] that unless a person works full-time in a trade, profession, vocation, office or employment, he cannot bring himself within the ambit of TA 1988 s 335. The fact that a person may so work is, however, not sufficient, on its own, to guarantee his inclusion within the ambit of the section, for there is an additional condition which must first be fulfilled.

In the case of a person working full-time in a trade, profession or vocation, that condition is that no part of the trade, profession or vocation is carried on in the United Kingdom. If any part of it is carried on then the person is beyond the scope of the section and the question of whether he himself ever actually works in the United Kingdom is completely irrelevant.

The consequences of this may be severe. Anyone who carries on a trade, profession or vocation partly in the United Kingdom and partly overseas will, if he

93

is attributed with United Kingdom residence status, find himself chargeable to tax under Schedule D, Case I or II, on the *whole* of his profits or gains irrespective of whether they have arisen from activities inside the United Kingdom or abroad.[2] Only if he is able to obtain or maintain non-resident status will assessments under Schedule D, Case I or II be restricted to such of his profits or gains as may be attributed to activities in the United Kingdom.[3]

In order to determine where a trade is carried on, one must ask the question: 'Where do the operations take place from which the profits in substance arise?'.[4] If the answer to that question is: partly within and partly outside the United Kingdom, then it follows that 'part of the trade . . . is carried on in the United Kingdom' within the meaning of TA 1988 s 335.

The test is a very broad one and necessitates a detailed examination of all the facts in any particular case, but a number of decided cases have given rise to certain general principles. In *Sully v A–G*,[5] for instance, it was decided that merely contracting to purchase goods in the United Kingdom for subsequent resale abroad cannot constitute the carrying on of trade in the United Kingdom. Nor, according to the decision in *Grainger & Son v Gough*,[6] can the mere soliciting of sales orders which are then actually entered into overseas amount to trading in the United Kingdom. (In that case, the now-familiar distinction between trading *in* the United Kingdom and trading *with* the United Kingdom was drawn.) Similarly, in *Smidth & Co v Greenwood*,[7] it was decided that assistance given in the United Kingdom in relation to the negotiation and execution of sales contracts concluded overseas did not amount to trading here. Where, however, contracts are actually and habitually made in the United Kingdom, by a person not resident here, he may, according to the decision in *Erichsen v Last*,[8] be regarded as trading in the United Kingdom, even though the fulfilment of the contracts made in the United Kingdom takes place overseas. The importance which the place of the making of sales contracts has assumed in these matters may be traced back to *Werle & Co v Colquhoun*[9] where Esher MR said:

> the contract is the very foundation of the trade. It is the trade really . . . If the trade consists in making contracts which are profitable contracts, if those contracts are made in England, then the trade is carried on in England, because the making of the contracts is the very substance and essence of the trade.[10]

It must be remembered, however, that those words were spoken in the context of a case which concerned the merchanting of wine, and that even there, the place of delivery and the place of payment were held to be important matters for consideration. Where the trade involves manufacture, and the manufacture takes place in the United Kingdom, the place at which contracts of sale are made will be of much less significance. As Atkin LJ said in the *Smidth* case:[11]

> The contracts in this case were made abroad. But I am not prepared to hold that this test is decisive. I can imagine cases where the contract of re-sale is made abroad and yet the manufacture of the goods, some negotiation of the terms and complete execution of the contract take place here under such circumstances that the trade was in truth exercised here.[12]

This provides a salutary check to the widespread belief that, provided no sales contract is ever signed in the United Kingdom, trading cannot be held to be taking place here. That is simply not so. The identification of the place of trade will invariably necessitate an analysis of the nature and scope of a person's activities in the various territories concerned, with particular reference to where, in relation to those activities, the profits, in substance, arise.

1 At **4.17** above.
2 TA 1988 s 18(1)(a)(ii).
3 Ibid, s 18(1)(a)(iii).
4 *Smidth & Co v Greenwood* (1922) 8 TC 193 at 204, per Atkin LJ.
5 (1860) 2 TC 149.
6 (1896) 3 TC 311.
7 (1922) 8 TC 193.
8 (1881) 1 TC 351.
9 (1888) 2 TC 402.
10 Ibid, at 410–412.
11 *Smidth & Co v Greenwood* (1922) 8 TC 193.
12 Ibid, at 204.

4.19 Employments

The condition which must be fulfilled before a person who works full-time in an office or employment will become entitled to have his residence status decided without regard to any place of abode which he maintains in the United Kingdom is contained in TA 1988 s 335(1)(b) and is that 'all the duties of the office or employment are performed outside the United Kingdom'.

The condition contained in TA 1988 s 335(1)(b) must be interpreted in the light of TA 1988 s 335(2) which modifies the condition in two ways. First, the office or employment must be 'in substance one of which the duties fall . . . to be performed outside the United Kingdom', and, secondly, 'duties performed in the United Kingdom the performance of which is merely incidental to the performance of the other duties outside the United Kingdom' must be treated as performed outside the United Kingdom.

In *Robson v Dixon*,[1] Pennycuick V-C expressed doubt as to whether the first requirement had any meaning if viewed as anything but an adjunct of the second requirement:

> The words 'in substance' are extremely vague in their import. Moreover, it is extremely difficult to see in what circumstances that requirement could be of any significance independently of the second requirement in the subsection. The Special Commissioners skated over the first requirement. I think they were quite right to do so, and I propose to follow their example. The sole question is whether the second requirement is performed.[2]

It is suggested, however, that that opinion (and its last sentence in particular) should not be taken as an absolute dismissal of the term 'in substance' but merely as the Vice-Chancellor's own assessment of its relevance in the context of the *Robson* case, coloured as that case was by his own particular interpretation of the word 'incidental'. The Inland Revenue would seem to have indicated a way in which the term might well be of significance independently of the second requirement of TA 1988 s 335(2) when it states in its guidance notes:

It is normally the nature of the duties performed in the UK, rather than the amount of time spent on them, that is important, but if the total time you spend working in the UK is more than 91 days a year, the work you do will not be treated as incidental.[3]

The Inland Revenue, it seems, regards the first requirement as establishing a *quantitative* trip-wire which will close the door to the benefits of TA 1988 s 335 if ever United Kingdom duties *qualitatively* incidental to overseas duties occupy a disproportionate amount of a person's time. In the Board's eyes, an employment of which duties other than overseas duties involve periods in the United Kingdom amounting to 91 days or more in the year is not 'in substance one of which the duties fall . . . to be performed outside the United Kingdom', and, once that is the case, no concession can be made under TA 1988 s 335 even if the United Kingdom duties are, in qualitative terms, 'merely incidental' to the overseas duties.

---

1 (1972) 48 TC 527.
2 Ibid, at 534.
3 Appendix IR 20 (11 April 2000), para 5.7.

4.20 Incidental duties

The discussion in the previous paragraph brings us to the words 'merely incidental' which are central to the second requirement of TA 1988 s 335(2). Unfortunately for the taxpayer, these words have been given a judicial definition which is not only exceedingly narrow but which must surely be at variance with the understanding of that term in the mind of 'the man on the Clapham omnibus':[1]

> The expression 'merely incidental to' is a striking one, and effect must be given to the natural meaning of those words. The words 'merely incidental to' are upon their ordinary use apt to denote an activity (here the performance of duties) which does not serve any independent purpose but is carried out in order to further some other purpose.[2]

Although that definition must presently be adhered to, it is interesting to compare it with the definition of 'incidental' provided by *Chambers Twentieth Century Dictionary*[3] – 'liable to occur: naturally attached: accompanying: concomitant: occasional, casual' – and to observe, as this discussion proceeds, that had any one of those meanings been adopted by Pennycuick V-C in the *Robson* case, its outcome would undoubtedly have been quite different.

Having said that, it must be admitted that Pennycuick V-C's understanding of the term does not actually invalidate the examples of 'incidental duties' offered by the Royal Commission on the Taxation of Profits and Income when, in 1955, it recommended that 'there should be a saving qualification to the effect that work is not the less to be treated as performed wholly in one country because certain merely incidental duties such as returning for report, to collect samples, etc., are carried out in another'.[4] In parliamentary debate, however, it was said that:

> if a man were in this country, perhaps on leave, for a month during the year, and was called to the London office to give an opinion on something, or received instructions,[5]

his performance of those duties could be regarded incidental to the duties he performed abroad. That first example is surely beyond the narrow scope of the Vice-Chancellor's definition, for the giving of an opinion would surely serve a purpose independent of the purpose of the person's overseas duties.

It should also be noted that all the examples given concern occurrences of short *duration* which merely break briefly into the long-term pattern of overseas activity. This could be taken as indicating that Parliament, at least, understood the word 'incidental' to be expressive of temporariness, and it was this factor that was, Mr Robson argued, of paramount importance in deciding whether or not duties performed in the United Kingdom were merely incidental to duties performed abroad.

Mr Robson was a pilot employed by KLM, a Dutch airline, and was based at Schipol Airport in Amsterdam though he and his wife and children had their home in Chorleywood, Hertfordshire. So far as his employment allowed him to do so, he commuted between Chorleywood and Schipol, travelling at preferential rates on passenger flights to and from Heathrow Airport. During the years 1961–62 to 1966–67 (for which he had been assessed to tax as a person resident in the United Kingdom), his regular duty was to fly aircraft on scheduled journeys between Amsterdam and various world-wide locations, in particular North and South America. Of the 811 take-offs and landings which he made during the years in question 38 landings took place in the United Kingdom, but none related to flights beginning here and of the 38 landings 16 were on charter services which were outside his regular duties. Landings in the United Kingdom generally involved a wait of 45 to 60 minutes before taking-off again, though there would be a further hour or so delay if refuelling was necessary. In each of the relevant years, Mr Robson spent less than 60 days in the United Kingdom, excluding days on which he had landed here as described, and he contended, therefore, that his residence status should have been decided without regard to his home in Chorleywood. As he saw it, he worked full-time in an employment of which all the duties were performed outside the United Kingdom apart from duties which 'were of short duration by contrast with the substantial periods spent outside the United Kingdom'[6] and which were therefore merely incidental to the performance of his duties outside the United Kingdom. Accordingly, in his opinion, he came within the ambit of FA 1956 s 11 (now TA 1988 s 335). Pennycuick V-C could not agree:

> With the best will in the world, I find it impossible to say that the activities carried on in or over England are merely incidental to the performance of the comparable duties carried on in or over Holland or in or over the ultimate destination in America. The activities are precisely co-ordinate, and I cannot see how it can properly be said that the activities in England are in some way incidental to the other activities. Going back to the words of the section, when one asks, 'What exactly are the other duties outside the United Kingdom to which the performance of the duties are incidental?' no satisfactory answer can be given. The other duties are simply co-ordinate duties.[7]

If one were to take the dictionary definition of 'incidental' quoted earlier, one could retort, 'But co-ordinate duties *are* incidental duties; no satisfactory answer can be given to your question because of the particular way in which you have chosen to define the word "incidental"; and you are not "going back to the words of the section" but to the extremely narrow interpretation you have given to the words of the section.' It is, however, no part of the Inland Revenue's duties to dilute the strength of a favourable judicial decision, however open to criticism that decision might be, and, accordingly, it has merely taken-up and amplified the Vice-Chancellor's dicta in its guidance notes relating to this matter.[8]

Commenting on the construction of TA 1970 s 50(3) (now TA 1988 s 335(2)) advanced by Mr Robson, the Vice-Chancellor said:

> I think it is impossible to construe subsection three . . . as indicating merely relatively short periods of employment in the United Kingdom in relation to the period of employment outside the United Kingdom. It would have been quite simple for the section so to provide; and it may well be that if the condition were imported only by the expression 'in substance' that would be the result. But the second requirement is expressed in quite different terms and cannot, I think, be treated as referring merely to what has been described as a quantitative, in contradistinction to a qualitative, basis.[9]

Again it must be said that, had the Vice-Chancellor attached a more usual meaning to the word 'incidental', there would have been no divergence between the words of the first and second requirements and Mr Robson's contention could have been upheld. As matters now stand, however, the amount of time occupied by duties performed in the United Kingdom must be regarded as being of no significance for the purpose of deciding whether or not those duties are 'merely incidental', and, in consequence, great care will need to be taken by anyone who works full-time abroad to ensure that he does not inadvertently place himself beyond the ambit of TA 1988 s 335 by allowing his normal duties to bring him, however fleetingly, into the United Kingdom. Having said that, it must, however, be added that an isolated performance of duties in the United Kingdom which are qualitatively no different from the duties performed overseas will not always preclude the operation of TA 1988 s 335. In the *Robson* case, the Vice-Chancellor made it clear that, so far as a pilot is concerned,

> it is accepted on behalf of the Crown that a landing in the United Kingdom by reason of some emergency, such as weather conditions or mechanical trouble, might be regarded as incidental to the performance of duties outside the United Kingdom,[10]

and he not only thought that was right but outlined other situations which, though he could express no view on them, clearly commended themselves to him as cases for leniency:

> the position of *de minimis* – a single landing . . . the position if a pilot's normal route did not touch on the United Kingdom but on one or two occasions he had landed in the United Kingdom while acting as a substitute for some other pilot who was ill. Those might well be borderline questions.[11]

In the event, the Crown accepted that the *de minimis* principle[12] should be applied as regards 1961–62, a year in which Mr Robson made only one landing and take-off in the United Kingdom, and, three years after the Robson case, it was confirmed in an answer to a parliamentary question concerning airline pilots that:

> In practice, where only a single take-off and landing in this country occurred in a year, the Inland Revenue would normally disregard this on *de minimis* grounds in considering whether any duties were performed in this country.[13]

Although the circumstances in the *Robson* case served to highlight the particular problems which airline pilots may encounter in attempting to fulfil the 'incidental duties' requirement of TA 1988 s 335, there would seem to be no obvious argument which the Inland Revenue could advance were the *de minimis* principle to be pleaded in relation to a single transgression of the rules by a member of any other class of overseas employee.

One further point remains to be made in this connection and that is that, under TA 1988 s 335(2), any incidental duties which, though performed in the United Kingdom, are to be regarded as performed outside the United Kingdom are to be so regarded only 'for the purposes of this section'. Clearly, this will prevent them being so regarded for the purposes of TA 1988 s 336 and, accordingly, if incidental duties performed in the United Kingdom exceed the 91 days which the Inland Revenue regard as the maximum permissible average length of a temporary annual visit,[14] the Inland Revenue will treat such persons as having become resident on those grounds alone. In such circumstances the disregarding of any place of abode in the United Kingdom will become irrelevant. As it is now common practice for companies to allow such of their senior employees as are engaged in full-time work overseas to take between two and three months' leave each year (particularly if their work is performed in some insalubrious or undesirable location), periods of leave spent in the United Kingdom may alone be sufficient to take such employees dangerously near to the 91 days and incidental duties may well take them beyond it.

1 An expression coined by Lord Devlin.
2 *Robson v Dixon* (1972) 48 TC 527 at 534, per Pennycuick V-C.
3 1983 edn.
4 Final Report, 1955, Cmd 9474, para 300.
5 Hansard, 7 June 1956, col 1456.
6 *Robson v Dixon* (1972) 48 TC 527 at 530.
7 Ibid, at 534.
8 Appendix IR 20 (11 April 2000), paras 5.7, 5.8, 5.5.
9 *Robson v Dixon* (1972) 48 TC 527 at 535.
10 Ibid.
11 Ibid.
12 *De minimis non curat lex*: the law does not concern itself with trifles.
13 Hansard, 28 October 1975, vol 898, no. 187, col 431.
14 See **4.03** above.

4.21 Revenue practice

Although the Inland Revenue agrees that, as has been explained at **2.05** above,

> You are taxed as a UK resident for the whole of a tax year,

the rule is, in practice, relaxed in certain circumstances.[1] This latest booklet also sets out the Revenue's guidance rules regarding persons who, in a variety of circumstances, leave the United Kingdom[2] or come to the United Kingdom.[3]

1 Appendix IR 20 (11 April 2000) paras 1.5, 1.6, 1.7.
2 Ibid, Ch 2; see also **4.22** below.
3 Ibid, Ch3; see also **4.22** below.

4.22   Capital gains tax: Temporary non-residence

Section 127(1) of the Finance Act 1998 introduced a new section 10A to the TCGA Act 1992 amending the capital gains tax rules where taxpayers go abroad for temporary periods in order to sell assets which would otherwise be chargeable to capital gains tax. The new rules apply to individuals who cease to be resident or ordinarily resident in the United Kingdom on or after the 17 March 1998 or to those who become resident or ordinarily resident on or after 6 April 1998.

In future, individuals who have been tax resident in the United Kingdom for any part of, at least, four out of seven tax years immediately preceding the year of departure, and became not resident and not ordinarily resident for a period of less than five tax years, and own assets before they leave the United Kingdom will be liable to tax on any gains realised on those assets after departure from the United Kingdom. Gains made by such an individual in the year of assessment in which he or she leaves the country will be chargeable for that year. Gains made after that will be chargeable in the year of assessment in which the taxpayer resumes residence in the United Kingdom. Losses will be allowable on the same basis as gains are chargeable.

Extra-statutory Concession D2, which enables the years of commencement and cessation of residence in the United Kingdom to be split for capital gains tax purposes, has been amended to take account of the new rules.

CHAPTER 5

Residence of partnerships and trusts

One likes to do business with a British firm. One knows where one is, if you see what I mean.

Graham Greene *Our Man in Havana* Ch 1

5.01 Introduction

As the foregoing chapters have made clear, residence is a personal attribute – a quality which a person attracts to himself by virtue of the strength of his association with a particular place or country. That being so, we might have expected that Parliament would have prescribed some other more objective determinant of chargeability to tax so far as partnerships, trusts and corporations are concerned, but it has seen fit not to do so. Partnerships, trusts and corporations are treated in tax law as possessing a personality independent of that possessed by their members (even though only corporations are true legal entities) and they are, therefore, treated in tax law as being capable of possessing resident or non-resident status in just the same way as may a natural person. The tests by which their residence status is to be determined are, however, somewhat different from the tests applying in the case of an individual, and those relating to partnerships and trusts are considered below. The tests whereby corporate residence is determined are considered in Chapter 6.

Partnerships

5.02 The general meaning of partnership

Partnership is the relationship which subsists between persons carrying on a business in common with a view of profit.[1] In England and Wales, a partnership has no existence independent of its constituent members but, in Scotland, it is 'a legal person distinct from the partners of whom it is composed'.[2]

---

1 Partnership Act 1890 s 1.
2 Ibid, s 4(2).

5.03 The tax meaning of partnerships from 5 April 1994

Taxes Act 1988 s 111 was repealed by FA 1994 s 215 and replaced by a new s 111. The new s 111 was in turn repealed and FA 1995 s 117 substituted another 'new' s 111.

The changes mentioned above contained in the new TA s 111 and inserted by FA 1995 s 117 represent a fundamental change in the taxation of partnerships. Partnerships will no longer be assessed jointly in the partnership name as they were in the 'old' TA s 111. Generally a partner will be responsible for his own taxation in connection with his share of the partnership's profits and losses. A partnership is not to be treated for tax purposes as an entity separate and distinct from the partners. The assessment of profits in the partnership name will cease.[1]

The new s 111 of TA 1988 applies for the year 1994/95 and subsequent years of assessment in relation to partnerships whose trades, profession or business are set up and commenced after 5 April 1994 (but from 1995–96 for such partnerships which are controlled abroad). In relation to partnerships set up and commenced before 6 April 1994 the new version has effect from 1997/98 and subsequent years of assessment.[2]

1 TA 1988 s 111(1).
2 FA 1994 s 215(4)(5).

5.04 Control and management

The question whether the control and management of a partnership carried fully or partly outside the United Kingdom is situated outside the United Kingdom for the purposes of section 112 (1A) of TA 1988 is the test which the courts have formulated for ascertaining the residence status of companies. In *De Beers Consolidated Mines Ltd v Howe*,[1] Loreburn LC said:

> The decision of Kelly CB and Huddleston B in the *Calcutta Jute Mills v Nicholson*[2] and the *Cesena Suphur Co v Nicholson*,[3] now thirty years ago, involved the principle that a company resides for purposes of income tax where its real business is carried on. Those decisions have been acted upon ever since. I regard this as the true rule, and the real business is carried on where the central management and control actually abides.[4]

In seeking to ascertain where control of a company is situate, Kelly CB was of the firm opinion that one has to look at

> where its governing body meets in bodily presence for the purposes of the company, and exercises the powers conferred upon it by statute and by the articles of association.[5]

That principle is not without its difficulties when applied to partnerships, however. A company is an entity in which the members place management and control of the company's trade or business in the hands of a board of directors who, although they themselves will usually be numbered among the members, occupy a position which is clearly distinguishable from that which the members occupy. A partnership, however, is an entity in which *all* the members are, *de jure*, 'directors'.

It is true that, in some large partnerships, control and management of the trade or business is placed in the hands of a committee drawn from among the partnership members, but this is the exception rather than the rule. In such cases, the place where control and management of the partnership is situate will be the place where the committee 'meets in bodily presence' for the purpose of the partnership, and exercises the powers conferred upon it by the Partnership Act 1890, by the partnership agreement and by any mandate given it by the other partners. In other cases, however, the place of management and control will, it is suggested, be the place where a *majority* of the partners meet. The primary meaning of the verb 'control' is 'to check, to restrain, to govern'[6] and a partnership's trade and business is checked, restrained or governed by *majority* decision:[7]

> I call that the act of all, which is the act of the majority, provided all are consulted and the majority are acting bona fide, meeting, not for the purpose of negativing what any one may have to offer, but for the purpose of negativing what, when they are met together, they may after due consideration, think proper to negative.[8]

It must be emphasised that what is in question is where the *de facto* control and management of the trade or business which the entity carries on is located. The amount of capital contributed by individual partners and the degree to which individual partners are to participate in profits is of no relevance to the determination of this question, nor is the *de jure* share in control which each partner possesses. *De facto* control lies with the decision-makers – however great or small their individual stakes in the funding of the entity might be and however open to veto by the other members their decisions might in principle, be.

It follows from this that a partnership agreement will not in itself be determinative of the location of management and control. If an agreement provides that partnership meetings are to be held in, say, Paris, but control and management of the partnership business is actually exercised from, say, Manchester, the control and management of the trade or business is situated in Manchester. Only if the control and management of the partnership business is, in fact, exercised overseas will the partnership be deemed to reside outside the United Kingdom.

Although, therefore, in theory, it is possible for a partnership of which all the members are resident in the United Kingdom to be resident abroad by virtue of all partnership meetings being held abroad and the day-to-day running of the trade or business being carried out only in accordance with decisions which have been taken abroad, it will, in practice, be difficult to support the claim unless there is at least one non-resident partner who fully participates in the control and management of the partnership's trade or business. Although not essential, it will, of course, help to allay Revenue scepticism if a majority of the partners reside outside the United Kingdom or a non-resident partner or partners are (subject to safeguards concerning the division of profits) given voting control.

---

1   (1906) 5 TC 198.
2   (1876) 1 TC 83.
3   (1876) 1 TC 88.
4   *De Beers Consolidated Mines Ltd v Howe* (1906) 5 TC 198 at 213.
5   (1876) 1 TC 83 at 95, per Kelly CB.
6   *Chambers Twentieth Century Dictionary*.
7   See PA 1890 s 24(8).
8   *Const v Harris* (1824) Turn & R 496 at 525, per Lord Eldon LC.

5.05 The significance of partnership residence

Finance Act 1995 s 125 has amended the law regarding the residence of partnerships and the income tax consequence. It has done so by substituting a new TA 1988 s 112 for the old version with regard to partnerships controlled abroad. The new version applies to the year 1997–98 and subsequent years of assessment but where the partnerships were set up and commenced after 5 April 1994 it applies to the years 1995–95 and 1996–97.[1]

Section 112(1) of TA 1988 provides that in computing the profits of a non-resident partner under TA 1988 s 111 (new version), the profits of the partnership are computed as if the partnership were an individual not resident in the United Kingdom. The effect is to limit the charge on the non-resident, where the partnership carries on a trade partly in the United Kingdom and partly outside the United Kingdom, to his share of the profits of the trade carried on in the United Kingdom.

Section 112(1A) of TA 1988 provides that where the partnership is a trade, profession or business carried on fully or partly outside the United Kingdom; where the control and management[1] of the partnership is situated outside the United Kingdom; where any individual partner who is resident[2] in the United Kingdom can satisfy the Board of Inland Revenue that he is not domiciled[3] in the United Kingdom or that, being a Commonwealth citizen or a citizen of the Republic of Ireland, he is not ordinarily resident[4] in the United Kingdom, then the partnership interest which entitles him to a share of the profits or gains arising from the carrying on of the trade etc otherwise than in the United Kingdom[5] is treated for the purposes of Case V of Schedule D as if it were a possession outside the United Kingdom, and such profits or gains will be taxable on the remittance basis.[6]

---

1 **5.04** above.
2 Chapter 2.
3 Chapter 7.
4 Chapter 3.
5 TA 1988 s 112(1)(A).
6 Ibid, s 18(3).

Trusts

5.06 Dual approach

A trust, like an English partnership, is, in law, a relationship rather than an entity. It is the equitable obligation which is created when one person (the settlor) transfers assets (the trust property) to another person (the trustee) who is to hold, control and deal with those assets for the benefit of third parties (the beneficiaries or *cestuis que trust*) of whom the trustee himself may be one and any one of whom may enforce the obligation. If the trust is created by the settlor *inter vivos* it is usually referred to as a settlement and the trust property is known as settled property.

Despite the fact that a trust or settlement is not a legal entity, however, it is to be treated as one for certain specific purposes under the Taxes Acts and, insofar as it is so treated, may possess both residence and ordinary residence status. TCGA 1992 s 69(1) provides that:

In relation to settled property, the trustees of the settlement shall for the purposes of this Act be treated as being a single and continuing body of persons (distinct from the persons who may from time to time be the trustees), and that body shall be treated as being resident and ordinarily resident in the United Kingdom unless the general administration of the trusts is ordinarily carried out outside the United Kingdom and the trustees or a majority of them for the time being are not resident or not ordinarily resident in the United Kingdom.

The 'purpose' of TCGA 1992 is to charge a person to capital gains tax in respect of chargeable gains accruing to him in a year of assessment during any part of which he is resident in the United Kingdom, and it is for the purposes of capital gains tax only, therefore, that a trust is, under TCGA 1992 s 69(1), to be treated as a person distinct from the persons who may from time to time be the trustees. The residence status of trusts and settlements for capital gains tax purposes is considered in more detail at **5.07** below.

Before the year 1989–90, there was no specific legislation dealing with the place of residence of a trust for income tax purposes. If all the individual trustees were United Kingdom resident, then income tax liability arose on foreign source and United Kingdom source income. If all the individual trustees were non-resident, income tax liability was regarded as arising only on United Kingdom source income.

Where the trustees included both a United Kingdom resident and a non-resident, the Revenue's view was that liability depended upon whether the proper law of the trust was English law or foreign law. If the proper law was English law, an income tax liability arose on the total income. If the proper law was a foreign law, the trustees were liable on United Kingdom source income only.

However, this view was rejected by the courts in *Dawson v IRC*.[1] In that case it was held by the House of Lords that where the general administration of the trust was ordinarily carried on outside the United Kingdom and a majority of the trustees was non-resident, a United Kingdom resident trustee was not assessable under Schedule D in respect of income derived from sources outside the United Kingdom. It was held that the trust income did not accrue to an individual trustee in his personal capacity and that he had no right of control over it except, in conjunction with his co-trustees, to see that it was applied in accordance with the terms of the trust.[2]

It was in response to the House of Lords decision in *Dawson v IRC* that statutory rules[3] were introduced for determining the residence status of a trust for income tax purposes, where the trustees include at least one United Kingdom resident and one non-resident trustee. In those circumstances the trustees are all treated as United Kingdom resident if the settlor was resident, ordinarily resident or domiciled in the United Kingdom at the time when the trust was set up or at any later time when he provided funds for the trust.[4]

Conversely, if the settlor was not resident, not ordinarily resident and not domiciled in the United Kingdom at any of those times, the trustees are treated as non-resident.

In the case of a trust set up on the settlor's death, the trustees are treated as United Kingdom resident unless the settlor was neither resident, ordinarily resident nor domiciled in the United Kingdom at the time of his death.[5]

For this purpose the term 'settlor' includes any person who has provided funds directly or indirectly for a trust.[6]

The statutory rules apply generally for income tax purposes for the year 1989–90 and subsequent years of assessment.[7] However, as a transitional measure, all the trustees were treated as non-resident for the year 1989–90 if none of them was United Kingdom resident at any time during the period 1 October 1989 to 5 April 1990, regardless of the residence status of the settlor.[8]

1 [1989] STC 473.
2 Ibid at 479, per Lord Keith.
3 FA 1989 s 110.
4 FA 1989 s 110.
5 FA 1989 s 110(2), (3).
6 FA 1989 s 110(4).
7 FA 1989 s 110(6).
8 FA 1989 s 110(7).

5.07 Residence for capital gains tax purposes

In order for a trust to be attributed with non-residence status for the purposes of capital gains tax, TCGA 1992 s 69(1) requires two conditions to be satisfied. The general administration of the trust must be 'ordinarily carried on outside the United Kingdom' and the trustees 'or a majority of them for the time being' must be 'not resident or not ordinarily resident in the United Kingdom'.

In the context of TCGA 1992 s 69(1), the word 'majority' is strictly construed. No concession is made where the number of trustees who are not resident or not ordinarily resident in the United Kingdom is merely equal to the number of trustees who are resident and ordinarily resident here and, in any such case, the trust will be regarded as resident in the United Kingdom.

In order to determine whether or not a majority of the trustees of a trust are not resident or not ordinarily resident in the United Kingdom, the residence and ordinary residence status of each individual trustee will need to be determined in accordance with the principles discussed in Chapters 2 and 3 except where any particular trustee is 'a person carrying on a business which consists of or includes the management of trusts' and he is acting as a trustee of the trust 'in the course of that business'.[1] Under TCGA 1992 s 69(2), the actual residence status of any such trustee is to be disregarded and he is to be

> treated in relation to that trust as not resident in the United Kingdom if the whole of the settled property consists of or derives from property provided by a person not at the time (or, in the case of a trust arising under a testamentary disposition or on an intestacy or partial intestacy, at his death) domiciled, resident or ordinarily resident in the United Kingdom.

It is understood that the Inland Revenue will regard a trust company, a bank, a solicitor, an accountant and, in some instances, a stockbroker as 'a person carrying on a business which consists of or includes the management of trusts', but not a director of a trust company or an employee of a bank, solicitor, accountant or stockbroker.

Where TCGA 1992 s 69(2) applies, the general administration of the trust is to be treated as ordinarily carried on outside the United Kingdom[2] – even where this is not, in fact, the case – and the trust will be treated as non-resident. The location of the general administration of a trust will, in all other instances, be a question of fact to be determined in the light of evidence as to where the day-to-day management of the trust is exercised. It should be noted, however, that TCGA 1992 s 69(1) does not require that the general administration of a trust should be exclusively carried on abroad but only that it is 'ordinarily' so carried on. As we have noted in a different connection,[3] 'ordinary' contrasts with 'special or occasional or casual', and it would seem, therefore, that where, exceptionally, the general administration of a non-resident trust is carried on within the United Kingdom, its non-resident status will not be jeopardised.

The wording of the second of the two conditions under which a trust will be regarded as non-resident – ie that the majority of its trustees 'are not resident or not ordinarily resident in the United Kingdom' – may give rise to difficulties of interpretation where some trustees are resident but not ordinarily resident, others are ordinarily resident but not resident, others are neither resident nor ordinarily resident, and others are both resident and ordinarily resident. Does the wording permit a finding of non-residence where a mixture of not resident but ordinarily resident trustees and not ordinarily resident but resident trustees form a majority, or must all the trustees forming a majority belong to one group or the other? It is the author's view that the language used does permit a mixture since the 'are' which links the subject and the predicate clearly indicates that 'majority' is being used in its plural sense of 'more people than not out of those concerned' and not in its singular sense of 'the more numerous party'.[4] Had 'majority' been used in its singular sense, the alternatives in the predicate would necessarily have been exclusive but, as it is, they are clearly inclusive.

A further complication is introduced into the question of the residence of trusts for capital gains tax purposes when, upon the creation of a trust different assets are vested in different sets of trustees, or when, at a later stage, assets are added to an existing trust and vested in trustees other than the original trustees. In either situation, it must first be established whether the facts reveal the existence of a single settlement or of two or more separate settlements. If there is but a single settlement, TCGA 1992 s 69(3) will be of application, for s 69(3) provides that:

> where part of the property comprised in a settlement is vested in one trustee or set of trustees and part in another . . . they shall be treated as together constituting . . . a single body of trustees.

The residence status of the trust will then fall to be determined under TCGA 1992 s 69(1) and (2) as described above, ie by a consideration of both the location of the general administration of the trust and the residence and ordinary residence status of each individual trustee belonging to the 'single body' of trustees.

Arguments that the application of TCGA 1992 s 69(3) should be confined to situations where each part of the property comprised in a settlement is held on identical trusts[5] or where there is a unity of beneficial interests[6] must be rejected on the grounds that the language used in s 69(3) is 'deliberately wide and plain in its scope'.[7]

---

1 TCGA 1992 s 69(2).
2 Ibid.
3 See **3.02** above.
4 See Fowler's *Modern English Usage* (2nd edn. Oxford University Press) under the heading 'majority'.

5 *Roome v Edwards* [1921] STC 96 at 100, per Lord Wilberforce.
6 Ibid at 104, per Lord Roskill.
7 Ibid.

5.08 Scottish Parliament

Under the Scotland Act 1998 a Scottish Parliament is set up with the power to vary the basic rate of income tax set by the United Kingdom Parliament by three per cent either way. On the 23 February 1998 the Inland Revenue published a technical paper on the tax consequences of this power. Paragraphs 9–22 of that paper sets out the Inland Revenue's views on the possible effect of the exercise of that power on the taxation of trusts which are 'resident' in Scotland. The proposals in the technical paper, if adopted, may require legislation.

CHAPTER 6

Residence of corporations

A Company Limited? What may that be?
The term, I rather think, is new to me.

Sir W. S. Gilbert *Utopia Limited* Finale

6.01 Introduction

Unlike a trust or an English partnership, a corporation is a true legal entity. It is, under the law, an artificial person, separate and distinct from its members and endowed with an existence independent of their existence.[1]

Although a corporation's personality is artificial, it is not fictitious. Since 1889 the word 'person' in any Act of Parliament has included 'a body of persons corporate' unless the contrary intention appears,[2] and a corporation may, accordingly, be fined for contempt of court,[3] be convicted of an offence involving a fraudulent intent,[4] and be a 'respectable and responsible person' to whom to assign a lease.[5] More to the point, it may possess the status of residence and ordinary residence:

> Now the definition of the word 'residence' is founded upon the habits and relations of the natural man, and is therefore inapplicable to the artificial and legal person whom we call a corporation. But for the purpose of giving effect to the words of the Legislature an artificial residence must be assigned to this artificial person, and one formed on the analogy of natural persons.[6]

A corporation may be a corporation sole (eg a bishopric, a rectorate and a public trusteeship) or a corporation aggregate (eg a municipal corporation, a building society and a limited company), but it is only in connection with the taxation of this second type of corporation, and with limited companies in particular, that questions of residence arise. The reason is not difficult to find. Although it is through the medium of the limited company (or its foreign equivalent) that by far the greater part of the world's business and commerce is transacted, 'a company not resident in the United Kingdom shall not be within the charge to corporation tax unless it carries on a trade in the United Kingdom through a branch or agency' and, even where it does so, it is chargeable to corporation tax only on 'trading income arising directly or indirectly through or from the branch or agency' and on certain income and chargeable gains relating to assets used or held by or for the branch or agency.[7]

1 *Salomon v Salomon & Co* [1897] AC 22.
2 Interpretation Act 1978 s 5 and Sch 1.
3 *R v J G Hammond & Co* [1914] 2 KB 866.
4 *R v ICR Haulage Ltd* [1944] KB 551.
5 *Ideal Film Renting Co v Nielson* [1921] 1 Ch 575.
6 *Calcutta Jute Mills Co Ltd v Nicholson* (1876) 1 TC 83 at 103, per Huddleston B.
7 TA 1988 s 11(1) and (2). The term 'company' is not, of course, descriptive only of a limited company but, under TA 1988 s 832(1), must be taken to mean, in this context, 'any body corporate or unincorporated association' excluding 'a partnership, a local authority or a local authority association'.

6.02 UK registered companies

Section 66 of the Finance Act 1988 provides that as from 15 March 1988 any company incorporated in the United Kingdom is conclusively presumed to be resident in the United Kingdom. The case law which determined the test of residence on the basis of the location of a company's central control and management is of no relevance to any company which has been or is incorporated in the United Kingdom. The test of central control and management is now only applicable to foreign registered companies.[1]

There is an exception to the incorporation rule. This exception operates if the company was carrying on business before 15 March 1988 and had become non-resident before then pursuant to a general or a specific Treasury consent obtained under what is now TA 1988 s 765.

If the consent was a specific consent, the company can remain non-resident regardless of where it is based, and it only becomes United Kingdom resident if it in fact becomes resident under the central management and control test.

If the consent was a general consent, a further condition has to be satisfied. This condition is that a company was taxable in a foreign territory. By 'taxable' is meant being liable to tax on income by reason of domicile, residence or place of management but not simply being liable to a flat rate sum or fee. Provided that a company which registered before 15 March 1988 pursuant to general consent was taxable in a foreign state it may remain non-resident, but only so long as it is so taxable.

The exception for companies which become non-resident pursuant to a specific consent applies also to companies which registered after 15 March 1988 pursuant to a specific consent applied for before then. Such a company does however have to have commenced business before then.

1 **6.03** below.

6.03 Foreign registered companies

A foreign registered company will be deemed to be resident in the United Kingdom if the central management and control of the company is exercised in the United Kingdom.

The phrase 'central management and control' was coined not by Parliament but by Lord Loreburn in one of the earliest of all the cases concerning company residence.[1] In *Bullock v Unit Construction Co Ltd*,[2] Lord Radcliffe summarised the position as it existed in 1959 and as it still exists today:[3]

the necessity of establishing some common standard for the treatment of different tax-payers meant that the Courts of Law were bound in course of time to produce and apply some general principle of their own to form an acceptable test of residence . . . [T]he prin-ciple was adopted that a company is resident where its central management and control abide: words which, according to the decision of the House of Lords that finally pro-pounded the test, *De Beers Consolidated Mines Ltd v Howe*,[4] are equivalent to saying that a company's residence is where its 'real business' is carried on.

1 *De Beers Consolidated Mines Ltd v Howe* (1906) 5 TC 198 at 213.
2 (1959) 38 TC 712.
3 Ibid, per Lord Radcliffe at 738.
4 (1906) 5 TC 198.

6.04 A question of fact

The ultimate confirmation that corporate residence is a conclusion of fact came in *Bullock v Unit Construction Co Ltd*.[1] There, Unit Construction Company Ltd, a United Kingdom resident subsidiary of Alfred Booth & Co Ltd, a United Kingdom resident parent company, made subvention payments to three of its fellow subsidiary companies in Kenya and claimed that those payments were, under FA 1953 s 20, permissible deductions in arriving at its profits for tax purposes. This would have been so only if the three Kenyan subsidiaries also were resident in the United Kingdom, but the Inland Revenue contended that they were not. The three subsidiaries had been incorporated in Kenya and their articles of association expressly placed their management and control in the hands of their directors and required directors' meetings to be held outside the United Kingdom. That being so, the three Kenyan subsidiaries must, said the Revenue, be resident outside the United Kingdom. The Commissioners found as a *fact*, however, that, due to trad-ing difficulties which the subsidiaries had encountered,

at the material times . . . the boards of directors of the African subsidiaries . . . were standing aside in all matters of real importance and in many matters of minor importance affecting the central management and control, and . . . the real control and management was being exercised by the board of directors of Alfred Booth & Co Ltd in London.[2]

Accordingly, the Commissioners found that each of the African subsidiaries was resident in the United Kingdom, and their finding was ultimately upheld in the House of Lords. Referring to the reversals the decision had suffered at the hands of the High Court and the Court of Appeal, Viscount Simonds said:

the contention of learned Counsel for the Crown which has so far found favour with the courts is no less than this, that if by the constitution of the company, that is, by its mem-orandum and articles of association interpreted in the light of the relevant law, that is, in this case the law of Kenya, the management of the company's business is contemplated as being exercised, and ought therefore to be exercised, in Kenya or at any rate outside the United Kingdom, then for the purpose of British Income Tax law the facts are to be dis-regarded and the control and management which as a fact are found to abide in the United Kingdom are to be regarded as abiding outside it. There is no doubt, I think, that the management of the African subsidiaries, which were incorporated in Kenya under the Kenya Companies Ordinance and registered in Nairobi, was placed in the hands of their directors and that their articles of association expressly provided that directors' meetings might be held anywhere outside the United Kingdom. Nor can there be any doubt – for this is the unchallengeable finding of the Commissioners – that the management of the business of the companies was not exercised in the manner contemplated. Whence it follows that the business was conducted in a manner irregular, unauthorised and perhaps unlawful . . .

My Lords, I should certainly be prepared to admit that the many Judges who in the past have pronounced upon this question had not in mind such a case as this. But, with great respect to those who take a different view, the present case does not seem to lie outside the principle underlying their judgment. Nothing can be more factual and concrete than the acts of management which enable a Court to find as a fact that central management and control is exercised in one country or another. It does not in any way alter their character that in greater or less degree they are irregular or unauthorised or unlawful. The business is not the less managed in London because it ought to be managed in Kenya. Its residence is determined by the solid facts, not by the terms of its constitution, however imperative. If indeed I must disregard the facts as they are, because they are irregular, I find a company without any central management at all. For, though I may disregard existing facts, I cannot invent facts which do not exist and say that the company's business is managed in Kenya. Yet it is the place of central management which, however much or little weight ought to be given to other factors, essentially determines its residence. I come, therefore, to the conclusion . . . that it is the actual place of management, not the place in which it ought to be managed, which fixes the residence of a company.[3]

Because the residence of a company is to be determined by the location of its central management and control, and because that location is a question of fact, a finding by the Commissioners that a company is resident in this place or that will be unassailable provided the Commissioners have before them evidence from which their finding can be made and providing they do not misdirect themselves in law.[4] The court's approach is well-illustrated by Lord Loreburn's conclusion in the *De Beers* case:[5]

The Commissioners, after sifting the evidence, arrived at the two following conclusions, viz: . . . (2) That the head and seat and directing power of the affairs of the Appellant Company were at the office in London, from whence the chief operations of the Company, both in the United Kingdom and elsewhere, were, in fact, controlled, managed and directed. That conclusion of fact cannot be impugned, and it follows that this Company was resident within the United Kingdom for the purposes of Income Tax.[6]

---

1 (1959) 38 TC 712.
2 Ibid, at 721–722.
3 Ibid, at 735–736.
4 See **2.03** above.
5 *De Beers Consolidated Mines v Howe* (1906) 5 TC 198.
6 Ibid, at 213–214.

6.05 Delegated management and control

Delegated management and control and *central* management and control are mutually exclusive concepts.

In *Calcutta Jute Mills v Nicholson*,[1] Huddleston B held that the central management and control of the Calcutta Jute Mills, though ostensibly exercised by a director in India, was actually exercised from the company's office in London where the board of directors met:

From that office would issue all the orders to the managing director in Calcutta. No doubt, until he received orders to the contrary, he would have full power and discretion to do what he liked in Calcutta; but at any moment, from this head office, they might have revoked his authority, or altered any arrangement which he had made connected with the working of the company.[2]

The director in Calcutta was, for all his powers, a mere delegate and one had, therefore, to look beyond him to the delegators from whom his powers had been derived and by whom they were being sustained.

The situation was similar in *San Paulo (Brazilian) Rly Co Ltd v Carter*.[3] An English company with an English board of directors had, through a superintendent in Brazil and a workforce in his charge, built and was managing and working a railway in Brazil. Although it was admitted that the London board purchased materials for use in Brazil, it was contended that they did not actually interfere in the carrying on of the business and that the business was, therefore, carried on by the supervisor in Brazil. Lord Watson rejected that contention:

Apart from the authority, expressed or implied, which they have from the directors, neither the superintendent nor any other servant of the Company has any power to act in the carrying on of its trade . . . The only persons who can with propriety be described as carrying on the trade of the Company, are its directors. . . .[4]

In *American Thread Company v Joyce*[5] the delegation of powers was less obvious for the American Thread Co Ltd was ostensibly managed and controlled by an executive committee of directors in New York. The Master of the Rolls was, however, quite clear that central management and control lay in Manchester, England:

Now the current business the daily purchasing and selling of raw materials and making them into thread is, no doubt, carried out by the executive committee in New York, the executive committee of three. Who appoint them? The English board. It must be done by the English board where the majority of the directors, four out of seven, reside. They are appointed by them, their salary is fixed by them, in fact the whole control of the machine, so to say, is kept and carefully kept at Manchester.[6]

It should go without saying that the personal qualities and excellence of a person exercising delegated powers are quite irrelevant. The expression 'head and brain' is often used as an alternative to 'central management and control',[7] but, as Rowlatt J has said:[8]

I do not think when the head and brain are mentioned it is intended to allude to a clever manager. One might say in many businesses: 'The whole head and brain of this business are in the General manager; he knows all about it and far more than all the Directors put together'. Therefore they leave it to him, and they are well advised in doing so. It is not in that sense that the head and brain is meant. I do not think the cleverest servant in the world, although he possessed all the brains of the institution, could be said to be the head and brain. . . .[9]

What all these cases are illustrating, therefore, is that, in determining the location of a company's central management and control, it is necessary to ask of those who appear to be exercising such control, 'To whom do you look over your shoulder? From whom do you derive your powers and who is able to modify or withdraw them?' If the answer is, 'No-one. We derive our powers from the shareholders who appointed us and, short of the shareholders removing us from office, no-one can interfere with our powers', identification of those who exercise central management and control will have been made.[10] If the answer is otherwise it will provide a pointer either to those who truly exercise central management and control or to a person or persons who are one step nearer to the centre than those to whom the question was addressed.

1 (1976) 1 TC 83.
2 Ibid, at 107.
3 (1895) 3 TC 407. The central issue before the court in this case was not where the company resided – it was admittedly resident in the United Kingdom – but whether any part of its trade was carried on in the United Kingdom. Had it been possible to show that the trade was being carried on wholly abroad, the company would have been liable to tax under Schedule D, Case V only upon the amount of profits remitted to the United Kingdom. Because it failed to show that that was so, however, it became liable to tax under Schedule D, Case I on the whole of its profits.
4 Ibid, at 412.
5 (1913) 6 TC 1 and 163.
6 Ibid, at 29.
7 *San Paulo (Brazilian) Rly Co Ltd v Carter* (1895) 3 TC 407 at 410, per Halsbury LC.
8 (1926) 11 TC 372.
9 Ibid, at 411.
10 The distinction between shareholder control and central management and control is discussed at **6.07** below.

6.06 Shareholder control

It must be stressed that the test of corporate residence involves the identification of the place of central management *and* (not *or*) control. In other words, the control in question is that which relates to the highest level of management of a company's business and must not, therefore, be confused with the control which vests in a company's shareholders *per se*. The distinction was stressed by Moulton LJ in *Stanley v Gramophone and Typewriter Ltd*[1] when he said:

the individual corporator does not carry on the business of the corporation; he is only entitled to the profits of that business to a certain extent, fixed and ascertained in a certain way, depending upon the constitution of the corporation and his holding in it. This legal proposition . . . is not weakened by the fact that the extent of his interest in it entitles him to exercise a greater or lesser amount of control over the manner in which the business is carried on. Such control is inseparable from his position as a corporator, and is a wholly different thing both in fact and in law from carrying on the business himself. The Directors and employees of the corporation are not his agents, and he has no power of giving directions to them which they must obey. It has been decided by this court in the *Automatic Self-cleaning Filter Syndicate Co Ltd v Cunninghame*[2] that in an English Company by whose Articles of Association certain powers were placed in the hands of the Directors the shareholders could not interfere with the exercise of those powers by the Directors even by a majority in General Meeting. Their course is to obtain the requisite majority to remove the Directors and put persons in their place who agree to their policy. This shows that the control of individual corporators is something wholly different from the management of the business itself. Nor is this principle less true when the holding of the individual corporator is so large that he is able to override the wishes of the other corporators in matters relating to the control of the business of the Company. The extent but not the nature of his power is changed by the magnitude of his holding.[3]

It follows, therefore, that a company whose business is, in fact, managed and controlled by a board of directors in, say, London, will none the less be resident in England even if, say, 98 per cent of its shares are owned by an individual resident in France. This proposition was specifically approved by the Court of Appeal in *Bullock v Unit Construction Co Ltd*[4] and still stands. The Court of Appeal also assented to the proposition, however, that:

a shareholder who holds sufficient in a company can *de facto* control its affairs by his ability to remove directors who disagree with his policy and to vote others into their places.[5]

It should be noted that the word here is 'can' not 'will'. Only if (to continue with the example given above) the French resident shareholder, contrary to his rights, actually interferes with the board's exercise of its powers and, by the threat of removal which his 98 per cent shareholding tacitly poses, persuades or pressures the board into implementing his policies and carrying out his wishes will *de facto* control (and, consequently, the company's residence) be located not in England but in France.

The significance of a shareholder's power was given detailed consideration in *American Thread Co v Joyce*.[6] There, the Crown contended that the operations of the American company were controlled from Manchester not merely because a majority of directors met there but also because the English parent company owned the entire share capital of the American company.

In the Court of Appeal, Buckley LJ went to some lengths to emphasise that it was not shareholder control on which the finding that the American company was resident in the United Kingdom rested:

The shareholders can, no doubt, by virtue of their votes control the corporation; they can compel directors . . . to do their will, but it does not follow that the corporators are managing the corporation. The contrary is the truth; they are not. It is the directors who are managing the affairs of the corporation . . . [T]he executive committee in New York were in fact controlled . . . on this side in extraordinary sessions of the Board which were held once a fortnight, and the real control, the head and seat and directing power of the affairs of the Company were here. It was in that sense that the control was here. . . .[7]

The fact that, in some instances, however, it might be found that the central control and management of a company is being exercised unconstitutionally by a single shareholder or by a group of shareholders rather than by those who have the constitutional right to exercise management and control, adds point to Kelly CB's choice of the term 'governing body'[8] in preference to the term 'board of directors'. The central management and control of a company will usually, *de facto* and *de jure*, be in the hands of its board of directors but, as the Inland Revenue states in a statement of practice, it will not always be so:

In some cases . . . central management and control is exercised by a single individual. This may happen when a chairman or managing director exercises powers formally conferred by the company's Articles and the other board members are little more than cyphers, or

115

by reason of a dominant shareholding or for some other reason. In those cases the residence of the company is where the controlling individual exercises his powers.[9]

Before leaving the question of shareholder control, attention must – for the sake of completeness – be drawn to *Apthorpe v Peter Schoenhoffen Brewing Co Ltd*[10] which concerned the wholly-owned American brewing subsidiary of an English company. The directors of the English company had full power of management and control of the affairs of the American company but they delegated these powers to a committee of management in Chicago. The Commissioners found that:

> the head and seat and directing power of the [English] Company were at the [English] Company's registered office in the City of London, and that if the business at Chicago and the profits made thereby were technically the business and profits of the American company the American company was for such purpose the agent of the [English] Company.[11]

In its statement of practice, the Inland Revenue declares its position on wholly-owned subsidiaries to be as follows:

> It is particularly difficult to apply the 'central management and control' test in the situation where a subsidiary company and its parent operate in different territories. In this situation, the parent will normally influence, to a greater or lesser extent, the actions of the subsidiary. Where that influence is exerted by the parent exercising the powers which a sole or majority shareholder has in general meetings of the subsidiary, for example to appoint or dismiss members of the board of the subsidiary and to initiate or approve alterations to its financial structure, the Revenue would not seek to argue that central control and management of the subsidiary is located where the parent company is resident. However, in cases where the parent usurps the functions of the board of the subsidiary (such as *Unit Construction* itself) or where that board merely rubber stamps the parent company's decisions without giving them any independent consideration of its own, the Revenue draw the conclusion that the subsidiary has the same residence for tax purposes as its parent.[12]

This is all perfectly proper and fairly reflects the case law described in this chapter. However, the statement then goes on to say that:

> The Revenue recognise that there may be many cases where a company is a member of a group having its ultimate holding company in another country which will not fall readily into either of the categories referred to above. In considering whether the board of such a subsidiary company exercises central management and control of the subsidiary's business, they have regard to the degree of autonomy which those directors have in conducting the company's business. Matters (among others) that may be taken into account are the extent to which the directors of the subsidiary take decisions on their own authority as to investment, production, marketing and procurement without reference to the parent.[13]

It is with those last five words to which exception might be taken. As one critic of the Inland Revenue's statement has said:

> There will be relatively few boards of directors of subsidiary companies who make important decisions without any reference to the parent company. Very often a representative of the parent company will be a member of the board, and the parent company will

frequently make its wishes very plain. But provided the subsidiary company's minutes show that the directors did not consider themselves to be relieved of their duties as directors, and provided they have come to a decision that the parent company's suggestions are indeed in the best interest of the company, there should not be any doubt that the subsidiary company directors have continued to exercise central management and control. The real test is surely whether the subsidiary directors review the company's affairs and consider recommendations by the parent company rather than simply implement them without question.[14]

1   (1908) 5 TC 358.
2   [1906] 2 Ch 34.
3   (1908) 5 TC 358 at 376.
4   (1959) 38 TC 712 at 729–730, per Romer LJ.
5   Ibid, at 730.
6   (1913) 6 TC 1 and 163.
7   Ibid, at 32–33.
8   *Calcutta Jute Mills Co Ltd v Nicholson* (1876) 1 TC 83 at 95.
9   SP 1/90, para 13.
10 (1899) 4 TC 41.
11 Ibid, at 46.
12 SP 1/90, para 16.
13 Ibid, para 17.
14 Colin Sandy 'Company Residence: A Critical Look at the Recent Statement of Practice' *Taxation Practitioner*, January 1984, 12.

6.07   Policy-making

It is one thing to state that a company resides where its central management and control actually abides and quite another to identify the factors which will attest to, and reveal the location of, such management and control.

In the two cases in which the test was first established,[1] all business activities of the companies concerned were carried out, and largely controlled, overseas. Calcutta Jute Mills Co manufactured and sold jute in India and the Cesena Sulpher Co manufactured and sold sulphur in Italy. All Calcutta's property was situated in India – indeed the directors of Calcutta did not have even an office in the United Kingdom but met in that belonging to one of their number! – and Cesena's main books, accounts and banking accounts were maintained in Italy. Yet, on the basis of the 'real business' test, the court held that both companies were resident in the United Kingdom. Clearly, therefore, it cannot have been the day-to-day management and control of the business activities of those companies which Kelly CB and Huddleston B had in mind when they decided that the 'real business' of those companies was carried on, not overseas, but in the United Kingdom.

The clue as to what they did have in mind is provided by Kelly CB who said that:

the answer to the question, Where does a joint stock company reside? is, . . . where its governing body is to be met with and found, and where its governing body exercises the powers conferred upon it by the Act of Parliament, and by the Articles of Association, where it meets and is in bodily and personal presence for the purposes of the concern.[2]

The 'real business' of Calcutta Jute Mills Ltd and of Cesena Sulphur Co Ltd was, in other words, carried on, not in India or Italy, but in the place from which the decision to carry out operations in India or Italy had emanated. As Huddleston B said of the Cesena Sulphur Co Ltd's business:

> No doubt the manufacturing part may be done and was done in Italy; so supposing that in another part of the world they found sulphur and carried on their business there, the manufacturing part of the business would be carried on there, no doubt; but the administrative part of the business would be carried on at the place from which all the orders came, from which all the directions flowed, and where the appointments were made, where the appointments of the officers were revoked, where the agents were nominated, where their powers were recalled, where the money was received (whatever may have been sent), where the dividends were payable, and where the dividends were declared. We find that all these Acts are performed in London. I cannot help thinking that the main place of business of the Company is in England. . . .[3]

The place of central management and control is, then, not necessarily the place in which a company's manufacturing or trading activities take place but the place in which the parameters governing those activities are set and the place in which the fundamental policies to be implemented in the United Kingdom or elsewhere are conceived and adopted.

1 *Calcutta Jute Mills Co Ltd v Nicholson* (1876) 1 TC 83 and *Cesena Sulphur Co Ltd v Nicholson* (1876) 1 TC 88.
2 Ibid, at 95.
3 Ibid, at 107.

6.08 Finance

If, as has been demonstrated at **6.07** above, policy-making is the primary expression of central management and control, the raising and allocation of the funds without which a company's policies could not be implemented must be an almost equally important manifestation of such management and control.

In *American Thread Co v Joyce*,[1] for instance, the Master of the Rolls noted that the business of the New York company was one in which seasonable purchases of cotton had to be made, and commented:

> Those purchases of cotton necessarily involve considerable financing. The whole policy depends really upon aye or no, shall we finance to the extent of, I think in one case it appears, £300,000. The New York people cannot do that at all. The whole purse-strings in the sense of money coming in by borrowing are kept most zealously at Manchester, and by means of those purse strings they are able to control and do control the policy of the Company and the mode in which they carry on their business of buying and selling.[2]

Similarly, in *De Beers Consolidated Mines Ltd v Howe*,[3] the Lord Chancellor took as evidence that the company was resident in the United Kingdom the fact that:

> London has . . . always controlled . . . all questions of expenditure except wages, materials, and such like at the mines, and a limited sum which may be spent by the Directors at Kimberley.[4]

A further factor to be considered – though one which alone is not, it seems determinative of central management and control[5] – is the declaration of dividends. In *Calcutta Jute Mills Co Ltd v Nicholson*,[6] it was asserted (in support of the proposition that the company was resident in India) that the activities of the company in England were minimal, consisting of little more than the dividing between the English shareholders of the amount, less expenses, remitted to this country from India. Huddleston B refuted such a contention by pointing out that:

> The operation of the Company in London was, not to divide the amount sent among the shareholders, but it was to 'declare' the amount; and I apprehend that, within the meaning of that clause, the directors in London, who had full power, might say, 'Well, we do not approve of this system upon which the division has been made, and we shall require a different dividend for the future', or something of that kind, – showing plainly that they exercise the authority, and that they are the persons who are the principal body. . . .[7]

Similarly, in the *American Thread Company* case,[8] one of the factors which led Hamilton J to uphold the finding of the Commissioners that the central management and control of the American company rested with the English directors was that:

> In each year the directors, sitting in extraordinary session in England, recommend what the dividend on the common stock should be . . . But in the year 1904, when the dividend was 16 per cent, though the Board by resolution recommended that rate, the gentleman who sent the cablegram to the American directors said that the Board had decided that the dividend should be 16 per cent, and went on to say: 'Arrange for usual formal resolutions as regards dividends on preferred shares and common stock without delay'. Accordingly, the 16 per cent was announced. . . .[9]

These words of Hamilton J make it clear that, so far as dividends are concerned, what one must look for when one is seeking to locate the place of central management and control is the person or group of persons who actually decides upon the quantum of the dividend – not the persons who formally resolve to pay it or give their formal approval to its declaration.

---

1 (1913) 6 TC 1 and 163.
2 Ibid, at 29.
3 (1906) 5 TC 198.
4 Ibid, at 213.
5 In *Egyptian Hotels Ltd v Mitchell* (1914) 6 TC 542 at 552 Lord Sumner said that 'The mere declaration and payment of a dividend here out of profits earned in a business otherwise wholly carried on abroad, does not prevent the business in which the profits have already been earned from having been wholly carried on abroad. To say that part of a Company's business is to pay dividends, if it has earned them, seems to me to be a play upon words.'
6 (1876) 1 TC 83.
7 Ibid, at 107.
8 (1913) 6 TC 1 and 163.
9 Ibid, at 25.

6.09 Location of central management and control

Identification of the person or group of persons who exercise *de facto* central management and control of a company does not, of course, conclude the question of a company's residence. There remains the final step of identifying the place from which they exercise that central management and control.

Where, as will usually be the case, full powers of management and control are vested in the directors of a company and those powers are exercised by the directors or delegated to others under their control,[1] the place where the directors habitually meet to make their decisions on policy, finance and related matters will be the place of central management and control. This is stressed in case after case.

In *Calcutta Jute Mills Co v Nicholson*,[2] for example, Kelly CB says that a company resides

> where its governing body is to be met with and found, and where its governing body exercises the powers conferred upon it . . . where it meets and is in bodily and personal presence for the purposes of the concern . . . at the office or place of dwelling . . . where the directors meet,[3]

Similarly, in *De Beers Consolidated Mines Ltd v Howe*,[4] the Lord Chancellor said:

> it is clearly established . . . that the Directors' Meetings in London are the meetings where the real control is exercised in practically all the important business of the Company. . . .[5]

This recurrent emphasis on the place of directors' meetings must not, however, lead one to suppose that the location of directors' meetings is the test of company residence. As Lord Radcliffe pointed out in *Bullock v Unit Construction Co Ltd*:[6]

> the necessity of establishing some common standard for the treatment of different tax payers meant that the Courts of Law were bound in course of time to produce and apply some general principles of their own to form an acceptable test of residence. No doubt it might have taken a variety of forms . . . the site of meetings of the directors' board [was a] possible candidate . . . for selection as the criterion. In fact, as we know, the principle was adopted that a company is resident where its central control and management abide. . . .[7]

As the Inland Revenue statement of practice points out, therefore, where, for example, 'a chairman or managing director exercises powers formally conferred by the company's Articles and the other board members are little more than cyphers' or where 'central management and control is exercised by a single individual . . . by reason of a dominant shareholding or for some other reason', the residence of the company will not be where the directors meet but 'where the controlling individual exercises his powers'.[8]

Furthermore, even if central management and control is in the hands of the directors, their place of meeting will not determine the company's place of residence if their meetings there are merely a matter of form. As the Inland Revenue statement of practice puts it:

> In general the place of directors' meetings is significant only in so far as those meetings constitute the medium through which central management and control is exercised. If, for

example, the directors of a company were engaged together actively in the UK in the complete running of a business which was wholly in the UK, the company would not be regarded as resident outside the UK merely because the directors held formal board meetings outside the UK.[9]

Clearly, the residence status of individual directors will be of some significance in this connection. If, for example, a number of the directors of a company, sufficient to form a quorum within the terms of the articles of association, are resident in the United Kingdom but board meetings are held abroad, there will be a presumption that decisions binding on all the directors are being made in the United Kingdom and are merely being endorsed in the overseas location for the purpose of establishing or maintaining the company's non-resident status. If, however, an insufficient number of directors for that purpose are United Kingdom resident, that presumption cannot arise.

The word 'presumption' is used in the last paragraph because the fact that directors in sufficient number to form a quorum are resident in one country is by no means conclusive proof that the company whose affairs they manage and control is also resident in that country. In *John Hood & Co Ltd v Magee*,[10] for instance, the sole director of a company registered both in Ireland and in the United States was resident in New York. The Commissioners found that, though the company traded in both Ireland and America, it kept house and did its real business in Belfast where Mr Hood held his board 'meetings'. Kenny J said: 'It is a mere accident that Mr Hood resides in New York.'[11]

The Inland Revenue declines to lay down rigid guidelines on these matters because they would, it says, 'only be misleading'.[12] The guidance note does, however, lay down the Inland Revenue's approach:

(i) They first try to ascertain whether the directors of the company in fact exercise central management and control.
(ii) If so, they seek to determine where the directors exercise this central management and control (which is not necessarily where they meet).
(iii) In cases where the directors apparently do not exercise central management and control of the company, the Revenue then look to establish where and by whom it is exercised.[13]

---

1 See **6.05** above.
2 (1876) 1 TC 83.
3 Ibid, at 95–96.
4 (1906) 5 TC 198.
5 Ibid, at 213.
6 (1959) 38 TC 712.
7 Ibid, at 738.
8 SP 1/90 para 13.
9 Ibid, para 14.
10 (1918) 7 TC 327.
11 Ibid, at 358.
12 SP 1/90 para 14.
13 Ibid, para 16.

Dual residence

6.10 Divided management and control

Hitherto, there has been an underlying assumption in this chapter that, no matter how complex the affairs of a company or how dispersed over the face of the earth its activities might be, it will be possible to find, in one particular territory, the place of central management and control. Exceptionally, this will not be true. As Lord Radcliffe says in *Bullock v Unit Construction Co Ltd*:[1]

> the facts of individual cases have not always so arranged themselves as to make it possible to identify any one country as the seat of central management and control at all. Though such instances must be rare, the management and control may be divided or even, at any rate in theory, peripatetic. Situations of this kind do not arise just to tease the minds of Judges: they are the product of some peculiar necessity, political or otherwise.[2]

Such a division of management and control will necessitate a finding of dual residence, and, although the first such finding was not made until 1925, the possibility of such a finding had been admitted earlier.

In 1915, *Mitchell v Egyptian Hotels Ltd*[3] came before the court and, in an oblique way, the matter was moved forward a stage. Egyptian Hotels Ltd had admitted to being resident in the United Kingdom and its residence status was, therefore, not in question. It was held, however, that the company was managed and controlled in Egypt so as to be liable to tax on its profits under Schedule D, Case V. Viscount Cave saw this decision as being a tacit acceptance of the principle of dual residence:

> the facts . . . were sufficient . . . to establish residence in Egypt, so that, if a company can have but one residence – namely, the place where its control and management abides, it must have been held that the company being resident in Egypt was not resident here, and accordingly was not taxable at all; but no such suggestion was made either by counsel or by any member of the tribunals by which the decision was given and upheld. This being so, while the case does not expressly decide that a company may have two residences for income tax purposes, the decision appears to be inconsistent with any other view.[4]

This opinion was expressed by Viscount Cave LC in the context of his judgment in *Swedish Central Rly Co Ltd v Thompson*,[5] the first case in which an actual finding of dual residence was made and upheld. The decision in that case was, however, later described as 'unfortunate . . . having regard to the course of authority both before and after its date',[6] and the facts reveal why. The company concerned had been incorporated in England for the purpose of constructing, maintaining and leasing a railway between Frovi and Ludvika in Sweden. During the period with which the case was concerned the company had fulfilled all these objectives and was merely drawing an annual rental under a lease granted to a Swedish traffic company. The registered office of the company was maintained in London and there the company seal was kept, formal administrative business was dealt with by a committee of three directors, transfers of shares were made and registered, and the accounts were drawn up and audited. All directors' and shareholders' meetings were, however, held in Stockholm and there the minimal business activity of the company (the receipt of rents) was carried on. It was found as a fact by the Special

Commissioners that the central control and management was in Sweden but that the company was also resident in the United Kingdom, and their findings were upheld in the House of Lords. In another part of the speech from which the earlier quotation is taken, Viscount Cave LC said that:

> when the central management and control of a company abides in a particular place the company is held for the purposes of income tax to have a residence in that place; but it does not follow that it cannot have a residence elsewhere. An individual may clearly have more than one residence (see *Cooper v Cadwalader*[7]); and in principle there appears to be no reason why a company should not be in the same position. The central management and control may be divided and it may 'keep house and do business' in more than one place; and if so it may have more than one residence.[8]

The finding of the Commissioners, however, had been not that central management and control was divided, but that it lay in Sweden. Once upheld by the House of Lords, therefore, the case began to be regarded as an authority for the proposition that, while central management and control was one test of corporate residence, there was another test also: that of the location of administrative control. This was the approach taken by the Crown in *Egyptian Delta Land and Investment Co Ltd v Todd*,[9] but, there, in the House of Lords, Viscount Sumner went to great lengths to stamp out the idea and to forestall any endorsement of it by his brethren:

> All that was decided in the *Swedish Central Railway* case was that the company could have two residences, one in England as well as one in Sweden. Your Lordships were not asked to decide more. It is true that by admission the controlling power over the business was in Sweden, but other business was done in London the character and importance of which, though set out in the Case, was not discussed at the Bar. It was a matter of degree on the facts and your Lordships cannot be deemed to have come to some unexpressed conclusion on that ground merely because you did not for yourselves declare . . . that there was no evidence of business carried on in England . . . Nor is it decisive of the point to say now that the business done in England was only administrative. It was in fact a good deal more, and in the static condition of the company's affairs it was not much less important than the Swedish part. If new questions arose the Swedish directors could settle them, but as things were little had to be done anywhere except 'administration' . . . and that was fairly divided between the two countries.[10]

In other words, the question whether the Swedish Central Railway Co Ltd had more than one residence had been a question of fact for the Commissioners to determine, and the House of Lords, having held that there was some evidence on which the Commissioners' finding of dual residence could have been made, had felt itself unable to interfere with that finding. That did not mean, however, that the control of administrative duties (which was the only control the London board appeared to exercise) was an alternative test of residence. It was not, and the Law Lords had never said it was. Central control and management remained the only test and one must reconcile that with the Commissioners' decision by assuming a finding of divided central management and control.

Viscount Sumner's speech was a skilful piece of oratory – verbally shoring-up the meagre facts until they were able (if only just) to carry the weighty conclusion the Commissioners had placed on them – and it was much needed, for the facts in the *Egyptian Delta* case[11] then before the House of Lords, though not, on the face of it, dissimilar from the facts in the *Swedish Railway* case,[12] had led the Commissioners to find that Egyptian Delta Land and Investment Co Ltd was resident in Egypt only!

Viscount Sumner contrived a distinction between the two findings by declaring that such management and control as there was in the *Swedish Railway* case[13] was almost equally divided between London and Stockholm while, in the *Egyptian Delta* case,[14] the whole of the central management and control was situated in Cairo. This method of reconciling the apparently irreconcilable found such favour with Lord Radcliffe that, in *Bullock v Unit Construction Co Ltd*,[15] he declared:

> I am myself of the opinion that the best way of treating the matter is to regard the *Swedish Central Railway Company* and the *Egyptian Delta Land Company* decisions as if they were in effect one decision of the House and the speech of Viscount Sumner in the later case as affording an authoritative commentary on the significance of the earlier. He was party to both of them. If this is done much of the difficulty disappears; for it is clear that Lord Sumner wished it to be understood that the Swedish Central Railway Company's business and administration were of such a nature that what managing and controlling had to be done was in fact done as much on English as on Swedish soil. He regarded the key of the earlier decision as being contained in the words of Lord Cave: 'The central management and control of a company may be divided, and it may "keep house and do business" in more than one place; and if so it may have more than one residence'.[16] On this basis the 1925 decision of the House is . . . a decision on that special class of case[17] . . . where the facts themselves are genuinely such as to not to admit of a finding that central management and control are exercised in or from any one country.[18]

The second case in which a finding of dual residence was made was *Union Corpn Ltd v IRC*.[19] The case concerned a company which had been incorporated in South Africa but which carried on its activities partly in London and partly in South Africa. Management and control at the highest level was divided between the directors in the United Kingdom and those in South Africa but final and supreme authority lay with the directors in London. On those facts, therefore, the Commissioners found that the company was resident in the United Kingdom. That finding was rejected by the Court of Appeal as being wrong in law.

Sir Raymond Evershed MR found himself in difficulties but derived assistance from the Australian case of *Koitaki Para Rubber Estates Ltd v Federal Comr of Taxation*[20] in which Dixon J had said:

> a finding that a company is a resident of more than one country ought not to be made unless the control of the general affairs of the company is not centred in one country but is divided or distributed among two or more countries. The matter must always be one of degree and residence may be constituted by a combination of various factors, but one factor to be looked for is the existence in the place claimed as a residence of some part of the superior or directing authority by means of which the affairs of the company are controlled.[21]

In the light of this judgment, and of the English authorities, Sir Raymond Evershed MR rejected the Special Commissioners' view and arrived at the conclusion that:

> there must, in order to constitute residence, be not only some substantial business operations in any given country but also present some part of the superior and directing

authority . . . [T]he question of the extent of the superior or directing authority required (as well as of the business operations being performed) is one of fact to be determined by the Special Commissioners.[22]

In other words, final and supreme arbitrating authority is not the same thing as central management and control and if the latter is found to be divided to a significant degree between two or more territories a finding of multiple residence must be made – even if in one of those territories is a person or group of persons with the power of ultimate arbitrament.

It is important to understand that the decision in *Union Corpn Ltd v IRC*[23] has not established a new or modified test of residence but has merely provided a basis for decision where *the* test of residence (Where does the central control and management of this company abide?) will not admit of the single-territory answer which the word 'central' in the test question demands. Sir Raymond Evershed's solution was to 'fragment' the principle underlying the test of residence and to 'establish a residence for tax purposes wherever the exercise of some portion of controlling power and authority can be identified'.[24] Lord Radcliffe suggested this solution might still be open to question,[25] but the remainder of his dicta in *Bullock v Unit Construction Co Ltd*[26] make it clear that any basis for decision which involved a concept other than central management and control could never be countenanced.

1 (1959) 38 TC 712.
2 Ibid, at 739.
3 (1915) 6 TC 542.
4 (1925) 9 TC 342 at 374.
5 Ibid.
6 *Bullock v Unit Construction Co Ltd* (1959) 38 TC 712 at 740, per Lord Radcliffe.
7 (1904) 5 TC 101. See **2.08** above.
8 *Swedish Central Railway Co Ltd v Thompson* (1925) 9 TC 342 at 372.
9 (1929) 14 TC 119.
10 Ibid, at 143.
11 (1929) 14 TC 119.
12 (1925) 9 TC 342.
13 Ibid.
14 (1929) 14 TC 119.
15 (1959) 38 TC 712.
16 *Swedish Central Railway Co Ltd v Thompson* (1925) 9 TC 342 at 372.
17 Ibid.
18 *Bullock v Unit Construction Co Ltd* (1959) 38 TC 712 at 740.
19 (1952) 34 TC 207.
20 (1940) 64 CLR 15.
21 (1952) 34 TC 207 at 241.
22 Ibid, at 275.
23 Ibid.
24 *Bullock v Unit Construction Co Ltd* (1959) 38 TC 712 at 739, per Lord Radcliffe.
25 Ibid.
26 (1959) 38 TC 712.

6.11 Fiscal residence

The purpose and effect of double taxation treaties has already been described at **2.21** above, but it must be noted here that such treaties generally make provision for determining in which of the two territories concerned a company resident in both is to be regarded as resident. The relevant article[1] in the OECD 1992 (as amended in 1994) Model Tax Convention states that:

> Where . . . a person other than an individual is a resident of both contracting States, then it shall be deemed to be a resident of the State in which its place of effective management is situated.

This *should* mean that a company regarded as resident in the United Kingdom under the municipal law of the United Kingdom continues to be regarded as resident here (to the exclusion of the residence status with which it has been attributed by the foreign state concerned[2]) since the Inland Revenue regards 'effective management' as being a term synonymous with 'central management and control'.[3] The Revenue departments of some foreign states are, however, reluctant to accept that the two terms are identical in meaning and difficulties in reaching agreement on this matter are frequently encountered.

---

1 Art 4, para 3.
2 Though, under the terms of most tax treaties, the foreign state will have the right to tax any profits arising from any 'permanent establishment' which the non-resident company has in the foreign state. A permanent establishment is 'a fixed place of business through which the business of an enterprise is wholly or partly carried on' (OECD Model Convention, art 5, para 1). It will generally include 'a place of management, a branch, an office, a factory, a workshop, and a mine, an oil or gas well, a quarry or any other place of extraction of natural resources' (art 5, para 2). A building site or construction or installation project will generally constitute a permanent establishment only if it lasts more than twelve months (art 5, para 3). The term 'permanent establishment' will not normally include the use of facilities solely for the purpose of storage, display or delivery of goods or merchandise belonging to the enterprise; the maintenance of stocks of such goods or merchandise for the purpose of storage, display or delivery, or for the purpose of processing by another enterprise; the maintenance of a fixed place of business solely for the purpose of purchasing goods or merchandise or of collecting information, for the enterprise, or for carrying on, for the enterprise, any other activity of a preparatory or auxiliary character, or for any combination of any of the activities mentioned provided the overall activity resulting from the combination is of a preparatory or auxiliary character (art 5, para 4). An enterprise will normally be deemed to have a permanent establishment in the foreign state if a person there (other than a broker, general commission agent or any other agent of independent status, acting in the ordinary course of his business) acts on its behalf and has, and habitually exercises, an authority to conclude contracts in the name of the enterprise (art 5, paras 5 and 6). The control of a company in one state by a company in another is not of itself sufficient to render either one a permanent establishment of the other (art 5, para 7).
3 This latter term is actually used instead of 'effective management' in some early double tax treaties.

6.12 Transfer of residence abroad

Following the decision of the courts that the place of a company's central management and control was the sole determinant of its place of residence, it became commonplace for companies engaged extensively in overseas activities to amend their articles of association and to transfer their central management and control abroad once the burden of United Kingdom taxation became significantly greater than that which would be imposed were they to be resident overseas. Of the companies involved in the cases discussed in this chapter, two, at least, changed their place of residence in this way: The Cesena Sulphur Company became resident in Italy and The American Thread Company became resident in America;[1] and, in 1928, when the validity of The Egyptian Delta Land and Investment Co

Ltd's change of residence was being challenged, Viscount Sumner was able to affirm that:

> Many companies have, at the cost of some trouble and expense, transferred their control and management abroad on the faith of decisions, or if you will, *dicta*, to the effect that by so doing they could legitimately reduce the burden of their taxation.[2]

As tax rates increased, however, the loss to the Exchequer through company migration reached unacceptable levels and, in FA 1951 s 36, Parliament enacted a measure which made it unlawful 'for a body corporate resident in the United Kingdom to cease to be so resident' unless the change was made with the consent of the Treasury. This provision was re-enacted as TA 1970 s 482(1)(a).

Taxes Act 1970 s 482(1)(a) and (b) was repealed by section 105(6) and (7) of FA 1988 with effect from 15 March 1988 although the repeal does not affect an application for Treasury consent made before that date or a consent already granted. Consent is now only required under TA 1988 s 765 for 'a body corporate resident in the United Kingdom to cause or permit a body corporate not resident in the United Kingdom over which it has control to create or issue any debentures'[3] or 'except for the purpose of enabling a person to be qualified to act as a director, for a body corporate so resident to transfer to any person, or cause or permit to be transferred to any person, any shares or debentures of a body corporate not so resident over which it has control, being shares or debentures which it owns or in which it has an interest'.[4] The above consents are not required where the transaction involves movements of capital between residents of member states of the EC.[5]

There are penalties for carrying out the transactions at s 765 without Treasury consent.

A person guilty of an offence is liable to 'imprisonment for not more than two years or to a fine, or to both' or 'where the person in question is a body corporate which is or was resident in the United Kingdom, to a fine not exceeding an amount equal to three times the corporation tax, capital gains tax and income tax paid or payable which is attributable to the income profit or gains (including chargeable gains) arising in the 36 months immediately preceding the commission of the offence of £10,000 whichever is the greater;'.[6] No proceedings shall however be instituted without the consent of the Attorney General.

Taxes Act 1988 s 765 includes no criteria by reference to which a decision as to whether consent should be given or withheld might be made, but, in practice, such criteria are provided under the terms of reference of an extra-statutory advisory committee which advises the Chancellor of the Exchequer on applications from which the Treasury consider consent should be withheld. Those criteria include the commercial justification (if any) for the proposed transaction, the amount of tax likely to be lost if consent were to be given, and the dictates of the wider national interest.

Under TA 1988 s 765(4) the Treasury consent referred to above may be special, in respect of a particular transaction or company, or general.

---

1 See paras 3 and 4 of the case stated in *Bradbury v English Sewing Cotton Co Ltd* (1923) 8 TC 481 at 482.
2 *Egyptian Delta Land and Investment Co Ltd v Todd* (1929) 14 TC 119 at 156.
3 TA 1988 s765(1)(c).
4 Ibid, s 765(1)(d). Section 765(2) and (3) excludes non-resident companies from this provision in

respect of loans raised on security from banks or insurance companies in the ordinary course of their business as bankers or fund investors.
5 TA 1988 s 765A.
6 Ibid, s 766(3).

6.13 Controlled foreign companies

Where a company which is resident outside the United Kingdom is controlled[1] by persons resident in the United Kingdom and is subject to a lower level of taxation in the territory in which it is resident[2] than it would be subjected to were it resident in the United Kingdom it is a 'controlled foreign company' within the terms of TA 1988 Chapter IV.

The consequences of acquiring such a status are serious in that, unless the company can pass various tests,[3] the Board of Inland Revenue may direct that the chargeable profits of the company for the accounting period to which the direction relates, and its creditable tax (if any) for that period, are each to be apportioned among the persons (whether resident in the United Kingdom or not) who had an interest in the company at any time during the accounting period.[4]

For the purpose of computing its chargeable profits, the company is to be regarded as resident in the United Kingdom, is to be assumed to have claimed all reliefs and capital allowances which, on that footing, it would have been eligible to claim, but is to be assumed to be neither a close company nor a member of a group.[5]

In order to determine whether a company is resident in a low-tax area, a company which is resident outside the United Kingdom is to be regarded as resident in the territory in which, throughout the accounting period concerned, it was liable to tax by reason of domicile, residence or place of management. If there were two such territories, a test of location of effective management is to be applied, followed (if necessary) by a test of location of assets with the highest aggregate market value at the end of the accounting period, in order to produce a single territory of residence, but, if those tests should fail, the Board will direct which territory is to be regarded as the country of residence. If there is no such territory, the company is to be conclusively assumed to be resident in a low-tax territory.[6]

'Interest' is widely defined and includes the possession of, or entitlement to acquire, share capital or voting rights; the right to receive or participate in distributions; the right to secure the direct or indirect application of income or assets for one's benefit; and the possession, alone or together with others, of control.[7]

Section 104 and Schedule 31 of the Finance Act 2000 introduce amendments to the previous legislation on controlled foreign companies.

Schedule 31 introduces four changes: to the meaning of control, to designer rates, to group service companies and to holding companies.

The new test for control includes a '40 per cent test' whereby a company is regarded as controlled by UK persons if it is at least 40 per cent controlled by a UK person and at least 40 per cent controlled by another person. The 40 per cent test will not apply where a foreign person in a joint venture holds more than 55 per cent of the interest, rights and powers.

Companies paying tax under 'designer rate tax provisions' are automatically treated as if they are subject to a lower level of taxation and the legislation also provides for regulations to be made specifying which provisions are to be regarded as designer rate tax provisions.

The list of businesses that are excluded from the exempt activities test is extended and the extension covers all types of predominantly intra-group service businesses that are not already excluded.

The income test in the local holding company exemption will only be met if the company receives the income in the territory in which it is resident. For other holding companies there are additional conditions.

The control changes come into effect from 21 March 2000 and the intra-group service company and holding company charges come into effect for CFC accounting periods beginning on or after that date.

The designer rate provisions have effect for CFC accounting periods beginning on or after 6 October 1999.

The Finance Act 2002 inserts a new TA 1988 s748A to enable the UK Treasury if necessary to specify jurisdictions for which controlled foreign company exceptions will not apply. These exercise of this power would require the express consent of the UK Parliament.

1 As defined in TA 1988 s 416.
2 A list of the territories which are not regarded by the Inland Revenue as low tax territories is reproduced in Inland Revenue Press Release of 5 October 1998.
3 TA 1988 s 748 and Sch 25 as amended by FA 2001 s 82. The tests concern distribution policy, profit levels, motive for being non-resident, extent of public ownership, and activities.
4 Ibid, s 747(3), (4) as amended by FA 1999 s 88.
5 Ibid, s 747(6) and Sch 24.
6 Ibid, s 749(1)–(4).
7 Ibid, s 749(5).

6.14 Dual resident companies

Under section 249 of the Finance Act 1994 a company which would otherwise be regarded as resident in the United Kingdom and is regarded for the purpose of any double taxation relief arrangements as resident in a territory outside the United Kingdom and not resident in the United Kingdom is treated as from 30 November 1993 as non-resident for all United Kingdom tax purposes.

CHAPTER 7

Domicile

If I should die, think only this of me:
That there's some corner of a foreign field
That is for ever England . . .

Rupert Brooke *The Soldier*

7.01 Introduction

It has been suggested earlier[1] that Parliament, in setting the determinants of liability to tax, chose residence in relation to the taxation of income, profits and gains but domicile in relation to the taxation of transfers of capital. That is, however, something of an over-simplification. Parliament has introduced domicile, as a modifying factor, into the law governing the taxation of income and gains also, so that, under TA 1988 s 65(4), for example, a person who is resident but not domiciled in the United Kingdom[2] is to be taxed only on *remittances* of foreign source income taxable under Schedule D, Case IV or V; and, under TA 1988 s 192 an employee who is non-domiciled and who works for a non-resident employer and whose duties are performed wholly abroad, receives complete exemption from liability. In the latter event any remittances of his emoluments will be taxed under Schedule E, Case III.

So far as gains are concerned, under TCGA 1992 s 12 a person who is resident or ordinarily resident but not domiciled in the United Kingdom is liable to capital gains tax only on the remittances of gains realised on foreign assets and not on the gain itself.

The purpose of this chapter, however, is to explore the actual concept of domicile, to show why Parliament chose it as a determinant of liability to inheritance tax and as a modifying factor in relation to other taxes, and to explain how a person's domicile may be identified.

---

1 At **1.13** above.
2 See **7.04** below as to whether 'not domiciled in the United Kingdom' means not domiciled in any of its three law districts.

The nature of domicile

7.02 Historical background

The concept of domicile (or domicil, as some prefer to call it) originated in the Roman Empire when, following the downfall of the Republic, Italy was divided into a number of individual townships known as *municipia* and the Empire was fragmented into numerous provinces. Each province and *municipium* possessed its own jurisdiction and, to a large extent, its own divergent internal law which was administered and enforced by magistrates. Most inhabitants of the Empire were connected by citizenship with one or more of these provincial or municipal communities and/or with Rome itself.

The link of citizenship could arise in various ways – by *origo* (the place within the Empire to which a person's father or, if he was illegitimate, his mother belonged), by adoption, by election or by manumission – and that presented three possibilities. A person might be a citizen of one place, a citizen of more than one place[1] or a citizen of none. This, inevitably, created difficulties. Given that, as stated, each province or *municipium* had its own system of law, to which system should a man in each of those situations be subject? The answer supplied by Rome was, in the first situation, the law of the man's place of citizenship, and, in the second situation, the law of his *origo*. In the third situation, however, a different determinant was needed and the determinant created was 'domicile' – the place in which a person had made his permanent home.

That concept of domicile was one of the concepts of Roman law, which, in the thirteenth century, was enthusiastically revived by the 'post-glossators' jurists who were attached to the Italian universities and who were engaged in developing the Roman law to meet the nation's changing needs.[2] Italy had by then emerged from the barbarism and feudalism into which the civilised world had been plunged following the fall of the Roman Empire in the fifth century and had become a land of independent, cosmopolitan cities: Bologna, Florence, Genoa, Milan, Padua, Pisa etc; all of which were subject generally to Roman law, but each of which had diverse laws of its own which gave rise to conflict as commercial intercourse between the cities increased. As a basis for the resolution of such conflicts, the post-glossators developed a set of principles, known to legal historians as 'statute theory', and it was into these that the revived concept of domicile was introduced.

A 'statute' in the terminology of the post-glossators was any legislative or customary local law which was found to be contrary to Roman law in general; and the statute theory proceeded from the premise that all such laws were either 'real', 'personal' or 'mixed'. A law which concerned things other than moveables was 'real',[3] a law which concerned persons and moveables was 'personal', and a law which concerned acts (such as the making of a contract) was 'mixed' as it generally concerned both persons and things. Real statutes were seen as essentially territorial and as having no application beyond the territorial bounds of the locality in which they were found. Mixed statutes were seen as partially territorial in that they applied to all acts done within the territorial bounds of the locality in which they were found but could give rise to litigation elsewhere. Personal statutes, on the other hand, were seen as non-territorial and as applicable to any person *domiciled* within the locality in which the laws were found, wherever that person might be.

Thus a Bologna-born merchant whose permanent home was in Florence would remain subject to Florentine personal laws while visiting, say, Padua, and neither Bolognan nor Paduan personal laws would apply to him.

The statute theory – the basis of today's 'private international law' or 'conflict of laws' as it is often called – was neither as simple nor as effective as it might appear and it was much refined by French jurists in the sixteenth century and Dutch jurists in the seventeenth century. Its subsequent development is beyond the scope of this work and it is sufficient to say that, despite all the changes which have taken place and despite the English and Scottish developments of the conflict of laws in the nineteenth century, the concept of domicile, and its use as the determinant of the system of personal law to which a person should be subject wherever he might be, has remained intact to the present day in the common law jurisdictions of the United Kingdom, the Commonwealth[4] and the United States of America. To such nations, possessing as they do within their territorial boundaries a number of diverse legal systems, domicile still presents, as it once presented to Italy, the best determinant of the relevant personal law. Ironically, in the nineteenth century, Italy itself and most other countries in Europe rejected the test of domicile in favour of the test of nationality, and Japan and many South American states followed suit.

---

1 St Paul, for example, was a citizen of Tarsus in Cilicia and a citizen of Rome (Acts ch 21, v 39 and ch 22, v 27).
2 In the eleventh century the jurists of Italy had taken the *Corpus Juris* – the Justinian code of Roman law – and added to it *glossae* – explanatory notes. The jurists themselves came to be known as the 'glossators' and the revived and expanded Roman law became the general law throughout Italy and the legal code on which the post-glossators then worked.
3 From late latin *realis* (Latin *res*), a thing.
4 Apart from Nauru which, in 1974, legislated for the replacement of domicile by habitual residence (Conflict of Laws Act 1974). See note 4 to **7.03** below.

7.03   The two roles of domicile

The brief picture of domicile's origins given at **7.02** above should have sufficed to show that domicile is essentially a conflict of laws concept employed in determining the system of personal law which should be applied where a person has connections with more than one jurisdiction. Personal law is that part of law which, to some degree, governs the validity of marriage, the effect of marriage on the proprietory rights of husband and wife, divorce and nullity of marriage, legitimacy, legitimation and adoption, wills of moveables and intestate succession to moveables. It follows, therefore, that, whenever a question arises in the English courts concerning any of these matters, it must be determined according to the law of the domicile of the person concerned and not (unless English law happens to be the law of his domicile) according to English law, the law of the territory in which he happens to be, or the law of the nation of which he is a citizen.

EXAMPLE

Alan, a citizen of Eriador (where wills require the attestation of three witnesses), dies on holiday in Mordor (where wills require the attestation of four witnesses) but, at the time of his death, is domiciled in Gondor under whose laws he has made a will attested by only one witness as is permitted under Gondorian law.

His will is contested in the English courts on the grounds that two witnesses are required under English law or, alternatively, that three are required under Eriadorian law or, alternatively, that four are required under Mordorian law. The suit fails.[1]

The rationale for this lies in the fact that (conceptually, at any rate) domicile, at any given moment in a person's life or at the moment of his death, singles out, from among all the territories in the world, the one territory in which – irrespective of where he happens to be or where he happens to reside or ordinarily reside – that person has his real home; and, once that person's real home has been identified, the law of that territory, and of no other, is the law which should be applied in all matters which relate to him as a person.

One of those matters is the transfer of capital to another – dispositions which reduce the value of a person's estate upon his death or, in certain circumstances, during his lifetime – and it is upon such transfers of value that, under United Kingdom revenue law, inheritance tax is charged. It is entirely appropriate, therefore, that – except as regards any part of a person's estate which is situated in the United Kingdom – the determinant of liability to tax on capital transfers should be the same as the determinant of the personal law governing those transfers, ie domicile.

There is, however, a second and more cogent reason why a person's domicile is a more appropriate determinant of liability to inheritance tax than residence. Inheritance tax is a cumulative charge on transfers of value made by a person upon his death *and* during the previous seven years, and there is also a seven year cumulation period in respect of chargeable transfers during his lifetime.[2] The effectiveness of the inheritance tax system depends, therefore, on a link of the greatest possible strength being used to attach a person to the United Kingdom, and domicile is just such a link. Residence may easily be snapped, ordinary residence is only a little stronger, but the bonds of domicile are very difficult to break – and, as is explained later,[3] even if a person should succeed in breaking those bonds, he may nonetheless find himself attributed with a *deemed* domicile under rules which Parliament has enacted to cover just such a contingency.[4]

The confinement of United Kingdom taxation of income and capital gains to the taxation of remittances in the case of income and gains generated overseas by a person who is not domiciled in the United Kingdom is further parliamentary recognition of the strength of the link between person and territory which domicile represents.

---

1 The territories used in this example are some of the fictitious territories created by J R R Tolkien as a setting for *The Lord of the Rings*.
2 IHTA 1984 s 7 as amended by FA 1986.
3 At **7.17** below.
4 Without doing so by name, these rules introduce into United Kingdom revenue law a highly-defined version of the concept known as 'habitual residence' which is increasingly being used as a territorial connecting factor in international conventions.

7.04 The five principles of domicile

Domicile, being a common law concept, is not defined in the Taxes Acts. In 1858, however, Lord Cranworth said:

> By domicile we mean home, the permanent home,[1]

and, ever since, that has been regarded as a basic (if deceptively simple) definition of the term. Although the idea of a permanent home is indeed central to the concept of domicile, the meaning of 'permanent home' in this context is not necessarily the meaning which the man on the Clapham omnibus would give to the term. There are, as will be shown, instances in which the courts will decide that a person's permanent home is in some far away territory in which he has never set foot and with which, so far as he is aware, he has never had any connection. This is because domicile, though founded on fact, is not merely a finding of fact but a conclusion of law which is reached by application of a set of legal principles.

The principles referred to are five in number, and the first is that no one shall, at any time, be without a domicile.[2] The necessity for this becomes apparent once we remind ourselves that domicile is, in English law, the sole determinant of the personal law to which a person is to be subject. Indeed, it is one of the weaknesses of legal systems which have opted for nationality as a determinant of the personal law that a person may be stateless and may thus not possess the required connecting link. This is not to say, of course, that assigning a domicile to every person never presents difficulties; it frequently does: but the courts have developed additional principles to overcome these problems.

The second principle is that no one can simultaneously have more than one operative domicile.[3] The justification for this is that domicile, being the sole determinant of the personal law, must, by its very nature, be exclusive, otherwise a further determinant will be needed. This exposes another weakness in systems which have taken nationality as the determinant of the personal law, for many persons have dual nationality. The adjective 'operative' has been introduced into the above statement of principle because, as will be explained,[4] there are three kinds of domicile and one of these, domicile of origin, will, if displaced by either of the others, become dormant but will, in the event of either of the others being lost, instantly revive. It should be noted that, in English law, domicile is regarded as a purely objective concept which remains unaffected by the subject matter of the point at issue.[5] In theory, therefore, there should be no question, in English law, of a person having one domicile for taxation purposes and another for, say, the purposes of divorce. As explained below, however, there are certain situations in which that may be possible – though not through any abandonment of the objective approach.

The third principle is said to be that domicile must relate to a territory subject to a single system of law, whether or not the limits of that territory coincide with national boundaries. This, so far as the United Kingdom is concerned, would mean that a domicile could arise only in Northern Ireland, Scotland or England and Wales.

However, the Taxes Acts speak not of domicile in Northern Ireland or Scotland or England and Wales but of domicile 'in the United Kingdom'.[6]

The fourth principle is that a change of domicile may never be presumed.[7] As Jenkins LJ has said:

Change of domicile, particularly where the change is from the domicile of origin to a domicile of choice (as distinct from a change from one domicile of choice to another) has always been regarded as a serious step which is only to be imputed to a person upon clear and unequivocal evidence.[8]

In other words, a change of domicile will always have to be proved and, as Lord Chelmsford has said:

the burden of proof unquestionably lies upon the party who asserts the change.[9]

The question of the degree of proof required is considered at **7.15** below.

The fifth principle is that domicile must be determined according to the English concept of domicile. As Lindley MR said in *Re Martin*:[10]

The domicil . . . must be determined by the English Court . . . according to those legal principles applicable to domicil which are recognised in this country and are part of its law.[11]

The significance of this rule lies in the fact that 'domicile' does not have a precise and universally accepted meaning. Not all jurisdictions accept the objective approach to domicile, others (such as Australia, New Zealand and the United States of America) do not accept English doctrines such as that of the revival of the domicile of origin,[12] and under some international conventions domicile is equated with habitual residence.[13]

---

1 *Whicker v Hume* (1858) 7 HL Cas 124 at 160.
2 *Udny v Udny* (1869) Lr 1 Sc & Div 441 at 457, per Lord Westbury.
3 *IRC v Bullock* [1976] STC 409 at 414, per Buckley LJ.
4 See **7.06** below.
5 It is understood that a subjective or 'multiple concept' view of domicile is increasingly being adopted in the United States of America.
6 Eg TA 1988 ss 65(4), 192, 207 and TCGA 1992 s 12(1).
7 See *Moorhouse v Lord* (1863) 10 HL Cas 272 at 286, per Lord Chelmsford.
8 *Travers v Holley* [1953] P 246 at 252.
9 *Moorhouse v Lord* (1863) 10 HL Cas 272 at 286.
10 [1900] P 211.
11 Ibid, at 227.
12 See **7.07** below.
13 Art 5 of the 1955 Hague Convention to regulate Conflicts between the Law of Nationality and the Law of Domicile attributes domicile with this meaning.

7.05 The need for reform

It will be apparent from the preceding section that the common law of domicile contains both gaps and anomalies. It was for this reason that, in 1952, a Private International Law Committee was established to consider what amendments were desirable. When the Committee reported in 1954,[1] it identified two particular defects which required remedial legislation: one concerning the revival of the domicile of origin[2] and the other concerning the level of proof required to establish a change in domicile.[3] In 1958, a Private Members' Bill designed to implement the Committee's proposals on these matters was introduced in the House of Lords, but this was opposed on behalf of the foreign business community who feared 'unforeseen and unpredictable consequences in the field of taxation'.[4] Accordingly, the Bill was withdrawn and replaced by a modified Bill in 1959. The earlier controversy had prejudiced the second Bill's chances of success, however, and so it too was withdrawn. The question of the reform of the law of domicile was thereupon referred back to the Committee and, in 1963, it again reported,[5] reiterating its original recommendations but making additional proposals which would cushion the foreign business community from the impact of any changes in the law. No parliamentary action has ever been taken on those recommendations. The Committee also considered, however, the reform of the law concerning the domicile of dependence acquired by women on their marriage, and, in 1972, a Departmental Committee proposed changes in this area which were subsequently enacted in the Domicile and Matrimonial Proceedings Act 1973 s 1. Other sections of that Act brought about minor reforms in relation to the domicile of dependence of children.

The latest call for reform has come from the Law Commission and the Scottish Law Commission which, in January 1984, set up a Joint Working Party to consider afresh the whole question of domicile. Their report was published in 1985[6] and its conclusions and proposals are noted where appropriate in the remainder of this chapter.

---

1 First Report of the Private International Law Committee (1954) Cmd 9068.
2 See **7.07** below.
3 See **7.15** below.
4 Hansard (HL) 1958, vol 211, cols 206–209.
5 Seventh Report of the Private International Law Committee: Law of Domicile (1963) Cmnd 1955.
6 The Law Commission Working Paper No. 88 and The Scottish Law Commission Consultative Memorandum No. 63, 'Private International Law, The Law of Domicile' (1985, HMSO).

Domicile of origin

7.06 Acquisition

English law recognises three kinds of domicile: domicile of origin, domicile of dependence and domicile of choice. Every person (including a corporation[1]) will possess the first of these, and any natural person may, at different times, possess either of the others.

The domicile of origin is the form of domicile which is imposed on every person at the moment of his birth. It is a link, forged by the law, which attaches a person to a particular system of law and which retains its hold on him throughout his life. Should he acquire a domicile of dependence or a domicile of choice, the link will be removed, but not destroyed; rather it will be held at readiness to re-attach him instantly to the original system of law should his domicile of dependence cease or his domicile of choice be abandoned.

Except in the case of a foundling (when the domicile of origin imposed is that of the place where the child is found), the basis of imposition of a domicile of origin is parentage. If a child is born legitimate and during his father's lifetime, the domicile of origin imposed on him is that of his father at the time of the child's birth.[2] If a child is born illegitimate,[3] or born legitimate but after his father's death,[4] the domicile of origin imposed on him is that of his mother.

One problem which could arise in this connection springs from the fact that the question of legitimacy is itself a matter of personal law. As the determinant of the appropriate person law is the child's domicile and as the child's domicile cannot be determined until the question of its legitimacy has been settled, it can be seen that, unless both parents are of the same domicile, an endless legal loop is created. Various solutions to the problem have been proposed[5] but there is no authority on the question in English law.

It seems clear that in the event of an illegitimate child being legitimated the child's domicile of origin will remain unaffected since, under the Legitimacy Acts, legitimation does not operate retrospectively.[6] In the event of a child becoming adopted, however, it would appear that a new domicile of origin will be acquired since adoption involves the complete severance of the legal relationship between parent and child and the establishment of a new one between child and the adoptive parent.[7]

The Law Commission and the Scottish Law Commission have recommended that the domicile of origin be abolished and that, in future, a child's domicile should be determined from the outset under revised domicile of dependence rules.[8]

1 See **7.18** below.
2 *Udny v Udny* (1869) LR 1 Sc & Div 441 at 457, per Lord Westbury.
3 Ibid.
4 This is apparently unsupported by any English authority.
5 Eg by R. H. Graveson *Private International Law* (7th edn, Sweet and Maxwell) at 195–196.
6 See **7.09** below for the domicile of dependence which legitimation creates.
7 *Bromley's Family Law* (18th edn) p 408.
8 The Law Commission Working Paper No. 88 and the Scottish Law Commission Consultative Memorandum No. 63, 'Private International Law, The Law of Domicile', 1985, para 4.22. See **7.09** below.

7.07 Displacement and revival

A domicile of origin, being a domicile imposed by operation of law independently of a person's will, can never be extinguished by an act of will or by mere abandonment. It will continue to be operative, whether its possessor wishes it to be operative or not, until it is displaced by the acquisition of either a domicile of dependency or a domicile of choice. This is well illustrated by the leading case of *Bell v Kennedy*.[1]

Mr Bell was born in 1802 of Scottish parents who were domiciled by choice in the island of Jamaica. Accordingly, he possessed a Jamaican domicile of origin. Following the death of his mother, Bell, at the age of two, was sent to Scotland to be cared for and educated. When he was ten years old his father died and left him his Jamaican estate. Mr Bell completed his education in Scotland, travelled for a while in Europe, then, shortly after reaching his majority, returned to Jamaica to cultivate the estate that had been left to him. The estate prospered and Mr Bell became a wealthy and important personage, attaining membership of the island's Legislative Assembly. He married and fathered three children. In 1834, however, the law was changed with regard to slavery and the change was to culminate in the complete emancipation of slaves in 1838. Mr Bell strongly disapproved of the change and that, coupled with his failing health, decided him upon a permanent return to the United Kingdom. Accordingly, in 1837, he sold the estate and left the island for good. Initially, he and his immediate family resided with his mother-in-law in Edinburgh and Mr Bell set about finding a suitable estate, preferably in Scotland but possible across the Border, in England, which he could purchase and in which he and his family could settle down. Before he had succeeded in this, however, his wife died. At that time, a woman acquired the domicile of her husband upon marriage and, accordingly, in order to resolve a dispute which had arisen concerning Mr and Mrs Bell's daughter's succession to Mrs Bell's share in goods held in common between Mr and Mrs Bell at the date of Mrs Bell's death, it became necessary to determine Mr Bell's domicile at the date of his wife's death. The court held that his domicile was his domicile of origin, ie Jamaica. Lord Cairns said:

> The birth-domicile of [Bell] in Jamaica continued, at all events till 1837, and the onus lies upon those who desire to shew that there was a change in this domicile . . . to prove that that change took place. The law is, beyond all doubt, clear with regard to the domicile of birth, that the personal status indicated by that term clings and adheres to the subject of it until an actual change is made by which the personal status of another domicile is acquired . . . It appears to me . . . that so far from [Mr and Mrs Bell's daughter and her husband] having discharged the onus which lies upon them to prove the adoption of a Scottish domicile, they have entirely failed in discharging that burden of proof, and that the evidence leads quite in the opposite direction. There is nothing in it to shew that [Bell's] personal status of domicile as a native and inhabitant of Jamaica has been changed on coming here by that which alone could change it, his assumption of domicile in another country.[2]

and Lord Colonsay had this to say:

> I think it is very clear that Mr Bell left Jamaica with the intention of never returning . . . But I do not think that his having sailed from Jamaica with that intent extinguished his Jamaica domicile . . . He could not so displace the effect which law gives to the domicile of origin, and which continues to attach until a new domicile is acquired *animo et facto*.[3]

Once a person has, however, *animo et facto* or through the act of the person on whom he is dependent, acquired a new domicile, his domicile of origin, though displaced, still does not die. It lives on within him, dormant but ready to awake and come back into operation in the instant any other domicile is voluntarily abandoned. As Lord Westbury has said in *Udny v Udny*:[4]

> When another domicile is put on, the domicile of origin is for that purpose relinquished, and remains in abeyance during the continuance of the domicile of choice; but as the domicile of origin is the creature of law, and independent of the will of the party, it would be inconsistent with the principles on which it is by law created and ascribed to suppose that it is capable of being by the act of the party entirely obliterated and extinguished.[5]

Colonel Udny acquired a domicile of origin in Scotland when he was born there of Scottish parents in 1779. His childhood was spent in Scotland but, after serving as an officer in the Guards, in 1812, he married and settled in London. There he resided for the next 32 years. In 1844, however, the Colonel 'having been involved for some time in pecuniary difficulties (owing chiefly to his connection with the turf) was compelled to leave England in order to avoid his creditors'.[6] He first went to Scotland and from there he arranged for the sale of the lease of the London house and 'everything that was in the house, including what had belonged to his mother, his sister, and his . . . wife';[7] and then he fled to Boulogne. It was in Boulogne that he formed the illicit attachment that resulted in the birth of child whose legitimation was in question.

Some doubt was expressed by the court whether Colonel Udny had ever, in fact, acquired an English domicile of choice. Nevertheless, the Lord Chancellor was of the opinion that:

> the English domicil of Colonel Udny, if it were ever acquired, was formally and completely abandoned in 1844 when he sold his house and broke up his English establishment with the intention never to return. And, indeed, his return to that country was barred against him by the continued threat of process by his creditors. I think that on such abandonment his domicil of origin revived. It is clear that by our law a man must have some domicil, and must have a single domicil. It is clear, on the evidence, that the Colonel did not contemplate residing in France . . . Why should not the domicil of origin cast on him by no choice of his own, and changed for a time, be the state to which he naturally falls back when his first choice has been abandoned *animo et facto*, and whilst he is deliberating before he makes a second choice.[8]

Both the Private International Law Committee[9] and now The Law Commission and the Scottish Law Commission[10] have recommended that the principle of revival be discarded and that an existing domicile should continue until a new domicile is acquired. This is the rule in the United States of America,[11] New Zealand[12] and Australia.[13]

The question of the precise point at which the domicile of origin will revive upon a domicile of choice being abandoned is fully discussed at **7.16** below.

---

1 *Bell v Kennedy* (1868) LR 1 Sc & Div 307.
2 Ibid, at 310, 316–317.
3 Ibid, at 323.
4 (1869) LR 1 Sc & Div 441.
5 Ibid, at 458.
6 Ibid, at 445.
7 Ibid.
8 Ibid, at 448.
9 First Report (1954) Cmd 9068, para 14.
10 The Law Commission Working Paper No. 88 and The Scottish Law Commission Consultative Memorandum No. 63, 'Private International Law, The Law of Domicile', 1985, para 5.22.
11 *Re Jones' Estate* 192 Iowa 78, 182 NW 227 (1921).
12 Domicile Act 1976 s 11 (New Zealand).
13 Domicile Act 1982 s 7 (Australia).

Domicile of dependence

7.08 Married women

Until 1 January 1974 there were three classes of persons who could or would acquire a domicile of dependence: children, mentally disordered persons and married women. Now, only the first two classes remain, for, by the Domicile and Matrimonial Proceedings Act 1973 s 1, – the rule at common law that every woman acquired from her husband his domicile immediately upon her marriage – was swept away. The Act provides that the domicile of a married woman as at any time on or after 1 January 1974

> shall, instead of being the same as her husband's by virtue only of marriage, be ascertained by reference to the same factors as in the case of any other individual capable of having an independent domicile.[1]

So far as any woman who married on, or has married since, 1 January 1974 is concerned, the position is quite straightforward. As the subsection quoted makes plain, the woman has the same capacity as her husband or any other non-dependent person for acquiring a domicile of choice. It will, of course, usually be the case that the domicile of a husband and his wife will be the same, but this will now merely be because of their independent choice to live together permanently in the same place. Such a choice is not always made at the time of the marriage, or if made then, may not be implemented by residence until later. In that event, each may, under the Act, retain different domiciles.

EXAMPLE

Marie-Louise is domiciled in Belgium. While attending art college in Manchester in 1985 she marries a fellow student. Henri, who is domiciled in France. Upon the completion of their respective courses they are resolved to settle permanently in Monaco. Until that decision is implemented by residence in Monaco, Marie-Louise will retain her Belgian domicile and Henri will retain his French domicile. Thereafter they will each acquire a Monagesque domicile of choice. Had they married before 1 January 1974, Marie-Louise would, upon her marriage, have acquired a French domicile of dependence and then, when they settled in Monaco, a Monagesque domicile of dependence.

The position of a woman who married before 1 January 1974 is set out in subsection (2) of the Act:

> Where immediately before [1 January 1974] a woman was married and then had her husband's domicile by dependence, she is to be treated as retaining that domicile (as a domicile of choice, if it is not also her domicile of origin) unless and until it is changed by acquisition or revival of another domicile on or after [1 January 1974].[2]

The principal difficulty to which this provision gives rise was dealt with in *IRC v Duchess of Portland*.[3] In 1948, the taxpayer, a Canadian citizen with a domicile of origin in Quebec, married Lord William Cavendish-Bentinck (subsequently the Duke of Portland) in England and became Lady William Cavendish-Bentinck (subsequently the Duchess of Portland). Thereupon she acquired from her husband an English domicile of dependence which displaced her Quebec domicile of origin, but she was resolved to return to live in Canada should her husband predecease her and she hoped to persuade him to live in Canada on his retirement. Throughout her marriage, the Duchess of Portland maintained her links with Canada, returning there to visit friends and relatives for between ten and twelve weeks each year and (since about 1964) owning and maintaining there at her own expense her family home in Metis Beach, Quebec. The Duchess of Portland's first visit to Canada following the enactment of the Domicile and Matrimonial Proceedings Act 1973 was in July 1974, and following that visit she claimed that, under section 1(2) of the Act, her domicile of dependence had been changed by the revival of her Quebec domicile of origin. Had her claim succeeded she would have become exempt under TA 1970 s 122(2)(a) from liability to tax on income accruing to her in Canada but not remitted to the United Kingdom.

The basis of the Duchess of Portland's claim was that the domicile of choice which, under DMPA 1973 s 1(2), she acquired on 1 January 1974 was merely a *deemed* domicile of choice and that the strict test applicable to the abandonment of a true domicile of choice should not be applied in deciding whether or not her deemed domicile of choice had been abandoned. Instead, she claimed, the more lenient test applicable to the abandonment of a domicile of dependency was appropriate. Nourse J agreed that DMPA 1973 s 1(2) was a deeming provision but said:

> that which is deemed in a case where the domicile of dependency is not the same as the domicile of origin is the retention of the domicile of dependency as a domicile of choice. I think that that must mean that the effect of the subsection is to reimpose the domicile of dependency as a domicile of choice. The concept of an imposed domicile of choice is not one which it is very easy to grasp, but the force of the subsection requires me to do the best I can. It requires me to treat the taxpayer as if she had acquired an English domicile of choice, even though the facts found by the commissioners tell me that that would have been an impossibility in the real world. In my judgment it necessarily follows that the question whether, after 1 January 1974, the taxpayer abandoned her deemed English domicile of choice must be determined by reference to the test appropriate to the abandonment of a domicile of choice and not by reference to the more lenient test appropriate to the abandonment of one of dependency.[4]

It was pointed out in *IRC v Duchess of Portland* that, if the Duke and Duchess had married on or after 1 January 1974 the effect of DMPA 1973 s 1(1) would have been to preserve the Duchess's domicile of origin. Nourse J admitted that it was so and said:

> It seems clear that a woman living in England with her husband who was married before 1 January 1974 can only free herself from the shackles of dependency by choosing to leave her husband for permanent residence in another country. That is a very limited freedom and it is less than that available under s 1(1) to those who marry on or after 1 January 1974. Be that as it may, Parliament did not, as it might have done, provide that a woman who was married before 1 January 1974 was to be treated as if she had never acquired her domicile of dependency. Section 1(2) having taken the form which it has, by treating the married woman as retaining her domicile of dependency as a domicile of choice, I regret that I have no choice but to attach to it all the consequences which the law has long recognised the latter domicile to have.[5]

A second difficulty which arises in relation to DMPA s 1(2) concerns the position after 1 January 1974 of a woman who, having married before that date, had left or had been abandoned by her husband before that date and had settled permanently in some country other than that of her domicile of dependence. In the absence of some new act on her part on or after 1 January 1974, does the woman retain her domicile of dependence as her domicile of choice or does she immediately acquire as her domicile of choice the country in which she settled permanently during her domicile of dependency? This question was also answered, albeit *obiter*, in *IRC v Duchess of Portland*. The problem, said Nourse J, is to be resolved 'consistently with the rule which would have applied if the husband had died before 1 January 1974.[6] The rule he referred to was established in *Re Cooke's Trustees*[7] and *Re Scullard*[8] and is that where a husband and wife have been living apart, the intent and act of the wife in permanently making her home elsewhere creates a domicile of choice upon the death of her husband without the need for any additional act on her part, or, if the country in which she has settled is her domicile of origin, revives her domicile of origin without the need for any such act. The application of the rule is straightforward.

EXAMPLE

In 1952, Tom, who was, and continued to be, domiciled in England, married Ingrid, who had a domicile of origin in Germany. In 1968 Ingrid left Tom and made her permanent home in Switzerland. Upon her marriage, Ingrid acquired an English domicile of dependence. This endured until 1 January 1974, but, on that date, in accordance with the rule in *Re Scullard's Estate*,[9] she automatically acquired a domicile of choice in Switzerland. Had Ingrid, upon leaving Tom, made her permanent home in Germany rather than Switzerland, her domicile of origin would have automatically revived on 1 January 1974.

Nourse J summed up as follows the procedure which DMPA 1973 s 1(2) requires one to adopt in determining the domicile of a woman who was married before 1 January 1974:

> first . . . look at the state of affairs prevailing on 1 January 1974 to see whether there has been any automatic change on that date [as in the above example]. If there has not . . . look at events after that date in order to see whether any change has occurred subsequently.[10]

---

1 Domicile and Matrimonial Proceedings Act 1973 s 1(1).
2 Ibid, s 1(2).
3 [1982] STC 149.
4 Ibid, at 154.
5 Ibid, at 156.
6 Ibid, at 155.
7 (1887) 56 LT 737.
8 [1956] 3 All ER 898.
9 Ibid.
10 *IRC v Duchess of Portland* [1982] STC 149 at 155.

7.09 Children

Until 1 January 1974, it was the rule at common law that a minor, whether married or not, was totally incapable of acquiring by his own act an independent domicile of choice.[1] A female child who, before then, married before attaining her majority acquired her husband's domicile as a domicile of dependence and, if widowed before that date, reacquired the domicile she had immediately before her marriage.[2]

On 1 January 1974, however, the Domicile and Matrimonial Proceedings Act 1973 came into effect and, with application only to England and Wales and Northern Ireland,[3] confined this rule to unmarried children under the age of 16.[4] Since then, any child reaching the age of 16 or marrying under that age, has been capable of acquiring an independent domicile of choice; and the same applied to any child who, at that date, was already over the age of 16 or, if then still under the age of 16, was then already married.[5]

The present position is, then, that every child acquires at birth a domicile of origin[6] and cannot, so long as he remains unmarried and below the age of 16, displace that domicile of origin by a domicile of choice acquired by his own act of will. There is, however, nothing to prevent his domicile of origin being displaced by an act of will on the part of one of his parents, and if this occurs the new domicile he acquires will be a domicile of dependence.

The primary rule is that, upon any change in the domicile of a child's father after the child's birth, a legitimate or adopted child will acquire his father's new domicile as a domicile of dependence unless his parents[7] are living apart and he either has then a home with his mother and not with his father or having had a home with his mother has not since then had a home with his father.[8] This is because, upon a separation, a child acquires a domicile of dependence from the parent with whom he makes his home and, should he subsequently make his home with the other parent, he will (subject to a mother's right *not* to communicate her domicile to a child who is dependent upon her – see next paragraph) acquire a new domicile of dependence from that parent, but, should he cease to have a home with either parent, his last-acquired domicile of dependence will continue. A legitimate, legitimated or adopted child who shares his time between the homes of both parents will acquire and retain throughout the arrangement the domicile of his father.

Where a child is illegitimate or was born after the death of his father, he will prima facie acquire as a domicile of dependence any new domicile acquired by his mother whether he has a home with her or not,[9] unless the mother elects, bona fide and in the interests of the child, that the child's domicile shall not change with her domicile.[10]

Where one or both of a child's parents die during a child's period of dependency, the rules are as follows.

Where a legitimate or adopted child's father dies after the child is born, the child acquires (if he has not acquired it already[11]) the domicile of his mother as a domicile of dependence[12] which will then change as her domicile changes – subject, as explained above, to her right to elect that it shall not be so. The same will be true of an illegitimate child who, before his father's death, has been legitimated, for such a child will, upon legitimation, have received his father's domicile as a domicile of dependence. The death of the father of an illegitimate child who has not been legitimated will have no effect.

Where a child's mother dies, the death will have no effect on the child's domicile unless the child was either born illegitimate and has never been legitimated or has (or last had) a home with his mother following a separation of his parents. In either event, the child will continue to have his dead mother's domicile as a domicile of dependence unless and until, in the case of a legitimate or legitimated or adopted child only, he makes a home with his father.[13]

143

Where a child's parents both die, the domicile of dependence which the child possessed at the date of their deaths will continue; though a child's guardian has no capacity to change the domicile of his ward.[14]

A domicile of dependence will continue until *animo et facto* he abandons the country of that domicile. Thereupon his domicile of origin will revive until it is displaced by a domicile of choice.[15]

EXAMPLE

Susan is born of an English domiciled father and thus acquires an English domicile of origin by operation of law. When she is eight years old she and her parents move to Denmark and her father acquires there a domicile of choice which is then automatically communicated to Susan as a domicile of dependence. Susan continues to live with her parents until she is 24 when she marries a Norwegian and moves to Oslo where she intends to spend the rest of her life. Her Danish domicile of dependence will endure until she leaves Danish territorial waters, whereupon her English domicile of origin will revive. Upon arriving in Norway, however, her domicile of origin will be displaced by her Norwegian domicile of choice.

It should be noted that it is usually easier to establish the abandonment of a domicile of dependence than to establish the abandonment of a domicile of choice.[16]

The Law Commission and the Scottish Law Commission have proposed that the domicile of any person under the age of 16 should be determined according to where the child has his home. If his home is with both parents, his domicile, they say, should be the same as, and change with, that of his parents if their domiciles are the same, or with that of his mother if their domiciles are different. If his home is with only one parent, his domicile, they say, should be the same as, and change with, the domicile of that parent. And in any other case, the child's domicile should, they say, be the country with which he is, for the time being, most closely connected.[17]

---

1 *Forbes v Forbes* (1854) Kay 341; *Harrison v Harrison* [1953] 1 WLR 865.
2 *Shekleton v Shekleton* [1972] 2 NSWR 675.
3 Not Scotland. Under Scottish law the relevant respective ages are 14 in the case of a boy, 12 in the case of a girl.
4 DMPA 1973, s 3.
5 Because no English domiciled child has the capacity to marry below that age, however, the parts of the rule which relate to persons who are married under the age of 16 is of application only to foreign domiciled children whose marriages are recognised by the courts in this country – as, for example in *Mohamed v Knott* [1968] 2 All ER 563.
6 See **7.06** above.
7 Adoptive parents in the case of an adopted child (Children Act 1975 Sch 1, para 3 as repealed and re-enacted in the Adoption Act 1976 s 39(1) and the Adoption (Scotland) Act 1978 s 39(1)).
8 *D'Etchegoyen v D'Etchegoyen* (1888) 13 PD 132, DMPA 1973 s 4(1)–(2).
9 DMPA 1973, s 4(4) and *Johnstone v Beattie* (1843) 10 Cl & Fin 42.
10 In *Re Beaumont* [1893] 3 Ch 490 at 496, Stirling J said, 'Change in the domicile of an infant which . . . may follow from a change of domicile on the part of the mother, is not to be regarded as the necessary consequence of a change of the mother's domicile, but as the result of the exercise by her of a power vested in her for the welfare of the infants, which in their interest she may abstain from exercising, even when she changes her own domicile.' Where, however, a mother exercises her power in her own interest, eg to take advantage of a law of succession more beneficial to herself,

such an exercise of her power will be ineffective (*Potinger v Wightman* (1817) 3 Mer 67).
11 The child might already have acquired his mother's domicile as a domicile of dependence if his parents had separated before his father's death and if the child had, upon the separation, made his home with his mother.
12 *Potinger v Wightman* (1817) 3 Mer 67.
13 DMPA 1973 s 4(3).
14 See Dicey and Morris, *The Conflict of Laws* (13th edn), Sweet & Maxwell, Vol 1. p 141.
15 *Re Macreight, Paxton v Macreight* (1885) 30 ChD 165.
16 *Harrison v Harrison* [1953] 1 WLR 865.
17 The Law Commission Working Paper No. 88 and the Scottish Law Commission Consultative Memorandum No. 63, 'Private International Law, The Law of Domicile', 1985, HMSO, para 4.18.

7.10 Persons suffering from mental disorder

The position of a person suffering from mental disorder is lacking in direct authority so far as the question of his domicile is concerned. Until a child reaches the age of 16 or marries under that age, the rules governing his domicile will be those already discussed at **7.06** and **7.09** above. If, however, a child becomes insane and his insanity continues beyond his sixteenth[1] birthday, the law would appear to be that his domicile will continue to change with the parent from whom he last acquired a domicile of dependence, but that where he becomes of unsound mind after he has attained the age of 16 or married under that age, he will permanently retain whatever domicile he then possessed and that domicile will be incapable of change either by his own act or by that of those who are entrusted with his care.[2] The degree of mental unsoundness which is required before these rules will have effect is not settled, but it is arguable that the test to be applied should be whether or not the person is capable of forming the necessary intention to bring about a change in domicile.[3]

The Law Commission and the Scottish Law Commission have recommended that the domicile of an adult *incapax* should not be frozen at the onset of his incapacity but should be changed as necessary so that his domicile is always that of the country with which he is at any time most closely connected.[4]

1 In Scotland, 14 in the case of a boy, 12 in the case of a girl.
2 *Sharpe v Crispin* (1869) LR 1 P & D 611 at 615, per Sir J. P. Wilde.
3 See **7.13** below.
4 The Law Commission Working Paper No. 88 and the Scottish Law Commission Consultative Memorandum No. 63, 'Private International Law, The Law of Domicile', HMSO, para 6.9.

Domicile of choice

7.11 Acquisition

As has been explained at **7.08** to **7.10** above, a domicile of choice can be acquired only by a person who is not incapacitated either by age or by unsoundness of mind. There are no formal steps to be taken for a person of full age and capacity to acquire a domicile of choice. As the Inland Revenue guidance note puts it:

To do so, you must broadly leave your current country of domicile and settle in another country. You need to provide strong evidence that you intend to live there permanently or indefinitely.[1]

In *Udny v Udny*,[2] Lord Westbury described a domicile of choice as:

> a conclusion or inference which the law derives from the fact of a man fixing voluntarily his sole or chief residence in a particular place, with the intention of continuing to reside there for an unlimited time.[3]

Both elements must be present. As Lord Chelmsford put it in *Bell v Kennedy*:[4]

> a new domicile is not acquired until there is not only a fixed intention of establishing a permanent residence in some other country, but until also this intention has been carried out by actual residence there.[5]

These two elements are known, respectively, as the *animus manendi* (the intention to remain) and the *factum* (the fact of residence) and, as foregoing dicta make clear, both are essential. Before considering each element individually, however, one point must be made. The 'country' to which both the *animus* and the *factum* relate must, for the purpose of determining whether a domicile of choice has been acquired under common law, be

> a territory subject to a distinctive legal system.[6]

This follows from the third principle of domicile discussed at **7.04** above but, as explained there, the problem which arises when discussing domicile in the context of United Kingdom taxation is that, under the Taxes Acts, the question to be determined is whether a person is domiciled 'in the United Kingdom', ie a territory which is *not* subject to a distinctive legal system. It is important to refer to the earlier discussion, therefore, and to bear in mind that where a reference is made to a 'country' or 'territory' in the following paragraphs, it is possible that, for the purposes of this work, the country or territory referred to may be the United Kingdom collectively and not necessarily Northern Ireland, Scotland or England and Wales individually.

---

1 Appendix IR 20 (11 April 2000), para 4.5.
2 (1869) LR 1 Sc & Div 441.
3 Ibid, at 458.
4 (1868) LR 1 Sc & Div 307.
5 Ibid, at 319.
6 *Re Fuld's Estate (No. 3)* [1968] P 675 at 684, per Scarman J reiterating the formula in *Henderson v Henderson* [1967] P 77 at p 79.

7.12 Residence

The meaning of the term 'residence' has already been explored at some depth in the earlier chapters of this work but here a distinction must be drawn between residence as a connecting factor in its own right for the purposes of United Kingdom taxation and residence in the context of the acquisition of the connecting factor of domicile. In *IRC v Duchess of Portland*,[1] Nourse J said:

Residence in a country for the purposes of the law of domicile is physical presence in that country as an inhabitant of it . . . [I]n a case where the domiciliary divides his physical presence between two countries at a time . . . it is necessary to look at all the facts in order to decide which of the two countries is the one he inhabits.[2]

The Duchess of Portland had claimed that, by spending some ten to twelve weeks each year in Quebec visiting relatives and maintaining her links with Canada (the land of her birth and the country to which she hoped eventually to return), she had acquired a domicile of choice in Canada. She spent the rest of her time living with her husband in England. Nourse J said:

On those facts it appears clear to me that since 1948 the taxpayer has been physically present in this country as an inhabitant of it. Her physical presence in Quebec has been for periods of limited duration and for the purpose of maintaining her links with the country to which it is her intention ultimately to return. That is not enough to have made her an inhabitant of Quebec. In my judgment it is clear that she was resident in England on 1 January 1974 and that that residence was not displaced when she went to Canada in July 1974 or at any other time during the material period.[3]

It has been shown that residence for tax purposes, ie as a territorial connecting link *per se*, is a quality of the person which – despite judicial asseverations to the contrary – may be attributed to a person not according to its ordinary meaning in the speech of plain men but according to a special, forensic meaning derived from case law precedents and Revenue practice. It will be recalled, for instance, that the celebrated Mr Lysaght, who had a settled place of residence in Ireland, was attributed with United Kingdom residence status merely by reason of his regular monthly business trips to the United Kingdom during the course of which he stayed with his brother or at the Spa Hotel in Bath.[4] It has also been demonstrated that, because residence in its taxation context is a qualitative attribute, a person may (as in the case of Lysaght) be resident in two or more countries at the same time.[5] It is clear from the judgment of Nourse J, however, that neither of these possibilities is open so far as residence in the context of the acquisition of a domicile of choice is concerned. A person *may* be resident in a particular country for both taxation purposes *and* domicile purposes, but he will not necessarily be so. Residence for domicile purposes involves actual inhabitance of a country,[6] dwelling within its borders rather than merely paying it visits, however extensive and regular those visits might be: and where a person inhabits two different countries, the only one in which he will be regarded as resident for domicile purposes is the one in which, on the balance of the facts, he is shown to have his 'chief residence'.[7]

The length of a person's residence in a particular country may be of great importance in determining whether or not a person has acquired a domicile of choice in that country, but it is not in itself determinative of the matter. As Lord Chelmsford said in *Bell v Kennedy*:[8]

It may be conceded that if the intention of permanently residing in a place exists, a residence in pursuance of that intention, however short, will establish domicile.[9]

This principle was reiterated (with the insertion of an interesting additional clause) by Nourse J in *Re Clore No 2*:[10]

if the evidence [of intention] is there, particularly perhaps where the motive is the avoidance of taxes, the necessary intention will not be held to be missing merely because the period of actual residence is a short one.[11]

The fact of residence does, however, raise a presumption of domicile in the country of residence[12] and this presumption grows with the length of the period of residence so that, in some instances, it will be sufficient to override declarations of contrary intention[13] and will require a person's actual removal elsewhere if it is to be rebutted.[14] In *Udny v Udny*,[15] Lord Chelmsford said:

Time is always a material element in questions of domicil; and if there is nothing to counteract its effect, it may be conclusive upon the subject.[16]

Anderson v Laneuville[17] provides an interesting illustration of the point. The case concerned Anderson, a person born in 1768 with an Irish domicile of origin who, at the age of 67 (by which time he had acquired an English domicile of choice) traced, and thereafter until his death some 24 years later, cohabited with, in France, a widow, Madame Laneuville, who, some 46 years earlier, had risked her life in helping him to escape the Terror of the revolution in France where he was then being educated. Anderson had, it seems, expressed some intention of returning to England should Madame Laneuville have predeceased him, but on appeal from the Prerogative Court of Canterbury, that one fact was held to carry insufficient weight to counteract the effect of the length of Anderson's residence in France, and that long period of residence was held to lead inevitably to the conclusion that Anderson had died domiciled in France.

Thus it was in the more recent case of *Re Furse, Furse v IRC*.[18] William King Furse was born in Rhode Island in 1883 and had a Rhode Island domicile of origin. At the age of four, he was brought to England by his father but, after completing his education here, he returned to America, married and remained in employment there until 1916. He then left America to serve in the British army in the 1914–18 war. Upon demobilisation in 1919 he returned to New York where his wife had purchased a house and he found employment there. In 1923 Furse and his wife and children moved to England and bought a farm in West Hoathly. There Furse lived until his death 40 years later. From time to time between 1923 and the early 1950s, Furse and his wife contemplated a return to America and in the 1940s actually inspected a farm in Maryland. In the early 1950s Furse decided, however, that he would not return to America unless he became incapable of leading an active life on his farm in England. Fox J, declaring that Furse died domiciled in England, said:

the facts . . . show a man deeply settled in England. He came to England at the age of four; he died in England at the age of 80. Of the intervening 76 years he spent 58 in England (in the sense that England was his normal place of abode in those years) and three or four in the British army. . . [He] was wholly integrated into the English community in which he lived. There is no doubt at all, as I see it, that the life which he was living in England was the life he wanted to go on living to the end of his life . . . In my view, by the time of his death, the balance of probabilities is that he can have had no real intention of leaving; a fact which is emphasised by the vagueness of his expressed intentions. . . .[19]

There was, to use Lord Chelmsford's words, nothing (or nothing sufficiently concrete in the way of intention or surrounding circumstances) to counteract the effect of time, and time was, therefore, conclusive on the subject. This is not to say, however, that residence of long duration will alone suffice to establish domicile. It will not. As the Inland Revenue guidance note points out:

> Living in another country for a long time, although an important factor, is not enough in itself to prove you have acquired a new domicile.[20]

This follows from what Cottenham LC said in *Munro v Munro*:[21]

> Residence alone has no effect, per se, though it may be most important as a ground from which to infer intention.[22]

In both *Anderson v Laneuville*[23] and *Re Furse, Furse v IRC*,[24] that was where the significance of the long residence of Anderson and Furse lay. All the evidence suggested that, despite their vague assertions of a possible return to their native lands, Anderson and Furse would have remained where they were, however long they had lived; and the courts, therefore, permitted the *animus* of true intention to be inferred from the *factum* of residence.

Where, however, there is evidence to the contrary – something sufficiently concrete to counteract the effect of the duration of residence – the duration of residence will not be conclusive upon the subject as *Ramsay v Liverpool Royal Infirmary*[25] illustrates. George Bowie (the validity of whose will was in question) was born in Glasgow in 1845 and acquired from his father a Scottish domicile of origin. Upon reaching the age of 37 he gave up his employment as a commercial traveller and steadfastly refused to work again throughout the remainder of his life. For ten years he 'lived on the bounty' of his mother and sisters in Glasgow, then, in 1892, he moved to lodgings in Liverpool and for the next 21 years sponged instead on his brother. Upon his brother's death, Bowie moved into his brother's house and for the next eight years sponged on his sister until she died in 1920. He remained at his brother's house and died in Liverpool (where he had arranged to be buried) seven years later. Bowie boasted of being a Glasgow man but during the 36 years he lived in England he refused to return to Scotland, even for his mother's funeral. He left England only twice, once to visit America and once to holiday in the Isle of Man. On those facts, the House of Lords held unanimously that Bowie had *not* acquired a domicile of choice in England but that his Scottish domicile of origin was still operative at the date of his death. Their lordships were convinced that declarations by Bowie to the effect that he would never return to Scotland were mere posturing and that, had Bowie's source of funds dried up, he would, in fact, have gone back there. That, plus the fact that there was no evidence to show that Bowie had made his permanent home in England was, in their view, sufficient to quash the inference of intention to which Bowie's 36 years of residence in England would otherwise have given rise. Lord Macmillan said:

> Prolonged actual residence is an important item of evidence of . . . volition, but it must be supplemented by other facts and circumstances indicative of intention. The residence must answer a qualitative as well as a quantitative test.[26]

IRC v Bullock[27] provides a modern (and much more convincing) illustration of the application of this principle. Group Captain Bullock had a domicile of origin in Nova Scotia but came to England in 1932 and joined the Royal Air Force. He intended to return to Canada on completing his service but, in 1946, he married an Englishwoman some three years his junior. Between then and 1960, Bullock and his wife made several trips to Canada and, upon leaving the RAF in 1959, Bullock would have liked them to move there permanently. His wife did not wish to do so, however, so Bullock took up civilian employment in England until 1961 when an inheritance enabled him to retire completely. Until 1966, Bullock continued to try to persuade his wife to move with him to Canada, but thereafter resigned himself to the fact that she would never do so. In that year, however, he made a will under Nova Scotia law in which he declared that his domicile was and would continue to be the Province of Nova Scotia and that he would return and remain there upon his wife's death. Bullock retained his Canadian nationality and passport, never acquired British nationality or a British passport, refused to vote in local or parliamentary elections, maintained close contact with Canadian relatives and friends, and was a regular reader of a Toronto newspaper. On these facts the Commissioners found that Bullock was not domiciled in England and the Court of Appeal (reversing Brightman J's judgment in the High Court) upheld the Commissioners' finding. Bullock's residence in England, though over 40 years in duration, was accompanied at all times by a clear and definite intention to return to Canada upon the substantial possibility of his wife predeceasing him, and that was sufficient to counteract the effect of the element of time.

---

1   [1982] STC 149.
2   Ibid, at 155.
3   Ibid, at 155–156.
4   See **2.12** above.
5   See **2.08** above.
6   *IRC v Duchess of Portland* [1982] STC 149 at 155, per Nourse J.
7   *Re Fuld's Estate (No 3)* [1968] P 675 at 682, per Scarman J.
8   (1868) LR 1 Sc & Div 307.
9   Ibid, at 319.
10 [1984] STC 609.
11 Ibid, at 615.
12 *Bruce v Bruce* (1790) 2 Bos & P 229; *Bempde v Johnstone* (1796) 3 Ves 198.
13 *Stanley v Bernes* (1830) 3 Hagg Ecc 373; *Re Marrett, Chalmers v Wingfield* (1887) 36 Ch D 400.
14 *Hodgson v De Beauchesne* (1858) 12 Moo PCC 285.
15 (1869) LR 1 Sc & Div 441.
16 Ibid, at 455.
17 (1854) 9 Moo PCC 325.
18 [1980] STC 596.
19 Ibid, at 606.
20 Appendix IR 20 (11 April 2000), para 4.5.
21 (1840) 7 Cl & Fin 842.
22 Ibid, at 877.
23 (1854) 9 Moo PCC 325.
24 [1980] STC 596.
25 [1930] AC 588.
26 Ibid, at 598.
27 [1976] STC 409. See also *IRC v Cohen* (1937) 21 TC 301 where a person with an English domicile of origin who went to Australia at the age of 18 and did not return to England until 32 years later was nonetheless held to have retained his English domicile of origin throughout. Overturning the Commissioners' finding that Henry Cohen had acquired an Australian domicile of choice and never abandoned it, Finlay J held (at 315) that the true inference from the facts was that Henry

Cohen 'intended to reside and to reside for a long time in Australia, but . . . he intended to reside there so long only as his business made that necessary, and his business connection with Australia ceased in 1911.'

7.13 Intention

The acquisition of a domicile of choice requires not only residence (in the sense of actual habitation of the chosen territory) but also an intention to make that territory 'the permanent home'.[1] The problem of what is meant by 'permanent' has lain at the root of many a case concerning domicile. Lord Chelmsford took a strict view of the matter. In *Moorhouse v Lord*[2] he said:

> The present intention of making a place a person's permanent home can exist only where he has no other idea than to continue there without looking forward to any event, certain or uncertain, which might induce him to change his residence. If he has in contemplation some event upon the happening of which residence will cease, it is not correct to call this even a present intention of making it a permanent home. It is rather a present intention of making it a temporary home, though for a period indefinite and contingent.[3]

But others thought that far too strict. In *A-G v Pottinger*,[4] Bramwell B said:

> There is not a man who has not contingent intentions to do something that would be very much to his benefit if the occasion arises. But if every such intention or expression of intention prevented a man having a fixed domicil, no man would ever have a domicil at all, except his domicil of origin.[5]

The less absolute view of the nature of the necessary intention may be discerned in Lord Westbury's statement in *Udny v Udny*[6] that the residence which is the other necessary element in the acquisition of a domicile of choice

> must be a residence not for a limited period or particular purpose, but general and indefinite in its future contemplation.[7]

It emerged even more openly when, in *Gulbenkian v Gulbenkian*,[8] Langton J said:

> The intention must be a present intention to reside permanently, but it does not mean that such intention must be irrevocable. It must be an intention unlimited in period, but not irrevocable in character.[9]

And it is clearly discernible in the two widely-approved propositions concerning the acquisition of a domicile of choice made by Scarman J in *Re Fuld's Estate (No 3)*:[10]

> a domicile of choice is acquired when a man fixes voluntarily his sole or chief residence in a particular place with an intention of continuing to reside there for an unlimited time.[11]

> A domicile of choice is acquired only if it be affirmatively shown that the *propositus* is resident within a territory subject to a distinctive legal system with the intention, formed independently of external pressures, of residing there indefinitely.[12]

'Permanent', it will be noted, has become 'indefinite' or 'unlimited' and the difference that brings about may clearly be seen by comparing the dictum of Lord Cairns in *Bell v Kennedy*[13] and that of Buckley LJ in *IRC v Bullock*.[14] Lord Cairns said:

> The question . . . is . . . Whether [Bell] . . . had determined to make, and had made, Scotland his home, with the intention of establishing himself and his family there, and ending his days in that country.[15]

Buckley LJ said:

> I do not think that it is necessary to show that the intention to make a home in the new country is irrevocable or that the person whose intention is under consideration believes that for reasons of health or otherwise he will have no opportunity to change his mind. In my judgment, the true test is whether he intends to make his home in the new country until the end of his days *unless and until something happens to make him change his mind.*[16]

Buckley LJ had not only the authority of Bramwell B to rely on in adding those final eleven words. In *Aikman v Aikman*,[17] Campbell LC (another nineteenth-century judge) had said that a mere intention to return to a man's native country on a doubtful contingency would not prevent residence in a foreign country putting an end to his domicile of origin.

Given that Scarman J and Buckley J have accurately stated the current judicial view of intention for domicile of choice purposes, however, the question then arises: What constitutes a 'doubtful contingency'; what is the 'something' which a person might have in contemplation without the necessary intention of indefinite or unlimited residence being found lacking? Scarman J has answered the question thus:

> If a man intends to return to the land of his birth upon a clearly foreseen and reasonably anticipated contingency, eg the end of his job, the intention required by law is lacking: but if he has in mind only a vague possibility, such as making a fortune (a modern example might be winning a football pool) or some sentiment about dying in the land of his fathers, such a state of mind is consistent with the intention required by law. But no clear line can be drawn; the ultimate decision in each case is one of fact. . . .[18]

And Buckley LJ has answered it in a similar manner:

> No doubt, if a man who has made his home in a country other than his domicile of origin has expressed an intention to return to his domicile of origin or to remove to some third country on an event or condition of an indefinite kind (for example 'if I make a fortune' or 'when I've had enough of it'), it might be hard, if not impossible, to conclude that he retained any real intention of so returning or removing. Such a man, in the graphic language of James LJ in *Doucet v Geoghegan*,[19] is like a man who expects to reach the horizon; he finds it at last no nearer than it was at the beginning of his journey.[20]

In both these passages, however, the contingency contemplated is of a 'pipe dream' character. What if the contingency contemplated is something more specific? In the event, said Buckley LJ, the question to be asked is:

> is there a sufficiently substantial possibility of the contingency happening to justify regarding the intention to return as a real determination to do so on the contingency occurring rather than a vague hope or aspiration?[21]

The facts of the case of *IRC v Bullock*[22] in which that test was propounded, have already been set out at **7.12** above and it is clear from those facts that the single contingency upon which Group Captain Bullock intended to return to Canada was the death of his wife. It was only his wife's refusal to live in Canada which was keeping the Group Captain here, and, as his wife was only two or three years his junior, there was a substantial possibility that she would predecease him. Accordingly, Buckley LJ held that his test question could be answered affirmatively: Group Captain Bullock did not have the necessary intention to make England his domicile of choice. When applied to the facts in *Re Furse, Furse v IRC*[23] (also set out at **7.12** above), however, Buckley LJ's test produced the opposite answer. William Furse was happy and content in England and the only contingency upon which he intended to return to America was his becoming physically incapable of taking an active interest in his farm. Fox J said:

> It seems to me that the intention of [Furse] was indeed to continue to reside in England for an unlimited period. His intention was to continue to live here for the rest of his life, save on the contingency which he expressed. That contingency is so vague that I do not think it can be regarded as imposing any clear limitation on the period of his residence. I do not believe that he was ever prepared to face up to such a limitation. The contingency is of the sort which Simon P in *Qureshi v Qureshi*[24] described as 'open-ended' . . . I think that, when [Furse] died in his 81st year, still in England and still with no arrangements made for leaving England, one could not realistically regard his permanent home as other than in England. He intended to live out his days here, save on a contingency so vaguely expressed that I do not think, against the history of his life, it could be regarded for practical purposes as limiting that intention.[25]

It will have been noted that in many of the extracts from judgments given in this section the words 'present intention' are used. The force of the adjective 'present' emphasises that what must be considered is the state of a person's mind at the time when the acquisition of a domicile of choice is alleged to have taken place. Subsequent variations in that intention are irrelevant[26] unless accompanied or followed by appropriate action.[27]

It should not be overlooked, however, that evidence of a subsequent change of mind might, in some instances, lead the court to infer that the original intention to remain indefinitely in the country of choice was not as settled as the evidence of that original intention indicated.

Although actual residence and the intention to reside indefinitely must concur before a domicile of choice can be created, the intention may precede or succeed the commencement of residence. The person who decides to emigrate to Quebec will possess the intention which is one element in the creation of a Quebec domicile of choice before he establishes the residence which is the other essential element. The refugee escaping persecution may, on the other hand, establish residence before he acquires the intention to remain indefinitely in the land in which he resides.

The only remaining point to be made concerning intention is that it is only the intention to remain indefinitely in a country which is relevant to the acquisition of a domicile of choice. If a person has that intention and there comes a time when the intention coincides with actual residence, a domicile of choice is acquired whether it was also the person's intention to acquire a domicile of choice or not. Thus, in *Re Steer*,[28] Mr Steer, an Englishman who established his permanent home in

Hamburg and died there 50 years later, was held to have died domiciled in Germany even though, on one of his temporary visits to England, he had made a will in which he declared that although he was returning to Hamburg he had no intention of renouncing his English domicile of origin. The principle governing this matter was succinctly stated over a century ago:

> If the intention [to reside indefinitely in a particular country] exists and if it is sufficiently carried into effect certain legal consequences follow from it, whether such consequences are intended or not and perhaps even though the person in question may have intended the exact opposite.[29]

1   *Whicker v Hume* (1858) 7 HL Cas 124 at 160, per Lord Cranworth.
2   (1863) 10 HL Cas 272.
3   Ibid, at 285–286.
4   (1861) 30 LJ Ex 284.
5   Ibid, at 292.
6   (1869) LR 1 Sc & Div 441.
7   Ibid, at 458.
8   [1937] 4 All ER 618.
9   Ibid, at 627.
10   [1968] P 675.
11   Ibid, at 682.
12   Ibid, at 684.
13   (1868) LR 1 Sc & Div 307.
14   [1976] STC 409.
15   *Bell v Kennedy* (1868) LR 1 Sc & Div 307 at 311.
16   *IRC v Bullock* [1976] STC 409 at 415. Author's italics.
17   (1861) 4 LT 374 at 376.
18   *Re Fuld's Estate (No 3)* [1968] P 675 at 685, per Scarman J.
19   (1878) 9 Ch D 441 at 457.
20   *IRC v Bullock* [1976] STC 409 at 416.
21   Ibid.
22   [1976] STC 409.
23   [1980] STC 596.
24   [1971] 1 All ER 325 at 340.
25   *Re Furse, Furse v IRC* [1980] STC 596 at 606.
26   *Re Marrett, Chalmers v Wingfield* (1887) 36 Ch D 400.
27   See **7.16** below.
28   (1858) 3 H & N 594. See also *Re Lawton* discussed at **7.15** below.
29   *Douglas v Douglas* (1871) LR 12 Eq 617 at 644–645.

7.14   Motive as evidence of intention

It will have been noted that the first of Scarman J's two propositions concerning the acquisition of a domicile of choice, quoted at **7.13** above contains the words 'fixes *voluntarily* his sole or chief residence', and that the second contains the words 'with the intention, *formed independently of external pressures*, of residing'. Those words draw attention to the fact that the acquisition of a domicile of choice presupposes a freedom of choice. As Lord Westbury put it in *Udny v Udny*:[1]

> There must be a residence freely chosen, and not prescribed or dictated by any external necessity. . . .[2]

If it can be shown that a person resides where he does, not by choice but by constraint, the necessary intention will be lacking and no change of domicile will be imputed to the involuntary exile.

The most obvious example of residence by constraint rather than through choice is imprisonment in some country other than that of the existing domicile. No prisoner, during the term of his imprisonment, will acquire a new domicile in the country of his imprisonment, even if the imprisonment is for a very long term, for his residence is not a matter of choice.[3]

Another example of constraint is the persecution which may impel a person to flee his existing country of domicile for some other country. Although the residence in the country of refuge will be a matter of free choice, the inference at law will be that the refugee will return to his homeland upon it being safe for him to do so and he will, therefore, prima facie lack the intention to reside permanently in the country of refuge which would be necessary in order to attribute him with a domicile of choice in that country. It might be, of course, that a refugee will acquire such an intention during the course of his exile.[4]

A fugitive from justice is in much the same position as the refugee except that, if his crime is such that he will always (or for a very long time) be liable to proceedings in the country from which he has fled, there will be a presumption at law that he has selected his country of refuge with the intention of residing there indefinitely.[5] His departure will have been a matter of constraint but his establishment of residence elsewhere will have been a matter of free choice.

'The demands of creditors' was one of Lord Westbury's examples of an external necessity which might result in a person residing where he would not otherwise reside.[6] So it was with Colonel Udny and his residence in France. But the fact that a person has fled the country to escape his creditors will not necessarily mean that he cannot acquire a domicile of choice in the country to which he has fled. It will depend on circumstances: the size of the debts, the likelihood of them ultimately being met, how long their discharge is likely to take, and the imminence of recovery proceedings.

The invalid who, although in no immediate danger of untimely death, settles for the sake of his health in a country other than the country of his existing domicile is regarded at law as doing so out of choice rather than out of constraint. In the case of *Hoskins v Matthews*,[7] for example, Turner LJ said that Mr Matthews, an Englishman who, at the age of 60, had gone to Florence suffering from a spinal injury and had died there twelve years later, was not, when he first took up residence in Florence,

in any immediate danger or apprehension. He was, no doubt, out of health, and he went abroad for the purpose of trying the effect of other remedies and other climates. That he would have preferred settling in England I have little doubt, but I think he was not driven to settle in Italy by any cogent necessity. I think that in settling there he was exercising a preference, and not acting upon a necessity, and I cannot venture to hold that in such a case the domicil cannot be changed.[8]

If, however, the change of environment is a matter of life or death, or if, death being imminent and inevitable, the change of climate will alleviate suffering, there will, it seems, be no presumption of a change in domicile.[9]

The 'tax exile' who, in order to escape the incidence of taxation in the country of his existing domicile, settles in a country with a less harsh tax regime, will, it seems, be presumed to intend to remain in the new country permanently. In *Re Clore*

(No 2),[10] Nourse J said that even a short period of residence would be sufficient to establish a domicile of choice

> if the evidence is there, particularly perhaps where the motive is the avoidance of taxes.[11]

In the *Clore* case, there were, according to Nourse J, three areas where the evidence supported Sir Charles Clore's acquisition of a domicile of choice in Monaco. One was the severance of the more important of his connections with England where Sir Charles had his domicile of origin. Another was the establishment of connections with Monaco including residence there. But the most important, in Nourse J's eyes, was that:

> the professional advice which Sir Charles received was given not solely with the immediate object of his acquiring a non-resident status for income and capital gains tax purposes, but with the long-term objective of his acquiring a foreign domicile. Further, unless the operation was to be at least partially counter-productive, it was essential that the new country should be one where no tax was payable. Monaco was chosen because it was the only tax haven with which Sir Charles was familiar and the only one which could have been acceptable to him.[12]

Against the evidence in those three areas, however, was the evidence of four of his close friends who were unanimous in their testimony that Sir Charles was unhappy in Monaco and had never, in his heart of hearts, abandoned England. All his actions from mid-1978 until his death in London on 26 July 1979 were tentative and, right up to the time of his death, he was showing an interest in acquiring residential properties in France and Israel. Accordingly, Nourse J held that Sir Charles died domiciled in England. That decision must not, however, be allowed to obscure the fact that, because Sir Charles had resided in Monaco and his motive for residing there was tax avoidance, Nourse J accepted that there was a presumption at law that a domicile of choice had been acquired in Monaco. As with any presumption at law, however, the presumption to which a tax avoidance motive will give rise may be rebutted by other evidence, and in the *Clore* case it was rebutted by the evidence of parol declarations made by Sir Charles in his final years and testified to by his four friends.

It must finally be pointed out that the residence of a person in a country other than the country of his existing domicile will give rise to no presumption that a domicile of choice has been acquired in the new country if the person is there in pursuit of what Lord Westbury called 'the duties of office'.[13] These have been held to include the duties of a consul,[14] chief justice,[15] embassy attaché,[16] naval officer,[17] army officer.[18] Such a negative presumption may, of course, be rebutted by evidence to the contrary.[19]

---

1 (1869) LR 1 Sc & Div 441.
2 Ibid, at 458.
3 *Re the late Emperor Napoleon Bonaparte* (1853) 2 Rob Eccl 606.
4 *De Bonneval v De Bonneval* (1838) 1 Curt 856. See also *Steiner v IRC* (1973) 49 TC 13 where a refugee from the Nazi persecution of Jews made his home in England in 1939 but was held not to have acquired an English domicile of choice here until about 1950s when the facts were such as to indicate that he had formed the intention of remaining permanently in England.
5 *Re Martin, Loustalan v Loustalan* [1900] P 211.
6 *Udny v Udny* (1869) LR 1 Sc & Div 441 at 458.
7 (1856) 8 De GM & G 13.
8 Ibid, at 28–29.

9 See Lord Kingsdown's comments in *Moorhouse v Lord* (1863) 10 HL Cas 272 at 292.
10 [1984] STC 609.
11 Ibid, at 615.
12 Ibid, at 614.
13 *Udny v Udny* (1869) LR 1 Sc & Div 441 at 458.
14 *Sharpe v Crispin* (1869) LR 1 P & D 611.
15 *A-G v Lady Rowe* (1862) 1 H & C 31.
16 *A-G v Kent* (1862) 31 LJ Ex 391.
17 *Re Patten's Goods* (1860) 6 Jur NS 151.
18 *Firebrace v Firebrace* (1878) 4 PD 63.
19 *Donaldson v Donaldson* [1949] P 363.

7.15 Proof of intention

As Scarman J said in *Re Fuld's Estate (No 3)*:[1]

It is beyond doubt that the burden of proving the abandonment of a domicile of origin and the acquisition of a domicile of choice is upon the party asserting the change. But it is not so clear what is the standard of proof: is it to be proved beyond reasonable doubt or upon the balance of probabilities, or does the standard vary according to whether one seeks to establish abandonment of domicile of origin or merely a switch from one domicile of choice to another? Or is there some other standard? . . . The formula of proof beyond reasonable doubt is not frequently used in probate cases and I do not propose to give it currency. It is enough that the authorities emphasise that the conscience of the court . . . must be satisfied by the evidence. The weight to be attached to evidence, the inferences to be drawn, the facts justifying the exclusion of doubt and the expression of satisfaction will vary according to the nature of the case. Two things are clear – first, that unless the judicial conscience is satisfied by evidence of change, the domicile of origin persists: and secondly, that the acquisition of a domicile of choice is a serious matter not to be lightly inferred from slight indications or casual words.[2]

Those statements were later endorsed by Orr LJ who, in *Buswell v IRC*,[3] said:

I . . . accept the statements as accurate and would only add that in referring to the judicial conscience I am satisfied that Scarman J was not recognising the existence of some general standard of proof intermediate between the criminal and civil standards but was merely emphasising that in the application of the civil standard the degree of proof required will vary with the subject-matter of the case.[4]

If the judicial conscience is to be satisfied that a change in domicile has taken place, the courts must subject every department of a person's life to the most searching scrutiny. The length and nature of his residence in the country in which it is asserted that he has acquired a domicile will, of course, be a factor of particular interest since, as has been explained,[5] residence gives rise at law to a presumption of domicile, and intention may be inferred from residence if the residence is of sufficient length and there is other evidence to support such an inference. His motives too must be examined for, as has been explained at **7.14** above, a person's motive in taking up residence in a country other than that of his existing domicile may give rise to a presumption of, or against, a change in domicile. But the court's concern is never confined merely to residence and the motive for residence. As Lord Atkinson said of *Winans v A-G*[6] in *Casdagli v Casdagli*:[7]

> the tastes, habits, conduct, actions, ambitions, health, hopes, and projects of Mr Winans deceased were all considered as keys to his intention to make a home in England.[8]

It is often said that if a person wishes to ensure that his change of domicile will withstand the scrutiny of the courts he must not only take up residence in the country of choice but should purchase a property there and dispose of any property he has in the country he has abandoned, that he should apply for citizenship of the new country, obtain a passport in the new country and relinquish his existing passport, close all bank accounts in the abandoned country and open new accounts in the country of choice, relinquish credit cards and obtain new ones in the country of choice, resign any directorships in the country he has abandoned and acquire business interests in the country of choice, sever membership of clubs, societies, religious organisations etc in the abandoned country and join clubs etc in the country of choice, vote in the new country's elections, become involved in its politics and socially integrated into its life, educate his children in its schools, have his will drawn up under its laws and make arrangements to be buried or cremated there. Such a checklist has a certain value, being a list of factors to which particular significance has been attached in cases which have come before the courts at different times. But the approach is wrong. A person who has genuinely made his 'permanent home' in a new country will, in those and many other ways, manifest the reality of his intention to live out his days as an inhabitant of the land to which he has gone; but the person who is engaged in nothing more than a cosmetic exercise designed to conceal the fact that 'in spite of all temptations to belong to other nations, he remains an Englishman'[9] is likely to betray his lack of genuine intention no matter how scrupulously he adheres to a list of 'dos and don'ts'. No one factor will, in itself, be decisive, and even a factor which seems of supreme significance when viewed in isolation may carry little weight when set against all other factors. Thus, for example, in *Wahl v A-G*,[10] the fact that a person with a German domicile of origin and German nationality had become a naturalised British subject was not regarded as being at all conclusive:

> I am far from saying that an application for naturalisation is not a matter to be carefully considered as part of the evidence in a case of domicile, but it must be regarded as one of the totality of facts and it cannot assume the dominant importance attached to it in the judgment of the trial judge . . . It is not the law either that a change of domicile is a condition of naturalisation, or that naturalisation involves necessarily a change of domicile.[11]

In making his application for naturalisation, Wahl had made a statutory declaration to the effect that he intended to continue to reside permanently within the United Kingdom. That too formed part of the evidence of his intention and, since such declarations are frequently made by persons changing their domicile, their value must now be considered. In *F v Inland Revenue Commissioners*[12] the executor of F, a former Iranian national who had died in 1993, appealed against the determination of the Revenue that he had been domiciled in the UK for the years of assessment 1986/87 to 1992/93 inclusive. F had operated an accountancy business in Iran. He had brought land with a view to developing it, owned three houses and had constructed a large family home. At the time of the Iranian revolution he had sent his wife and children to live in the UK while remaining himself in Iran. At the time of the US hostage crisis F had decided to remain outside Iran at the same time he had been placed on an exit barred list due to alleged outstanding tax liabilities. In 1980 he had been granted indefinite leave to remain in the UK. He had subsequently applied for naturalisation, falsely claiming that he had left Iran to escape religious persecution. Up until the time of his death, F had made efforts at getting the exit bar removed. He had continued to consider Iran as his home. The Court in allowing the appeal held that the Revenue had not discharged the burden of proof to demonstrate that F had not abandoned his Iranian domicile. Having regard to the evidence, it had always been F's intention to return to Iran permanently during the relevant years for assessment. His acquisition of British citizenship and a British passport had not affected his domicile of origin in Iran, *Wahl v A-G* applied. He had been keen to gain the necessary documentation that would enable him to continue to travel freely in the furtherance of his business interests and had been willing to lie in order to gain such documentation. His return to Iran had been precluded by the exit bar. Such external pressures had prevented F from forming a free intention to acquire another domicile.

An example of the difficulties to which a written declaration might give rise is found in *Buswell v IRC*.[13] Leslie Buswell had a Transvaal domicile of origin acquired from his father who had a Transvaal domicile of choice. In 1928, when Buswell was seven years old, he and his parents moved to England so that Buswell could be educated here. Following his education and a brief period which Buswell spent as a teacher in Tenbury Wells, he was called-up in 1941 and served in the Royal Indian Navy. Upon demobilisation in 1945, he took employment in India and remained there until 1952 when he returned to England where his father was living in a poor state of health. Once in England, he took employment with a publishing firm for six months, then obtained a position with British Olivetti Ltd which he held until 1963. In 1955, Buswell obtained a South African passport and elected for South African nationality when South Africa left the Commonwealth, and, in 1958, wrote to a cousin in South Africa saying he intended to return there one day. In 1961, he married an Englishwoman of means who was agreeable to settling eventually in South Africa, and, by her, had children who were educated in England but were registered as South African nationals. In 1968, Buswell and his wife visited South Africa (Buswell's first visit there for 40 years) and bought a property in which they thereafter spent some three months of each year. Buswell claimed that, for the years 1961–62 to 1967–68, he was 'not domiciled in the United Kingdom' for the purposes of ITA 1952 s 132 (now TA 1988 s 65(4)). That claim was resisted by the Inland Revenue on the grounds that, on 11 November 1952, Buswell had completed a Revenue questionnaire (form P86) by answering 'Yes' to the question 'Do you propose to remain permanently in the United Kingdom?' and inserting a dash in answer to the next question. 'If not, how long do you expect to remain in this country?' The Commissioners attached great weight to those replies and accordingly found that Buswell had acquired an English domicile of choice. The High Court upheld the Commissioners' finding on appeal, but the Court of Appeal reversed it. Orr LJ said.

> The crucial question . . . is . . . whether the Commissioners, in coming to their conclusion, attributed to the answers on Form P86 a weight which in all the circumstances they could not reasonably bear. For this purpose it is necessary to consider both the terms of

the questions asked on the form and the circumstances in which it may reasonably be supposed that [Buswell] answered them . . . [T]he form was not intended by the Revenue to
ascertain domicile and it nowhere used that word . . . A person faced with . . . mutually
exclusive questions, would, I think, be very likely to consider that he was not expected to
say 'I do not know' in answer to the second question, an answer which would have to be
given if he said 'No' to the first . . . I find . . . that, in attributing a decisive importance to
[Buswell's] answers on the Form P86, given at a time when he had been back in this country for less than five months after an absence of ten years, and against the background to
which I have referred, the Commissioners acted 'upon a view of the facts which could not
reasonably be entertained'.[14]

Often a written declaration of intention will appear in a person's will, taking a form
similar to that appearing in the will of Frank Lawton in *Re Lawton*:[15]

Inasmuch as I am a British subject having my original domicile in England (which domicile I have never relinquished or abandoned) it is my wish and intention that this my
will . . . shall be construed and operate so far as the case admits as if I were now and
remained until my death domiciled in England.[16]

The value of such a declaration was assessed by Romer LJ in *A-G v Yule and
Mercantile Bank of India*[17] as follows:

For myself, I am not prepared to attach any importance to a declaration by a man as to
his domicile unless there is some evidence to show that the man knew what 'domicile'
means. A declaration by a man made orally or in writing that he intends to remain in a
certain country will, if not inconsistent with the facts, be of assistance in determining the
question whether he has become domiciled there. Domicile is, however, a legal conception
on which the views of a layman are not of much assistance.[18]

Lawton had, in fact, left England before he had attained the age of 21 and, having
lived and worked in Argentina and Spain, retired to France where he died some
63 years later. Upjohn J held that, despite the declaration in his will, Lawton died
domiciled in France.

Where the assertion of intention as to residence has been made orally, the
testimony of the person to whom it was made is admissible as evidence of intention
but, if made long after the assertion itself was made, will be treated with caution:

To entitle such declarations to any weight, the court must be satisfied not only of the
veracity of the witnesses who depose to such declarations, but of the accuracy of their
memory, and that the declarations contain a real expression of the intention of the
deceased.[19]

Where the assertion is actually made by the person whose domicile is being
determined during the court proceedings at which the determination of his domicile is to be made, the assertion will, of course, carry very little weight indeed. In
Bell v Kennedy[20] the Lord Chancellor said of Bell's own testimony:

it is to be accepted with very considerable reserve. An Appellant has naturally, on an issue
like the present, a very strong bias calculated to influence his mind, and he is, moreover,
speaking of what was his intention some twenty-five years ago.[21]

1   [1968] P 675.
2   Ibid, at 685–686.
3   [1974] STC 266.
4   Ibid, at 273.
5   See **7.11** above.
6   [1904] AC 287.
7   [1919] AC 145.
8   Ibid, at 178.
9   W. S. Gilbert, *HMS Pinafore*, Act II.
10 (1932) 147 LT 382.
11 Ibid at 385, per Lord Atkin.
12 (2000) 1 W.T.L.R 505.
13 (1974) 49 TC 334.
14 Ibid, at 362–363.
15 (1958) 37 ATC 216. See also *Re Steer* discussed at **7.13** above.
16 Ibid, at 218.
17 (1931) 145 LT 9.
18 Ibid, at 17.
19 *Hodgson v De Beauchesne* (1858) 12 Moo PCC 285 at 325.
20 (1868) LR 1 Sc & Div 307.
21 Ibid, at 313.

7.16   Change of domicile of choice

It should by now have become clear that the courts will not easily be satisfied that a domicile of origin has been replaced by a domicile of choice. The presumption of a domicile of origin's continuance is of the utmost strength and, compared with a domicile of choice:

its character is more enduring, its hold stronger and less easily shaken off.[1]

This is because a domicile of origin is conferred on a person by operation of law whereas, as has been explained,[2] a domicile of choice is acquired merely *animo et facto*. Once acquired, however, a domicile of choice may be extinguished *animo et facto* also, ie by an intention and an act. The act is the leaving of the country of the domicile of choice and the intention is the intention not to resume permanent residence there. This last is technically referred to as an *animus non revertendi*. Such an *animus* does not, it should be noted, include within it a decision to reside permanently elsewhere. In *Udny v Udny*,[3] the Lord Chancellor summed up the whole matter as follows:

if the choice of a new abode and actual settlement there constitute a change of the original domicil, then the exact converse of such a procedure, viz the intention to abandon the new domicil, and an actual abandonment of it, ought to be equally effective to destroy the new domicil. That which may be acquired may surely be abandoned, and though a man cannot, for civil reasons, be left without a domicil, no such difficulty arises if it be simply held that the original domicil revives. That original domicil depended not on choice but attached itself to its subject on his birth, and it seems to be consonant both to convenience and to the currency of the whole law of domicil to hold that the man born with a domicil may shift and vary it as often as he pleases, indicating each change by intention and act, whether in its acquisition or abandonment; and, further, to hold that every acquired domicil is capable of simple abandonment *animo et facto* the process by which it was acquired, without its being necessary that a new one should be at the same time chosen, otherwise one is driven to the absurdity of asserting a person to be domiciled in a country which he has resolutely forsaken and cast off, simply because he may (perhaps for years) be deliberating before he settles himself elsewhere.[4]

Just as a domicile of choice cannot be acquired *animo solo*, however, a domicile of choice cannot be abandoned unless the intention to leave the territory of the existing domicile of choice for good is accompanied by an actual departure from that territory. As Cotton LJ said in *Re Marrett*:[5]

in order to lose the domicil of choice once acquired, it is not only necessary that a man should be dissatisfied with his domicil of choice, and form an intention to leave it, but he must have left it, with the intention of leaving it permanently.[6]

The application of this principle is to be found in *Zanelli v Zanelli*.[7] The case concerned an Italian who, having married an Englishwoman and lived with her in England, deserted her and returned to Italy. The wife petitioned for divorce in England claiming that the English courts had jurisdiction because immediately before deserting her her husband was domiciled in England within the terms of the Matrimonial Causes Act 1937 s 13. The question before the court was whether that was so. It was accepted that, following the marriage, the woman's husband had acquired a domicile of choice in England and it was accepted also that, by the time of his desertion, he had formed the intention to return permanently to Italy. But did that bring about a loss of domicile of choice? Lord du Parq decided. No, it did not:

although the husband may have given up an intention to reside here, he certainly had not given up residence here. The *factum* had not occurred.[8]

Accordingly, the woman's petition was granted and her divorce (which would not have been permitted under Italian law) was granted under English law.

The question when the *factum* of departure does occur is not always an easy question to answer as *Re Raffenel's Goods*[9] illustrates. Madame Raffenel had a domicile of origin in England but, upon marrying a French naval officer, had acquired a French domicile of dependence. Following her husband's death, she decided to return permanently to England. She boarded ship at Calais with her children and baggage, having closed down her establishment in Dunkirk, but, before the ship left the harbour, became so ill that she had to disembark. She returned to Dunkirk where she later died. Sir Cresswell Cresswell said:

I cannot think that the French domicil was abandoned so long as the deceased remained in the territory of France. It must be admitted that she never left France, and that intention alone is not sufficient.[10]

Although that case was concerned with abandonment of a domicile of dependence, Lord du Parcq, in the case of *Zanelli v Zanelli*[11] which (as explained above) concerned the abandonment of a domicile of choice, expressly approved the decision in *Re Raffenel's Goods*[12] and drew no distinction between the two types of domicile in this connection. Speaking of Zanelli's desertion of his wife he said:

he cannot be said to have lost his domicile of choice even at the moment when he stepped into the train with his ticket in his pocket. Having regard to what was decided . . . in

Re Raffenel's Goods . . . I do not think that, even when he stepped on board the ship which was to carry him to the Continent, he had yet lost his domicile of choice.[13]

It should be noted, however, that in that case, Asquith LJ went even further:

To change an English domicile of choice there must be both *animus* and *factum*, the *animus* being the formation of the intention, and the *factum* consisting in some outward and visible act evincing it such as leaving this country or, *perhaps more accurately, arriving in another*.[14]

And on the strength of that dictum, Baker J held, in *Leon v Leon*,[15] that a person who had displaced his domicile of origin in British Guiana by a domicile of choice in England but had then left England for good and returned to British Guiana, had:

kept his English domicile until he reverted to his domicile of origin on his arrival in British Guiana in August 1964.[16]

This, it is suggested, was stretching Sir Cresswell Cresswell's dicta in *Re Raffenel's Goods*[17] too far. Surely, the domicile of origin of both Zanelli and Leon revived as soon as their respective ships left the territorial waters of the United Kingdom, not when they docked on the shores of their respective homelands.

It was said at the outset of this section that the *animus* required to effect the abandonment of a domicile of choice is an *animus non revertendi*, ie an intention not to return. It must now be emphasised that (despite recent indications of some relaxation in this view[18]) such an *animus* does *not* cover a case of mere irresolution (*sine animo revertendi*). A person who leaves the country of his existing domicile of choice in a state of indecision as to whether or not he will return there retains his existing domicile of choice until such time as his indecision hardens into a decision never to return. This is illustrated by *Fielden v IRC*.[19] Fielden had an English domicile of origin but, in or about 1935, this was displaced by a Michigan domicile of choice when he married a Michigan resident and settled in that state of America with the intention of remaining there permanently. In 1943, Fielden and his wife moved to Burnley in Lancashire with the intention of helping in his father's ailing business, and they bought a house there. In 1947, Fielden became a director of his father's company and later became chairman and managing director. It seems that he then decided that he owed it to his father to remain in England until he was satisfied the business could continue successfully without him, but he asserted that, upon his retirement, he would return to America, though not necessarily to Michigan. At the time the case was heard, however, he was still living in Burnley, 22 years after leaving America. The Commissioners decided that, by 1954–55, the first of the years for which his domicile was in question, Fielden's English domicile of origin had revived, but they also found that his Michigan domicile of choice had been retained for some years after his return to England, probably until 1947. This was, it is suggested, because for those years he was merely *sine animo revertendi* to Michigan, not *animo non revertendi* to Michigan. Later, however, his intention to return to America in general became too vague to prevent him being regarded as *animo non revertendi* and thereupon his domicile of origin revived. The Commissioners' findings were upheld by Cross J who said:

it is not necessary, in order to retain a domicile of choice after a change of residence, to have an unwavering intention of returning to live in the place of domicile in all circumstances . . . When [Fielden] came to England in 1943, he came under the stress of circumstances. He wanted to help his country and his father in the war; and the Commissioners have found – I think quite rightly found – that he did not there and then lose his Michigan domicile of choice. It would not, I think, matter for this purpose whether he then had an intention to go back as soon as possible to Michigan after the war, or simply to go back to some place in the United States after the war. But then one finds that after the war he buys a house here, that when he goes to the United States it is only for a short stay, and that he remains here continuously until the present time . . . [H]e re-acquired his English domicile of origin about 1947 . . . because . . . such intention as he may thereafter have had of going to live somewhere in the United States after his retirement was really too vague and uncertain to prevent the re-acquisition of his English domicile of origin.[20]

If a person leaves his domicile of choice *animo revertendi* but subsequently abandons his intention to return, his domicile of origin will, of course, thereupon revive.[21]

Finally, it should be noted that where a person *animo et facto* abandons one domicile of choice and *animo et facto* acquires another, his domicile of origin will revive for the duration of the interval, however brief, between the abandonment and the acquisition.[22]

---

1   *Winans v A-G* [1904] AC 287 at 290, per Lord Macnaghten; F *(F's Personal Representatives of F deceased) v CIR* (1999) Sp C 219, [2000] STC (SCD) 1.
2   See **7.11** above.
3   (1869) LR 1 Sc & Div 441.
4   Ibid, at 450.
5   (1887) 36 Ch D 400.
6   Ibid, at 407.
7   (1948) 64 TLR 556.
8   Ibid.
9   (1863) 3 Sw & Tr 49.
10 Ibid.
11 (1948) 64 TLR 556.
12 (1863) 3 Sw & Tr 49.
13 (1948) 64 TLR 556.
14 Ibid, at 557. Author's italics.
15 [1967] P 275.
16 Ibid, at 282. These words must not be taken as some sort of authority for the proposition that presence in the domicile of origin is necessary for that domicile's revival. As *Tee v Tee* [1974] 1 WLR 213 clearly shows, it is not.
17 (1863) 3 Sw & Tr 49.
18 In *Re Flynn* [1968] 1 WLR 103 Megarry J said (*obiter* at 113) that 'mere negative absence of any intention' to resume residence, rather than a positive intention not to return, would suffice to bring a domicile of choice to an end, and this was approved in *Qureshi v Qureshi* [1971] 2 WLR 518 at 530.
19 (1965) 42 TC 501.
20 Ibid, at 507–508.
21 *Tee v Tee* [1973] 3 All ER 1105.
22 *Harrison v Harrison* [1953] 1 WLR 865. The proposal of The Law Commission and the Scottish Law Commission is that this should cease to be so and that an abandoned domicile of choice should continue until a new domicile is acquired (Working Paper No 88 and Consultative Memorandum No 63, para 5.22).

7.17 Deemed domicile

In introducing the capital transfer tax (which has now been renamed 'inheritance tax'), the Finance Act 1975 s 45 provided that, under any of three sets of circumstances a person who was not domiciled in the United Kingdom under the common law rules described in this chapter was nevertheless to be treated as domiciled in the United Kingdom for most purposes of the tax. The provision relating to one of those three sets of circumstances was repealed by Finance (No 2) Act 1983 s 12 and the provisions describing the remaining two sets of circumstances have now been substantially re-enacted as the Inheritance Tax Act 1984 s 267(1)(a) and (b).

Section 267(1)(a) and (3) provides that a person not domiciled in the United Kingdom at the time of a transfer of value etc ('the relevant time') is to be treated as domiciled in the United Kingdom at that time if he was domiciled in the United Kingdom on or after 10 December 1974 and within the three years immediately preceding the relevant time.

In the absence of statutory definition to the contrary, 'year' means a period of twelve calendar months consisting of 365 days or 366 days in a leap year.[1]

The effect of this provision is to postpone (for inheritance tax purposes only) a person's acquisition of a domicile in some country outside the United Kingdom to a date three years after the date on which, according to common law rules, the acquisition of the new domicile actually took place. Thus any transfer of value made by the person within the three years immediately following his acquisition of an overseas domicile will remain potentially subject to inheritance tax regardless of the *situs* of the asset.

This rule has no rational basis and is a transparent piece of anti-avoidance legislation directed at keeping within the inheritance tax net anyone who, seeing a large inheritance tax bill appearing on the horizon, leaves the United Kingdom with the intention of avoiding it. Superficially, it parallels the Revenue rule of practice regarding the residence status of a person who leaves the United Kingdom for permanent residence abroad,[2] ie that a decision on that person's claim to have become non-resident and not ordinarily resident in the United Kingdom will be postponed for three years and that during those three years the person's tax liabilities will be calculated on the basis that he remains a United Kingdom resident; but, in the case of residence, a decision at the end of three years that the person had become non-resident on his departure is then applied retrospectively to the date of departure and all assessments are revised accordingly. There is, however, nothing similarly provisional about the three year postponement of non-domiciled status.

Unlike s 267(1)(a), s 267(1)(b) is a rational piece of legislation which is designed to place a non-domiciled person who has lived in the United Kingdom for a long number of years on an equal footing with the United Kingdom domiciled taxpayer.[3] It (and s 267(3)) provides that a person not domiciled in the United Kingdom at the time a transfer of value etc takes place ('the relevant time') is to be treated as domiciled in the United Kingdom at that time if he was resident in the United Kingdom on or after 10 December 1974 and in not less than seventeen of the twenty years of assessment ending with the year of assessment in which the relevant time falls. It should be noted, however, that, for the purposes of this provision:

the question of whether a person was resident in the United Kingdom in any year of assessment shall be determined as for the purposes of income tax.[4]

Chapters 2 and 4 should, therefore, be studied in this context, in particular sections **2.07** to **2.09** and **4.04** and **4.05** above. A person will thus be likely to acquire residence status if his presence in the United Kingdom is of sufficiently long duration during a tax year for a territorial link to be established (183 days or more in the opinion of the Inland Revenue) *or* if the pattern of his visits to the United Kingdom in years prior to and subsequent to the tax year in question, though not in themselves of significant length, nevertheless establish a similar territorial link (an average of three or more months a year over a period of four or more tax years in the Inland Revenue's view) *or* if visits to the United Kingdom which would otherwise be insignificant are given by ties such as nationality, family and business a significance sufficient to establish the kind of territorial link which residence status connotes.

The provision itself has two effects. The first is to bring persons who have never been domiciled in the United Kingdom into the inheritance tax net. The second (and often overlooked) effect is, unless the change of domicile takes place on 6 April, to keep a person who has been, but is no longer, domiciled in the United Kingdom within the inheritance tax net for up to almost a year longer than s 267(1)(a) will keep him there.

It should be noted that where (whether under these deemed domicile rules or not) a person is regarded under United Kingdom law as domiciled in the United Kingdom but is regarded under the law of a foreign state with which the United Kingdom has a double tax treaty covering estate and inheritance taxes as domiciled in that foreign state, the provisions of the treaty will apply so as to ensure that the person is treated by both the United Kingdom and the foreign state as being domiciled in one of the territories only.[5] Article 4(2) of the OECD 1982 draft double taxation convention on estates and inheritances provides for this to be achieved by a series of tests identical with those applied to determine fiscal residence as described at **2.21** above.

---

1 *IRC v Hobhouse* [1956] 1 WLR 1393.
2 See **4.21** above.
3 See Official Report, Standing Committee A, 13 February 1975, cols 1645-6.
4 IHTA 1984 s 267(4).
5 IHTA 1984 ss 158 and 267(2).

7.18 Appeals

As has been pointed out at **7.01** above, domicile may lie at the root of an assessment to income tax under Schedule E or Schedule D, to an assessment to capital gains tax, or to a determination of inheritance tax. Where it is necessary to appeal against any such assessment or determination, the procedure is as follows.

In the event of a dispute arising under Schedule E concerning a person's domicile,

> the question shall be referred to and determined by the Board, but any person who is aggrieved by their decision on the question may, by notice in writing to that effect given to them within three months from the date on which notice of the decision is given to him, make an application to have the question heard and determined by the Special Commissioners, and where an application is so made, the Special Commissioners shall hear and determine the question in like manner as an appeal.[1]

These provisions apply in their entirety to disputes concerning domicile which arise in connection with capital gains tax.[2]

Similarly, there is a right of appeal to the Special Commissioners against a decision or determination of the Revenue as to a person's domicile for the purpose of TA 1988 s 192 (Relief from tax for foreign emoluments).

In the event of a disagreement with a determination of inheritance tax payable, the person on whom the notice of determination has been served may, within 30 days of the service, appeal against it to the Special Commissioners by notice in writing given to the Board and specifying the grounds of appeal.[3] However:

> Where it is so agreed between the appellant and the Board, or the High Court, on an application made by the appellant, is satisfied that the matters to be decided on the appeal are likely to be substantially confined to questions of law and gives leave for that purpose, the appeal may be to the High Court.[4]

It might well be that where the matter to be decided is a question of domicile, leave will be given for such a direct appeal, but, where leave is not granted and the appeal is heard by the Special Commissioners, an appeal may then (as it may in all cases coming before the Special Commissioners) be made to the High Court on a point of law.[5]

---

1 TA 1988 s 207.
2 TCGA 1992 s 9(2).
3 IHTA 1984 s 222.
4 Ibid s 222(3).
5 TMA 1970 ss 44, 46 and 56A.

CHAPTER 8

Compliance and enforcement

'The bell', said Noggs, as though in explanation; 'at home?'
'Yes.'
'To anybody?'
'Yes.'
'To the tax-gatherer?'
'No! Let him call again.'

Dickens *Nicholas Nickleby* Ch 2

8.01 Introduction

The problem alluded to in this Chapter is that of ensuring compliance with, and obtaining enforcement of, United Kingdom revenue laws where the person subject to those laws (whatever his residence, ordinary residence or domicile status might be) has, by leaving the territory of the United Kingdom and remaining outside it, placed himself beyond the jurisdiction of the United Kingdom courts. The problem may be broken down into two questions: What are the legal obligations imposed on a person outside the United Kingdom as regards returns, payment of tax etc, and what power has the Inland Revenue to assess and collect tax from such a person? The following paragraphs will attempt to supply some answers.

Notices, returns and assessments

8.02 Notice of chargeability

In order that assessment to tax might take place, the law imposes an obligation on any person chargeable to income tax or capital gains tax for a year of assessment and who has not received a notice from the inspector of taxes under TMA 1970 s 8 requiring a return for that year of his total income and charge to give to an officer of the Board of Inland Revenue notice that he is so chargeable within six months from the end of that year.[1] Notice is not required in respect of certain classes of income.[2] The point to be made here is that that obligation extends to residents and non-residents alike and knows no territorial bounds. In *Whitney v IRC*,[3] Lord

Wrenbury considered the obligation which ITA 1918 s 7(3) imposed on every person chargeable with super-tax (a form of income taxation which no longer exists) to give notice that he was so chargeable, and said of Mr Whitney, an American citizen and a resident of New York who had received dividends in respect of shares in a United Kingdom corporation:

> If . . . I am right in thinking that the non-resident alien is chargeable in respect of property in the United Kingdom, it was his duty to give that notice.[4]

---

1 TMA 1970 s 7. It is suggested that this obligation remains even where, because of the availability of allowances and reliefs, tax might not actually be payable: 'chargeable' probably means 'within the charge', ie caught by the schedules.
2 Ibid s 7(3).
3 (1925) 10 TC 88.
4 Ibid at 114.

8.03 Returns and assessments

Merely giving notice that one is chargeable to tax will not, however, be sufficient to enable an inspector to make an accurate assessment. A return will be needed and, accordingly, an inspector of taxes is empowered to require a person to deliver to him such a return.[1] Again, neither the notice requiring the return nor the obligation imposed by such a notice are subject to any territorial limitation, and the consequences of failing to comply with the requirement to render a return or of rendering a return which fails to satisfy an inspector are serious.

In either event, the inspector will then be acting within his powers if he makes an assessment to tax in an amount which ought in his opinion to be charged in order to make good to the Crown a loss of tax;[2] and the tax charged under such an assessment will, unless the assessment is successfully appealed against,[3] become due and payable on specified dates. If unpaid on those dates, the tax will be recoverable either by distraint (if the person assessed has property within the territory of the United Kingdom)[4] or by proceedings through the courts (if the person assessed is, or becomes, physically present in the territory of the United Kingdom).[5] Thus a person who decides to ignore the return requirements of United Kingdom income tax law on the grounds that he is safely beyond the jurisdiction of the United Kingdom courts may, if he should set foot in the United Kingdom at some future date, find himself liable to proceedings for the recovery of tax to which he has been assessed on an estimated basis in his absence.

Irrespective of whether a person is technically resident in the United Kingdom or not and irrespective of whether or not he is a United Kingdom national, his absence from the territory of the United Kingdom throughout the period over which the assessment process takes place will provide him with no defence against proceedings for the recovery of tax shown as due and payable under an assessment. In *IRC v Huni*,[6] for example, a Swiss national who was not resident in the United Kingdom argued that a notice to make a return for super-tax purposes served on him at his Paris address was invalid since it had been served outside the territory of the United Kingdom. It followed, he said, that he could not have failed to make a return within the terms of the legislation (FA 1910 in relation to super-tax) and that the Commissioners had, therefore, no jurisdiction to make an assessment to the

169

best of their judgment. Furthermore, he contended, irrespective of the validity of the assessment, the notice of assessment (also served on him at his Paris address) was as invalid (on the same grounds) as had been the notice requiring him to make a return. Rowlatt J did not agree. He said:

> A great deal has been said in the course of this argument about a non-resident and about an alien, but I think I am confronted with the question as to the operation of this Statute without the realm . . . In the words of the Statute there is no distinction drawn between aliens or residents or non-residents or anything of that sort; the question really is as to whether the Statute is to be cut down so as not to serve notices abroad. Now the principle involved here is the principle that Acts of Parliament are prima facie not to be construed so as to assume jurisdiction without the realm – extra-territorial jurisdiction – so as to make the jurisdiction extra-territorial. And of course where it comes to the case of creating a duty abroad or creating an offence abroad – both of which of course can be done by Parliament – . . . the Courts are bound to look narrowly at the Statute to see whether that is what is meant. But I apprehend there is no difficulty of that sort in the way if what the Statute really directs is the mere service of a notice, and that is all it is. There is no international difficulty in serving a notice abroad . . . It may have consequences, but it is a mere notice . . . I think there is involved in this machinery the mere giving of a notice as a preliminary to the Commissioners proceeding to do something which they are entitled to do . . . and that I ought not to limit the words of this Section so as to make this notice as a mere notice null and void.[7]

That being so, the assessment which followed Monsieur Huni's failure to make the return required of him was valid. Accordingly Rowlatt J turned to the question of the notice of assessment:

> The Respondent says that the notice of assessment is bad too, because it was served on him abroad. That I cannot think is bad. If a man has been validly assessed in England, what principle of international law is to be invoked by way of reflection to limit the words of the Statute which says that he may be told he has been assessed, I cannot conceive.[8]

This judgment was approved by the House of Lords in the *Whitney* case[9] where Mr Whitney had advanced arguments against his assessability similar to those which had been advanced by Monsieur Huni. Lord Wrenbury said:

> There was sent to the Appellant by post addressed to him in the United States a notice under Section 7(2) requiring him to make a return. It is contended that there was no right to send him a notice so addressed. The case, it is contended, is similar to the case of service of a writ out of the jurisdiction. I do not agree . . . It is not a step in a judicial proceeding, but a step which will create *inter partes* a state of things in which judicial proceedings can subsequently be taken in default of compliance. I think the notice was duly served. In my opinion *IRC v Huni* was rightly decided.[10]

If notice is to be served validly under the Taxes Acts, therefore, all that is required is that it be served at the 'usual or last known place of residence' of the person on whom it is served, whether that place of residence be in the United Kingdom or an address overseas.[11]

The provisions described above relate to income tax and capital gains tax, but similar provisions exist in relation to corporation tax and inheritance tax.

1   TMA 1970 ss 8(1) and 12.
2   Ibid, s 29.
3   Ibid, s 31.
4   Ibid, s 61.
5   Ibid, ss 65–68.
6   (1923) 8 TC 466.
7   Ibid, at 474.
8   Ibid.
9   (1925) 10 TC 88.
10 Ibid, at 113.
11 TMA 1970 s 115.

Assessment in the name of an agent

8.04 Introduction

Prior to the Finance Act 1995 the law governing the assessment of a non-resident in the name of a resident agent was contained in TMA 1970 ss 78–85. Those sections have been repealed by FA 1995 s 162, Sch 29 Part VIII(16) for the purposes of income tax and capital gains tax for the years 1996–97 and subsequent years of assessment, and for the purposes of corporation tax in relation to accounting periods beginning after 31 March 1996. The new rules are contained in FA 1995 ss 126, 127 and Sch 23.

8.05 United Kingdom representatives of non-residents

A branch or agent[1] in the United Kingdom through which a non-resident carries on, whether solely or in partnership, any trade profession or vocation is made the United Kingdom representative of the non-resident for income tax and corporation tax in relation to: the amount of any income from the trade profession or vocation arising directly or indirectly from the branch or agency; to income from property or rights which are used by, or held for, that branch or agency; to amounts which by reference to that branch or agency are charged to capital gains tax under TCGA 1992 s 10 or fall under that section to be included in the chargeable profits of the non-resident; where the non-resident is an overseas life insurance company the chargeable profits subject to tax under TA 1988 Sch 19 AC, para 3.[2]

These rules only apply where the non-resident (either solely or in partnership) carries on a trade, profession or vocation.[3] The obligations of the non-resident to make returns, to conform to the new rules of self-assessment and to pay the tax, interest, and penalties, if any, apply as if they were also the joint obligations of the United Kingdom representative.[4]

1   TMA 1970 s 118(1).
2   FA 1995 s 126(2).
3   FA 1995 s 126(2).
4   FA 1995 Sch 23.

8.06 Persons not treated as United Kingdom representatives

The new rules decree that certain categories of persons are not capable of being treated as United Kingdom representatives of non-resident persons for the purposes of FA 1995 s 126 and Sch 23:[1] an irregular agent not carrying on a regular agency for the non resident;[2] an agent acting as a broker where certain conditions are met;[3] an agent acting as an investment manager;[4] a member agent or a manager agent of a non-resident Lloyd's syndicate.[5]

---

1 FA 1995 s 127(1).
2 Ibid, s 127(1)(a).
3 Ibid, s 127(1)(b).
4 Ibid, s 127(1)(c).
5 Ibid, s 127(1)(d).

Collection of tax at source

8.07 The principle

It is a principle, deeply rooted in the United Kingdom income tax system, that, whenever possible, income tax should be collected at source (ie by the person making payments which become income in the hands of another) rather than by direct assessment on the recipient. The principle features prominently in the rules attaching to Schedule D, Case III, Schedule E and Schedule F, but it is extended into areas where it would not otherwise apply if a payment of income is being made to a person outside the United Kingdom who, because the source of income is within the United Kingdom, is nevertheless chargeable to tax in respect of that income.

Rents and other income from property are, for example, normally to be paid gross to their recipient who is then charged to tax by direct assessment. TA 1988 s 43 provides, however, in the case of rents paid before 6 April 1996 and where the 'usual place of abode' of the person to whom rents etc are paid is 'outside the United Kingdom', that TA 1988 s 349(1) is to be applied to those payments (whether they are made in the United Kingdom or elsewhere) as if they were an annual payment charged with tax under Schedule D, Case III and not payable out of profits or gains brought into charge to income tax. Section 349(1) directs that, where an annual payment is not payable out of profits or gains brought into charge to income tax, the person by or through whom the payment is made must, on making the payment, deduct out of it a sum representing the amount of income tax thereon and must forthwith deliver to the inspector of taxes an account of the payment and be assessed and charged to tax thereon.

Rent paid as from 6 April 1995 to a recipient whose 'usual place of abode' is outside the United Kingdom is governed by TA 1988 s 42A. TA 1988 s 43 is repealed as from 6 April 1995.[1]

This does not mean that the system of deducting tax at source from rents is to be abolished. TA 1988 s 42A is an enabling section permitting the Revenue to make regulations[2] to establish a new system which will provide for the deduction of tax at source from the rents, either by the agent of the property or where there is no agent the tenant.[3]

There is provision in the regulations to allow the rents to be paid gross where the non-resident chooses, by agreement with the Inland Revenue.[4] The Revenue will withdraw the authority to pay the rents gross if the non-resident fails to comply with his self-assessment obligations.

1 FA 1995 s 40(3) Sch 29 Pt VIII (16).
2 TA 1988 s 42A(1); Taxation of Income from land (Non-resident Regulations) 1995 No 2902.
3 Ibid, s 42A(2)(a)(b).
4 Taxation of Income from land (Non-resident Regulations) 1995 No 2902, para 17.

8.08　The meaning of 'usual place of abode'

The term 'usual place of abode' used in TA 1988 s 43 and the new s 42A is not defined in the legislation. While it may be true that a person whose usual place of abode is in the United Kingdom is resident in the United Kingdom,[1] it does not follow that a person whose usual place of abode is outside the United Kingdom is *not* resident in the United Kingdom.[2] In imposing a test of 'usual place of abode' (rather than a test of residence) in this context, Parliament is recognising that a person on whom it places the onus of applying the test (ie any person making payment of rent etc) will rarely be in possession of such facts as are required for the determination of the residence status of the person to whom payment is being made, whereas the determination of such a person's usual place of abode is capable of determination by mere inquiry and observation.

In *Haslope v Thorne*,[3] Lord Ellenborough CJ considered the term 'place of abode' in the context of a rule of court which required the place of abode of the deponent of an affidavit to be inserted in the affidavit and came to the conclusion that it meant 'the place where the deponent was most usually to be found'.[4] Thus, the place where a man 'lives with his family and sleeps at night' will always be 'his place of abode in the full sense of that expression'.[5] That does not presuppose, however, that the living and sleeping will take place in a house or flat or even an hotel room: a yacht,[6] a caravan,[7] a tent or bender,[8] and even a car[9] may constitute a person's place of abode!

1 See **2.07** above.
2 See **2.10–2.18** above.
3 (1813) 1 M & S 103.
4 Ibid, at 104. In accordance with that principle, the usual place of abode of a company will presumably be its principal place of business.
5 *R v Hammond* (1852) 17 QB 772 at 780, 781, per Lord Campbell CJ.
6 In *Bayard Brown v Burt* (1911) 5 TC 667, it was accepted that an ocean-going yacht anchored in territorial waters was the place of abode of Mr Bayard Brown, its owner and occupier.
7 In *Makins v Elson* [1977] STC 46, it was held that a wheeled caravan jacked up and resting on bricks, with water, electricity and telephone services installed, was a dwelling-house.
8 In *Hipperson v Electoral Registration Officer for the District of Newbury* [1985] 2 All ER 456, Sir John Donaldson MR (at 462) rejected the submission that ladies living in tents, vehicles and benders (a form of tent) on Greenham Common in furtherance of their protest concerning cruise missiles could not be said to have a home in the camp: 'It may be unusual to make one's home in a tent, bender or vehicle, but we can see no reason in law why it should be impossible.'
9 In *R v Bundy* [1977] 2 All ER 382, the motor car in which a certain Mr Bundy had been living rough was held to be his place of abode when sited but not while in transit. The court held, at 384, that the

term '"place of abode" . . . connotes, first of all, a site. That is the ordinary meaning of the word "place". It is a site at which the occupier intends to abide. So there are two elements in the phrase "place of abode", the element of site and the element of intention. When the appellant took the motor car to a site with the intention of abiding there, then his motor car on that site could be said to be his "place of abode", but when he took it from that site to move it to another site where he intended to abide, the motor car could not be said to be his "place of abode" during transit.'

8.09   The responsibility of the payer

It will be clear from what has been said at **8.10** above that the onus on any person paying rents etc is, therefore, to ascertain where the person to whom he is making payment is 'most usually to be found'. Is he usually in the United Kingdom or is he usually abroad? If the latter is the case, the obligation to deduct income tax at source is imposed, even if payment is made in the United Kingdom. If the former is the case, there is no obligation to deduct tax, even if payment is made abroad.

The payer is not to concern himself with whether or not the person to whom he is making payment is the person who is ultimately chargeable to tax in respect of the payment made. Even where it is transparently clear that the person to whom he is making payment is *not* the person chargeable, he must nevertheless deduct tax if the 'usual place of abode' of the person to whom payment is to be made is outside the United Kingdom. The question of chargeability lies with the Inland Revenue, not with the payer.

A person who refuses to allow the deduction of tax out of the payment of rents etc in accordance with provisions of TA 1988 s 43 or s 42A will incur a penalty of £50, and any agreement for the payment of the rent etc in full without allowing any such deduction will be void.[1] If, despite these provisions, no deduction is made in circumstances where it ought to have been made, the Inland Revenue may either assess the payer and collect from him the tax due as if he made the deduction[2] or assess the person chargeable in respect of the rents etc and collect from him the tax due.[3] As, however, the deduction at source obligation was imposed by TA 1988 s 43 or 42A to circumvent the difficulties which arise where the person from whom it is sought to collect tax is outside of the United Kingdom's jurisdiction, the Inland Revenue might normally be expected to take the first course of action.

Where the usual place of abode of the person to whom rents etc are paid is within the United Kingdom, no tax is to be deducted from the payment even if the person to whom the rents are paid is merely an agent and the usual place of abode of the person chargeable is outside the United Kingdom. If, however, the person chargeable is a person not resident in the United Kingdom, he may (and normally will be) assessed and charged to income tax in the name of the agent, in the same manner and to the same amount as he would be assessed and charged if he were resident in the United Kingdom and in actual receipt of the profits or gains.[4]

The foregoing has equal relevance where certain kinds of interest payments are made to a person who is usually to be found overseas. TA 1988 s 349(2) provides that 'where any yearly interest of money chargeable to tax under Case III of Schedule D is paid . . . by any person to another person whose usual place of abode is outside the United Kingdom, the person by or through whom the payment is made shall on making the payment, deduct out of it a sum representing the amount of income tax thereon for the year in which the payment is made' and, again, TA 1988 s 350(1) is to apply.

By virtue of TA 1988 s 536, 'where the usual place of abode of an owner of a copyright is not within the United Kingdom' TA 1988 s 349 is to apply to 'any payment of, or on account of, any royalties or sums paid periodically for or in respect of that copyright as it applies to annual payments not payable out of profits or gains brought into charge to income tax'; and, by virtue of TA 1988 s 537 those provisions of TA 1988 s 536 are to apply also to public lending right.

1 TMA 1970 s 106.
2 TA 1988 s 350(1). This subsection makes it clear that the assessability of the maker of a payment to which s 350(1) applies does not depend on his having deducted the tax which he was liable to deduct.
3 *Grosvenor Place Estates Ltd v Roberts* (1961) 39 TC 433.
4 See **8.08** above.

CHAPTER 9

Residence, nationality and discrimination in the European Union

To anyone who is somewhat familiar with tax law, it is clear that the concept of de facto non-discrimination could very easily result in the disintegration of national tax systems. Even were the court to limit itself to the elimination of the differences in tax treatment between taxpayers based on nationality or on residence, the resulting chaos in income tax would be considerable.

Vanistendael: 'The Limits of the New Community Tax Order', *CML Review*, 1994

9.01 Introduction

Direct taxation does not at present fall within the purview of the European Union, but the powers over direct taxation which are retained by member states must be exercised consistently with EU law.[1]

Since the early eighties the European Court of Justice (ECJ) has increasingly been called upon to hear cases where taxpayers who are resident in, or nationals of, member states have complained that the national tax laws of other member states in which they are non-residents have been applied in such a way as to discriminate against them thereby making them pay more tax than the residents of these member states or are denying them credits against tax or relief against losses.

In the main the discrimination is said to arise from the contravention of Article 48 of the Treaty of Rome establishing the European Community (the Treaty) which allows freedom of movement of workers or Article 52 which allows the unhindered freedom of establishment of businesses and commercial activities. Underlying these Articles is Article 6 of the Treaty which prohibits any discrimination 'on grounds of nationality'.

Usually the discrimination is alleged to be caused as a consequence of those laws of member states which provide for different tax treatment for residents and non-residents. A direct conflict can thus occur between the concept of residence and the concept of nationality.

The Treaty neither defines the word 'discrimination' nor describes what it means in the context of the above Articles. The ECJ, however, has consistently described 'discrimination' as consisting solely 'in the application of different rules to comparable situations or in the application of the same rule to differing situations'.[2]

An attempt is made below to analyse the leading cases. This will enable the reader to watch the developing jurisprudence of the ECJ in this area. Those readers whose training lies within the English legal system should bear in mind that while it is possible to extract principles from the decisions of the ECJ, that Court is not bound by its own previous decisions. Also it should be appreciated that the developing jurisprudence of the Court in these tax cases is affected by the tensions between 'state rights', that is the powers of the member states and the powers entrenched in the EU Treaties, as interpreted by the ECJ.

9.02   Analysis of recent ECJ cases

The first case on our journey is that of the *EC Commission v France.*[3] There the EC Commission complained that the French Republic had failed to fulfil its obligations under Article 52 (freedom of establishment) by refusing to offer a tax credit (*avoir fiscal*) to the branches and agencies established in France of insurance companies whose registered offices were located in other member states. While denying the tax credit to such branches or agencies, the French tax authorities gave the credit both to the branches and agencies of French registered companies and also to the French subsidiaries of companies registered in other member states.

The French Republic argued, inter alia, that the difference in treatment was as a result of an 'objective factor', that is, in the way most national tax systems distinguish between residents and non-residents; an essential distinction in tax law and one that is internationally recognised.

The ECJ, while not excluding the possibility that a distinction based on residence could serve as the justification for discrimination, was not impressed with the French government's arguments. The Court emphasised that companies registered in France, and the branches and agencies situated in France of companies whose registered offices were abroad, all paid French corporation tax on profits made in France. Accordingly, the French Government was not justified in treating them differently when it came to tax credits.

In the next case *Commerzbank*[4] the UK Inland Revenue found itself in the dock. Commerzbank AG was a company incorporated under German law with its registered office in Germany. It had a branch in the UK through which it granted loans to a number of United States companies and it paid tax in the UK on the interest received from those companies. It was discovered that because of a provision in the UK/USA Double Taxation Convention the interest was not properly taxable since Commerzbank was not resident in the UK. The tax was accordingly repaid to it.

Commerzbank then claimed a 'repayment supplement' under s 825 of TA 1988. That section enables taxpaying companies to recover interest on tax wrongly paid. The Inland Revenue refused the claim because the section applies only to resident companies. Commerzbank argued in the ECJ that the residency requirement was discriminating in that it rendered ineffective the right of establishment in Art 52 of the Treaty.

The UK government rejected the charge of discrimination arguing that Commerzbank was in a different position from a UK resident company since such a company would not have been exempt from tax on the interest; the exemption only arose because Commerzbank was non-resident. There was not therefore unequal treatment as between the non-resident Commerzbank and resident UK banks with regard to the entitlement to the repayment supplement.

The Court was not impressed. The true comparison should be made between a non-resident company and a resident company in regard to TA 1988 s 825. A resident company was entitled to the supplement, a non-resident was not. There was therefore discrimination which could fetter the application of Article 52.

In those tax cases that have reached the ECJ it is rare for the tax authorities of a member state to succeed. But one such case was *Bachmann*.[5] The taxpayer was a German national who worked in Belgium. He paid contributions to a German insurance company out of his salary under sickness and life assurance contracts which he had entered into before his arrival in Belgium. The Belgian authorities refused his claim to deduct those contributions from his total taxable income in Belgium because under Belgian tax law such contributions were only deductible when paid to Belgian companies and paid 'in Belgium'.

The ECJ held in the first place that there was discrimination for the purposes of Article 48 (freedom of movement of workers) since there was a risk that the refusal to allow the deductions would work against taxpayers who were nationals of other member states.

The Belgian government then argued that the discrimination was justified since if Mr Bachmann were allowed his deductions there was a danger that when the German insurance companies came to pay out, the Belgian authorities might be unable to recover tax on the moneys paid out since the companies were in Germany and Mr Bachmann was a German national. The corollary to allowing the deduction under Belgian law was the certainty that Belgian tax would be collected on moneys paid out by Belgian insurance companies. The cohesion of the Belgian tax system would be affected if Mr Bachmann was allowed the deductions.

The ECJ accepted that argument and held that the discrimination was justified. This was one of the first cases where the court was compelled squarely to face the argument that the cohesion of national tax systems had to be considered in weighing the provisions of the Treaty Articles against the tax laws of member states.

The cases which have given the ECJ most difficulties have been those involving taxpayers who were living in 'frontier areas' of member states.

One of the first such cases was *Schumacher*[6] where the taxpayer was a Belgium resident who in the relevant tax years had worked in Germany. He now lived with his wife in Belgium. His wife had no taxable income and 90 per cent of his income came from his employment in Germany.

Under German tax law, non-resident individuals were subject to German tax only on such of their income as arose in Germany (limited taxation). Persons resident in Germany were subject to German tax on all their income wherever it arose (unlimited taxation). Where a married couple was resident in Germany and thus liable to unlimited taxation, a 'splitting regime' was applied to their joint total income. This meant that their incomes were aggregated and then split, with each spouse being notionally attributed as to 50 per cent of their aggregated incomes and taxed accordingly.

Mr Schumacher claimed the benefit of the 'splitting regime' as between himself and his wife. If allowed to do so the regime would have taken him into a lower tax band in Germany. The German tax authorities refused the claim.

Before the ECJ, the taxpayer argued that the refusal represented discrimination within Article 48 of the Treaty. The Court decided in favour of the taxpayer and made a number of significant findings. First, it held that prima facie the principle of equal treatment as between different nationals would be rendered ineffective if it could be undermined by discriminatory national income tax provisions. Second, it reaffirmed the meaning of 'discrimination' as applied in previous cases.[3] Third, in relation to direct taxes such as income tax, the situations of residents and non-residents were not, as a rule, comparable, so that different treatment on the basis of residence and nonresidence is not in itself discriminatory since in general residents and non-residents are not in comparable situations.

Notwithstanding the findings above, the Court held that because Mr Schumacher's income arose 'entirely and exclusively' in Germany and because he did not have sufficient income in Belgium to utilise any allowances which otherwise would have been available in Belgium, he should be deemed to be a German resident and accordingly allowed to apply the splitting regime to his German income as if he were a German resident; but see *Gschwind*[7] where the German tax authorities were successful.

In *Wielockx*[8] the ECJ reaffirmed the three principles established in *Schumacher* but still decided for the taxpayer who was a Belgian national deriving his sole income from a partnership in the Netherlands. Under Netherlands tax law, resident self-employed persons were entitled to have their taxable income reduced by the amount of business profits they had added to their pension reserve. Taxation was thus deferred until such time as amounts were withdrawn from the pension reserve or the reserve was liquidated. Mr Wielockx appealed against the refusal of the Netherlands tax inspector to allow the deductions.

In a case with facts not dissimilar from *Bachmann*, the ECJ accepted the principle that different tax rules for non-residents do not amount to discrimination per se. However, notwithstanding that in *Bachmann* they had accepted the importance of national tax cohesion, they found this time against the Netherlands tax authorities.

The Court prayed in aid of the Double Taxation Convention between the Netherlands and Belgium. Under that Convention as under the OECD Model Convention, it was agreed that while a state taxed all pensions received by residents of its territory, it would conversely waive the right to tax pensions received abroad even if they derived from contributions paid in its territory which had been treated as deductible. The argument for fiscal cohesion as between tax deductible contributions and taxed receipts which won the day in *Bachmann* was therefore deemed not to be available to the Netherlands authorities because that cohesion had been 'negotiated away' in the Double Tax Convention.

The next case of *Werner*[9] forcibly demonstrates that the first requirement in all these cases involving income tax which come before the ECJ is that the taxpayer must convince the ECJ that the facts bring him squarely within one of the 'freedoms' contained in the Treaty such as, for example Article 48 (freedom of movement of workers) or Article 52 (freedom of establishment). In *Werner* the taxpayer failed so to do and lost the case.

Mr Werner was a German national who worked as a dentist in Germany but who lived with his wife in the Netherlands. Under German law, persons resident or ordinarily resident in Germany were liable to income tax on the whole of their income (unlimited taxation) and were entitled in the case of married taxpayers to a preferential regime known as a 'splitting tariff' and to certain deductions. The taxpayer claimed the benefit of the tariff and the deductions but was refused by the German authorities because he was not resident or ordinarily resident in Germany.

In finding against Mr Werner, the Court noted that he was a German national and he practised in Germany. The only foreign element was the fact of his residence in the Netherlands. Mr Werner had not been subject to any restrictions on his ability as a German national to establish himself in Germany. He was established in his own state. He did not at any time try to establish himself in a state other than his own. Article 52 only applies where there is some foreign element. The case was quite different from *Biehl*,[10] where Mr Biehl was a German national subject to Luxembourg legislation. It appears, therefore, that discrimination under Article 52 can only be shown where the taxpayer, as the national of one state, is discriminated against by the taxation legislation of another state.

The case of *Asscher*[11] was in a similar vein to *Bachmann* where the taxpayer lived in a frontier area. Mr Asscher was a Netherlands national who was resident for tax purposes in Belgium. He worked in the Netherlands as a director of a Netherlands private company and also in Belgium as a director of a Belgian private company. He was taxed in Belgium on his Belgian income and in the Netherlands on his Netherlands income where his income was less than 90 per cent of his total income from all sources.

Under the tax law of the Netherlands, residents of the Netherlands and those who although non-residents in the Netherlands received more than 90 per cent of their worldwide income from the Netherlands, paid tax on a tranche of income at the rate of 13 per cent. Other non-residents like Mr Asscher, whose income from the Netherlands was less than 90 per cent of their worldwide income were taxed on the same tranche of income at the higher rate of 25 per cent. Mr Asscher argued before the ECJ that he was thus discriminated against in that his freedom of establishment as provided by Article 52 of the Treaty was restricted.

The Court again accepted that residents and non-residents may be treated differently in principle without infringing the discrimination provisions of the Treaty and that such differences can be justified by the need to maintain the cohesion of member states' direct tax systems. However, it held in the Asscher case that there was no 'objective difference' between the situations of Mr Asscher and those non-residents who were deemed to be resident in the Netherlands because they received more than 90 per cent of their worldwide income from the Netherlands.

Another of the 'frontier cases' was *Gilly*.[12] Mr and Mrs Gilly resided in France, near the German border. Mr Gilly, a French national, taught in a state school in France. Mrs Gilly, a German national, but also a French national by marriage, taught in a state school in Germany but near the French border.

The taxation of Mrs Gilly's income was governed by the extremely complex provisions of the French/German convention for the avoidance of double taxation. The effect of those provisions was that initially she was taxed in both countries but then she was given a credit equal to the amount of the French tax on the relevant income received in Germany.

Since the German tax scale was more progressive than the French tax scale, and since Mrs Gilly's personal and family circumstances were not taken into account in Germany whereas they were taken into account in France, it turned out that the French tax credit was less than the tax actually paid in Germany.

Mrs Gilly contended before the ECJ that the provisions of the French/German convention caused discrimination and excessive taxation incompatible with Article 48 of the Treaty. She argued that if she had possessed only French nationality and not dual nationality, her tax liability would have been governed by a different Article of the convention whereby the income of 'frontier workers' was taxed in their state of residence, in her case in France.

The ECJ rejected her arguments. The French/German authorities, in framing their convention, had chosen the criterion of nationality for the purpose of allocating their powers of taxation as between themselves and to eliminate double taxation. That did not constitute discrimination. Also the Convention was based on international practice and on the OECD Model Convention. Further, whether the tax treatment of the taxpayer was favourable or unfavourable was governed not by which Article of the French/German convention imposed tax upon her, but by the differing levels of taxation in the two respective states, a matter within the competence of the state itself.

In *Zurstrassen*[13], Mr Zurstrassen, a Belgian National, worked in Luxembourg, where he earned 98 per cent of his income. His wife, from whom he was not separated or divorced, lived in Belgium, where he spent his weekends. Spouses residing in Luxembourg were assessed to tax jointly which was levied at a lower rate than for single persons. Mr Zurstrassen was assessed to tax at the single person's rate on the basis that he did not live with his spouse in Luxembourg. He appealed, arguing that the assessment was discriminatory as it placed him and his wife in a less advantageous position to couples that were resident in Luxembourg. The national court stayed the proceedings pending a reference to the ECJ for a preliminary ruling as to whether the EC Treaty Article 48(2) (now after amendment Article 39(2) EC), and Council Regulation 1612/68 Article 7(2) precluded income tax rules which stipulated that the applicable tax rate was conditional on both spouses being residents of the same Member State and which denied a tax advantage to a worker resident in the Member Sate where he earned virtually all his income on the basis that his spouse was resident in another Member State.

The Court held, giving a preliminary ruling, that the residence condition was contrary to Article 48(2) EC as it favoured Luxembourg nationals over nationals of other Member States who worked in Luxembourg, and that Article 48(2) EC and Article 7(2) of the Regulation precluded an income tax assessment that was conditional on both spouses residing in the same Member State where this meant that an advantageous tax rate was denied to a resident worker because his spouse resided in another Member State.

In *Imperial Chemical Industries plc v Colmer.*[14] ICI and Wellcome had formed a consortium in which ICI participated as to 49 per cent and Wellcome as to 51 per cent. The consortium owned the share capital of a trading company, CAHH, incorporated in the UK which held all the shares in 22 out of 23 subsidiary companies. Four of these subsidiaries were resident in the UK, six in other member states of the EU and the remainder outside the EU. One of the UK subsidiaries, CAHH purported to surrender to ICI substantial trading losses thus allowing ICI to claim group relief on its 49 per cent share under section 258(2) and (8) of the Income and Corporation Taxes Act 1970 (now ss 402–413 of TA 1988). The Inspector of Taxes refused the claim on the grounds that CAHH was not a holding company as defined in the legislation because its business did not consist wholly or mainly in the holding of shares or securities in trading companies resident in the UK.

The case went to the ECJ with ICI arguing that the Inspector's ruling and the terms of s 258(2) discriminated against the companies and infringed Article 52 of the Treaty (freedom of establishment).

The UK government argued that the discrimination was justified, first because the legislation was designed to reduce the risk of tax avoidance arising from the opportunity for members of a consortium to channel the charges of non-resident subsidiaries to resident subsidiaries; and second, to prevent the reduction in tax revenue caused by the existence of non-resident subsidiaries since the Revenue could not tax profits made by subsidiaries located outside the UK in order to offset the revenue lost by granting relief on losses incurred by resident subsidiaries.

The Court rejected both arguments pointing out that the establishment of a company outside the UK does not of itself entail tax avoidance and that diminution of a member state's tax revenue cannot be regarded as a matter of overriding general interest so as to justify treatment incompatible with Article 52 of the Treaty. In addition, while the ECJ accepted the need to maintain the cohesion of the tax systems of the member states, in the present case, unlike *Bachmann*, there was no 'direct link' between the consortium relief granted for losses incurred by a resident subsidiary and the taxation of the profits made by non-resident subsidiaries.

Following the above decision of the ECJ in *Colmer*, ICI returned to the English courts again to try to obtain group relief. The company failed in the House of Lords which held that since the majority of the subsidiaries of the holding company were resident in non-EU states EU law did not affect the application of s 258.[15]

The principle of the ECJ's decision in *Colmer* however stands and the UK Government's Finance Act 2000 contains a provision to change UK law to conform to that decision.[16]

That Finance Act also changes UK law[17] to comply with the ECJ's decision in the *St Gobain* case[18] where the ECJ held that there was discrimination within the EU Treaty where a German branch of a French company was treated less favourably in Germany in respect of foreign tax than a Germany-resident company. The change in UK law amends TA 1988 ss 790 and 794 to allow credit relief for foreign tax to non-resident persons who have branches or agencies in the United Kingdom.

In the *Royal Bank of Scotland plc v Greece*[19] the ECJ was asked whether the imposition of differential tax treatment on foreign companies was in conformity with the EC Treaty Art. 52. The Greek income tax code contained two levels of company taxation. Companies having their seat in Greece could be taxed at either 35 per cent or 40 per cent depending on their legal form and the nature of their issued shares, whereas companies having their seat outside Greece were taxed only at the higher rate.

The ECJ decided that (a) a difference in tax treatment between two categories of taxpayer may constitute discrimination where there was no objective difference to justify different treatment as between the two different categories. The Greek legislation introduced discrimination against companies having their seat in another member state in so far as it imposed on them, irrespective of their legal form and the nature of the shares issued, a rate of tax higher than the rate imposed on companies whose seat was in Greece, and (b) EC Treaty Art. 52 and Art. 58 were to be interpreted as precluding legislation of a member state which, in the case of companies with a seat in another member state and carrying on business in the first member state through a permanent establishment situated there, excluded the possibility, accorded only to companies with a seat in the first member state, of benefiting from a lower rate of tax, where there was no objective difference justifying such a different treatment.

In *Metallgesellschaft Ltd v IRC* and *Hoechst AG v IRC*[20] the question before the ECJ (by way of a preliminary ruling) was whether an EU parent company resident in a member state other than the UK, but with a UK resident subsidiary, had been discriminated against when the UK Inland Revenue refused to allow it to make a group income election for dividend payments in circumstances where a UK resident parent company would have been able to make such an election. Since the UK subsidiary was able to set off advance corporation tax against its mainstream corporation tax the only disadvantage, or discrimination as claimed by Hoechst, suffered by the UK resident subsidiary of the non-resident parent, as compared to a UK resident subsidiary of a UK parent, was that it paid its corporation tax earlier. Its claim therefore was for the loss of the use of the money, that is for interest.

The ECJ found for Hoechst and against the UK Inland Revenue on the ground that the UK's system of corporation tax provided a benefit to UK resident parent companies, which it denied to parent companies resident in another member state and thus discriminated against a national of another member state.

The Court rejected the argument based on the need to maintain the cohesion of the UK tax system and also held that it mattered not that the Hoechst claim was for financial loss arising from the loss of the use of the sums paid early.

1   *EC Commission v United Kingdom* [1991] ECR 4611 at para 12.
2   *Finanzant v Schumacher* [1995] STC 306 at 314.
3   [1987] 1 CMLR 401.
4   [1993] I ECR 4017.
5   [1994] STC 855.
6   [1995] STC 306.
7   [2001] STC 331.
8   [1995] STC 876.
9   [1996] STC 961.
10 [1991] STC 515.
11 [1996] STC 1025.
12 [1998] STC 1014.
13 [2001] STC 1102.
14 [1998] STC 874.
15 [1999] STC 1089.
16 Finance Act 2000 Section 97 and Schedule 27.
17 Ibid 2000 Schedule 30 para 4.
18 Compagnie de St Gobain Finanzamt Aachen Innenstudt (Case C-307/97).
19 [1999] 2 CMLR 973
20 [2001] STC 452

9.03 Conclusion

The ECJ will, in certain circumstances, strike down provisions in the income tax laws of member states notwithstanding that the Treaty establishing the European Community does not have a general jurisdiction in the area of income tax.

The ECJ will interfere where the income tax laws of member states are deemed to discriminate against certain 'freedoms' enshrined in the Treaty, such as the freedom of movement of workers (Article 48) and the freedom of establishment (Article 52). A national taxpayer who takes a case to the Court will need to show that his situation falls within one of the 'freedom' provisions of the Treaty as in the *Werner* case. If he fails to do so then the case falls at the first hurdle.

Discrimination can occur where the provisions of national tax laws treat residents and non-residents differently and these differences cause the kind of discrimination which is prohibited by one of the 'freedoms'.

The Court has now accepted that the different tax treatment of residents and non-residents is fundamental to national tax systems and a failure to recognise this could damage the cohesion of those systems.

However, mindful of its position as the guardian of the Treaty and the *acqui communitaire* of the EU, the Court will not be slow in accepting arguments which on the facts of the particular case indicate that if the court found for the taxpayer the cohesion of the member state's tax system would not be damaged (as in the *Bachmann* and *Gilly* cases).

So far the Court has refused to interfere where the taxpayer in effect complains that he has been discriminated against because of differing tax rates in member states (as in the *Gilly* case). How the jurisprudence of the Court develops in future will depend on the facts of the case before the Court, the *acqui communitaire* of the EU at the relevant time and the strength of political pressure for tax harmonisation within the EU.

CHAPTER 10

Residence and e-commerce

New technology

10.01 Introduction

In a discussion paper published in1996[1] the United States Treasury argues that the growth of e-commerce will increase the importance of residence-based taxation since identifying the location of the source of income becomes more difficult in cyberspace. The difficulties created for the tax system by the new technology become particularly acute when it is necessary to identify the source of trading income. Over the years it has been generally accepted that trading income should be taxed in the source country provided that the business and the income can be attributed to a certain level of physical presence in that country.[2] The concept of 'permanent establishment' which features in most double taxation treaties reflects this.[3]

---

1 Levine and Weintraub, The Importance of Treaties and the OECD in Electronic Commerce, Tax Planning International, 1 (9), 1999.
2 Maguire, Taxation of E-Commerce, International Tax Review, 10 (8), 1999.
3 See **10.06** below.

10.02 The website and its server

The problem of identifying the source of trading income is highlighted by the trading potential which is afforded by the use of a website and its server. An individual or a company resident outside the United Kingdom can obtain quick and easy access to the UK domestic market by acquiring a website and a server; the server hosts the website. The website would comprise a combination of software and electronic data which would be stored and operated by the server on a computer or on a number of computers. While the website is not tangible property, the server itself which hosts the website comprises equipment which has a physical location. The same non-resident individual or company which owns the website could own or alternatively rent or license the server equipment, although a more likely scenario is for the web-site to be hosted by an Independent Service Provider. The server might or might not be resident in the United Kingdom.

Old law

10.03 Non-resident individuals

A non-resident individual is chargeable to UK income tax on profits derived from a trade carried on within the United Kingdom.[1] The non-resident can be charged to income tax through a resident representative where that representative constitutes a 'branch or agency' within TA 1995 s 126. Both the individual non-resident and the resident representative can also be held jointly responsible. Where the non-resident is held not to have a resident representative, the non-resident is still chargeable to income tax but there could well be problems of enforcing the charge.[2]

1 TA 1988 s 18.
2 See **8.08** above.

10.04 Non-resident companies

A non-resident company trading in the United Kingdom is chargeable to corporation tax on the profits of that trade only if it is carrying on that trade through a branch or agency in the United Kingdom.[1] If there is no such branch or agency then the non-resident company will not be chargeable to corporation tax on the profits of that trade. TA 1988 s 834(1) defines a 'branch' as 'any factorship, agency, receivership, branch or management'.

1 TA 1988 s 11(1).

Old law meets new technology

10.05 Branch or agency

As explained at **10.03** and **10.04** above, trading through a branch or agency brings a non-resident company trader within the charge to tax and facilitates the collection of income tax in the case of a non-resident individual trader. A website could hardly come within the definition of a branch or agency but a website and its server could, it is submitted, come within that definition in certain circumstances; for example where the provision of the server facility was located in the UK and where the server authorised the contract with the consumer, processed the payment details and issued instructions for delivery.

10.06 Permanent establishment

Where a non-resident who trades in the United Kingdom is located in a country which has a double taxation treaty with the United Kingdom then the domestic law, such as explained at **10.03** and **10.04** above would usually be superseded by the law of the treaty. While the terms of such treaties may differ from country to country, treaties which are entered into between the developed countries usually follow the OECD Model Convention on Income and Capital.[1]

Article 7 of the OECD Model is concerned with business profits and provides that an 'enterprise of a Contracting State' shall be taxable only in that state unless it carries on business in the other contracting state through a 'permanent establishment' situated in that other contracting state.

Article 5 of the Model Convention defines 'permanent establishment' as including a place of management, a branch, an office, a factory, a building site, a workshop, a farm, or premises used as a sales outlet. A permanent establishment, as defined, requires a fixed place of business. The German Tax Court recently held that a remote-controlled pipeline located in Germany constituted a permanent establishment therein.[2] But what about a server used for electronic commerce, can it constitute a permanent establishment?

The UK Inland Revenue set out its view recently in a press release:[3]

'The Organisation for Economic Co-operation and Development has been reviewing with the business community the long term future of the 'permanent establishment' concept – the threshold in the Organisation for Economic Co-operation and Development's model tax treaty below which a country will not tax non-residents carrying on a business in that country . . .

Permanent establishment is a longstanding concept. It is tried and tested. And it is widely supported. As yet, we do not know enough about how e-commerce will develop for anyone to make reasoned decisions on whether or not to move away from it. But now is clearly the time for the debate to begin.

In the meantime, early decisions are needed on the status of websites and servers under the existing rules of permanent establishment. Businesses need to know where they stand in order to make investment decisions and calculate their tax liabilities . . .

In the United Kingdom, we take the view that a website of itself is not a permanent establishment. And we take the view that a server is insufficient of itself to constitute a permanent establishment of a business that is conducting e-commerce through a website on the server. We take that view regardless of whether the server is owned, rented or otherwise at the disposal of the business.'

While the press release attempts to give the impression of clarity and definitiveness, it is of little assistance to determine whether in a particular situation a non-resident is trading in the UK through a website and a server and whether the server in a particular situation constitutes a permanent establishment. The 'escape' words for the Inland Revenue are 'of itself' in the sentence – 'And we take the view that a server is insufficient of itself to constitute a permanent establishment'. But depending on the specific transactions it carries out a server could well be a fixed place of business within Article 5 of the Model Convention.

A better attempt to introduce some clarity is made by the OECD itself when it recently published new paragraphs to be added to its Commentary on Article 5 of the Model Convention. They are worth reproducing:[4]

1 There has been some discussion as to whether the mere use of computer equipment located in a country through which electronic commerce operations are carried on in that country could constitute a permanent establishment. That question raises a number of issues in relation to the provisions of the article.

2 First, whilst fixed automated equipment operated by an enterprise and located in a

country may constitute a permanent establishment in that country (see paragraph 10 [of the existing Commentary]), a distinction needs to be made between computer equipment, which could thus constitute a permanent establishment in these circumstances, and the data and software which is used by that equipment. For instance, an Internet website may be seen as a combination of software and electronic data which is stored on and operated by a server. The website itself does not involve any tangible property and therefore cannot itself constitute a 'place of business' ('installation d'affaires' in the French version) as there is 'no facility such as premises or, in certain circumstances, machinery or equipment' (see paragraph 2 [of the existing Commentary] above) as far as only the software and data constituting that website is concerned. On the other hand, the server through which that website is operated is a piece of equipment which itself needs a physical location and may thus, if it is fixed within the meaning of paragraph 1, constitute a 'fixed place of business' of the enterprise that operates it.

3   That distinction is important since the enterprise that operates a server on which a website is hosted is often different from the enterprise that carries on business through that website. Unless the server itself may be said to be a fixed place of business of the latter enterprise, e.g. where a server situated at a particular location is rented to the enterprise that carries on business through the website, the mere operation of the website of that enterprise from a server located in that country cannot constitute a permanent establishment for that enterprise. For example, it is common for the website through which an enterprise carries on its business to be hosted on the server of an Internet Service Provider (ISP). In that case, the server and its location are not at the disposal of the enterprise, even if the enterprise has been able to decide that its website should be hosted on that particular server; in fact, the enterprise does not even have a physical presence at that place since the website does not involve tangible assets. Thus, the enterprise cannot be considered to have acquired a place of business by virtue of that arrangement (the possible application of the provisions of paragraph 5 is discussed below).

4   Second, it is not relevant whether the equipment used for electronic commerce operations in a particular country is or is not operated and maintained by personnel who are residents of that country or visit that country for that purpose. Automated equipment that does not require on-site human intervention for its operation may still constitute a permanent establishment.

5   Third, computer equipment may only constitute a permanent establishment if it meets the requirement of being fixed. In the example referred to in paragraph 2, what matters is not the possibility of the server being moved around, but whether it is in fact so moved. Therefore, in order to constitute a fixed place of business, a server will need to be located at a certain place for a sufficient period of time so as to become fixed within the meaning of paragraph 1.

6   Fourth, as already noted, it is common that access to the Internet is provided by Internet Service Providers which, among the services that they provide, host websites of other enterprises on their own servers. In that case, the issue may arise as to whether paragraph 5 may apply to deem such ISPs to constitute permanent establishments of the enterprises that carry on electronic commerce through websites operated through the servers owned and operated by these ISPs. While this could be the case in very unusual circumstances, paragraph 5 will generally not be applicable because the ISPs will not constitute agents of the enterprises to which the websites belong, because these ISPs will not have the authority to conclude contracts in the name of these

enterprises and will not regularly conclude such contracts or because they will constitute independent agents acting in the ordinary course of their business, as evidenced by the fact that they host the websites of many different enterprises. It is also clear that since the website through which an enterprise carries on its business is not itself a 'person' as defined in Article 3, paragraph 5 cannot apply to deem a permanent establishment to exist by virtue of the website being an agent of the enterprise for purposes of that paragraph.

7 Finally, no permanent establishment may be considered to exist where the electronic commerce operations carried on through computer equipment located in a country are restricted to the preparatory or auxiliary activities covered by paragraph 4. The question of whether particular activities performed through computer equipment fall within paragraph 4 needs to be examined on a case-by-case basis having regard to the various functions performed by the enterprise through the software and electronic data stored or operated through that equipment. Where the functions performed through the computer equipment include activities that form in themselves an essential and significant part of the commercial activity of an enterprise as a whole, these would go beyond the activities covered by paragraph 4 and if the equipment constituted a fixed place of business of the enterprise (as discussed in paragraphs 1 to 5 above), this equipment would therefore be a permanent establishment of the enterprise.

10.07 Conclusion

The OECD's new paragraphs to the commentary to Article 5 of the Model Convention as reproduced at **10.06** above represent the best effort made so far to relate the 'old law' to the 'new technology' with regard to the concept of permanent establishment. The new paragraphs, it is submitted, provide useful guidance for deciding also whether a website and a server can constitute a 'branch or agency' for the purposes of domestic UK law.

1 Simon's Direct Tax Service F 4.402.
2 Federal Tax Bulletin, 1997 II p12.
3 IR press release, 11 April 2000.
4 Owens, Progress Report: Taxation and Electronic Commerce, European Taxation, November 1999; OECD website at www.oecd.org/daf/fa.

RESIDENTS AND NON-RESIDENTS – LIABILITY TO TAX IN THE UK

IR 20 (11 April 2000)

The text of this booklet is Crown copyright.

Contents

PREFACE

The notes in this booklet reflect the law and practice at October 1999. They are not binding in law and do not affect rights of appeal about your own tax.

You should bear in mind that the booklet offers general guidance on how the rules apply, but whether the guidance is appropriate in a particular case will depend on all the facts of that case. If you have any difficulty in applying the rules in your own case, you should consult an Inland Revenue tax office – see paragraphs 7, 9 of the Introduction on contacting the Inland Revenue.

Some practices explained in this booklet are concessions made by the Inland Revenue. A concession will not be given in any case where an attempt is made to use it for tax avoidance. Where the booklet mentions a concession, the reference given (for example 'Extra-statutory concession A11') is the number of the concession in booklet IR1 'Extra-statutory concessions', which provides further details.

INTRODUCTION

General

1   Broadly the United Kingdom (UK) charges tax on –

- income arising in the UK, whether or not the person to whom it belongs is resident in the UK;
- income arising outside the UK which belongs to people resident in the UK;
- gains accruing on the disposal of assets anywhere in the world which belong to people resident or ordinarily resident in the UK.

2   Special rules apply in some circumstances, but generally the amount of income tax and capital gains tax you have to pay depends on whether you are resident and/or ordinarily resident in the UK, and in some cases on your domicile.

3   The first part of this booklet explains what is meant by residence, ordinary residence and domicile. The second part explains how these factors affect how much income tax and capital gains tax you have to pay in the UK, and how the normal rules of taxation may be modified in some cases where a double taxation agreement applies.

4   The third part of the booklet outlines the rules for payment of UK national insurance contributions for individuals going abroad or coming to the UK.

5   The booklet is only concerned with individuals. It does not cover the position of companies, trusts, clubs, societies or other legal persons. Nor does it deal with inheritance tax. Booklet IHT 18 (Inheritance tax. Foreign aspects) explains how your domicile can affect the inheritance tax position if you transfer property, normally on or within seven years of death.

Definitions used in this booklet

6   Several terms used in this booklet have a particular meaning, as follows –

– Tax year	The 12 months starting with 6 April in one year and ending with 5 April in the following year. For example, the tax year 1999–2000 runs from 6 April 1999 to 5 April 2000.
– United Kingdom	England, Wales, Scotland and Northern Ireland, including the territorial sea (that is, waters within 12 nautical miles of the shore).
– Abroad/overseas	Anywhere outside the UK. The Channel Islands and the Isle of Man are abroad. (except in the limited context of certain bilateral Social Security Agreements – see paragraph 11.1)

Contacting the Inland Revenue

7 If you have any queries on your tax position, you should contact your tax office. Your employer will normally be able to tell you the address. If you have just come to the UK, or for any other reason you do not know which office deals with your tax affairs, you should write to your local tax office – the address is in the phone book under 'Inland Revenue'. If you have a national insurance number, please give it in your letter.

8 A system of self-assessment applies to individuals from 1996–97. This requires you to work out for yourself what tax you owe (calculating your own tax is, however, optional if you submit your tax return by a certain date, normally 30 September following the tax year). Initially, we will accept and process the figures in your return – except for any obvious mistakes, which we will correct. After processing, we will check all cases and select some for further examination.

We will provide guidance to help you calculate your tax liability or make any claim. We will ask you to give sufficient detail of your income and circumstances to allow us to check your tax return.

9 In a number of places this booklet refers to matters that are dealt with by specialist offices of the Inland Revenue. These offices and their addresses are as follows –

Financial Intermediaries and Claims Office (FICO), Bootle (Residence Advice and Liabilities – Unit 373), St John's House, Merton Road, Bootle, Merseyside, England L69 9BB (Telephone number 0151 472 6196. If phoning from abroad, 44 151 472 6196)

Financial Intermediaries and Claims Office (FICO), (Non-Resident Claims), Fitz Roy House, PO Box 46, England NG2 1BD (Telephone number 0115 974 2000. If phoning from abroad, 44 115 974 2000)

HM Inspector of Taxes Cardiff 4 (Foreign Section), Ty-Glas, Llanishen, Cardiff, Wales CF4 5GN (Telephone number 029 2023 5000)

Foreign Compliance, Compliance Centre 1, Queensway House, East Kilbride, Glasgow, Scotland G79 1AA (Telephone number 01355 275877/ 275733/ 275795)

Foreign Entertainers Unit, Prince's Gate, 2–6 Homer Road, Solihull, West Midlands, England, B91 3WG (Telephone number 0121 606 2861/2/3)

HM Inspector of Taxes Cardiff 1, Phase 2 Building, Ty-Glas, Llanishen, Cardiff, Wales CF4 5FN (Telephone number 029 2032 6077/8/9)

National Insurance Contributions Office, International Services, Benton Park Road, Newcastle upon Tyne NE98 1ZZ (Telephone number 06451 54811. If phoning from abroad, 44 191 2254811)

PART I
MEANING OF RESIDENCE, ORDINARY RESIDENCE AND DOMICILE FOR TAX PURPOSES

CHAPTER 1
RESIDENCE AND ORDINARY RESIDENCE

1.1 The terms residence and ordinary residence are not defined in the Taxes Acts. The guidelines to their meaning in this Chapter and in Chapters 2 (residence status of those leaving the UK) and 3 (those coming to the UK) are largely based on rulings of the Courts. This booklet sets out the main factors that are taken into account, but we can only make a decision on your residence status on the facts in your particular case.

As mentioned in paragraph 1.4, even if you are resident (or ordinarily resident) in the UK under these rules, the terms of a double taxation agreement with another country might affect your final tax position if, for example, you are resident in both that country and the UK.

Residence

1.2   To be regarded as resident in the UK you must normally be physically present in the country at some time in the tax year. You will always be resident if you are here for 183 days or more in the tax year. There are no exceptions to this. You count the total number of days you spend in the UK – it does not matter if you come and go several times during the year or if you are here for one stay of 183 days or more. If you are here for less than 183 days, you may still be treated as resident for the year under other tests (see Chapter 3, and in particular paragraph 3.3).

The normal rule is that days of arrival in and departure from the UK are ignored in counting the days spent in the UK, in all the various cases where calculations have to be made to determine your residence position – see for example paragraphs 2.2, 3.3 and 3.4 and the examples in 2.10 and 3.6. (This rule is not relevant to the concessionary split year treatment described in paragraphs 1.5 –1.6, where a person coming to or leaving the UK part way through a tax year is resident from the date of arrival or to the date of departure.)

Ordinary residence

1.3   If you are resident in the UK year after year, you are treated as ordinarily resident here. You may be resident but not ordinarily resident in the UK for a tax year if, for example, you normally live outside the UK but are in this country for 183 days or more in the year. Or you may be ordinarily resident but not resident for a tax year if, for example, you usually live in the UK but have gone abroad for a long holiday and do not set foot in the UK during that year

Residence in both the UK and another country

1.4   It is possible to be resident (or ordinarily resident) in both the UK and some other country (or countries) at the same time. If you are resident (or ordinarily resident) in another country, this does not mean that you cannot also be resident (or ordinarily resident) in the UK. Where, however, you are resident both in the UK and a country with which the UK has a double taxation agreement, there may be special provisions in the agreement for treating you as a resident of only one of the countries for the purposes of the agreement (see paragraph 9.2).

Leaving, or coming to, the UK part way through a tax year

1.5   Strictly, you are taxed as a UK resident for the whole of a tax year if you are resident here for any part of it. But if you leave or come to the UK part way through a tax year, the year may, by concession (Extra-statutory concession A11), be split. Where this applies, your tax liabilities on income which are affected by tax residence will be calculated on the basis of the period of your actual residence here during the year (see also paragraph 5.4). This has the same effect as splitting the tax year into resident and not resident periods.

1.6   Split year treatment applies where –

- you have been not ordinarily resident in the UK and you come to live here permanently or to stay for at least two years. You are taxed as a resident only from the date of your arrival; or
- you have been resident in the UK* and you leave to live abroad permanently or for a period of at least three years, and on your departure are not ordinarily resident in the UK. You are taxed as a resident only up to and including the date of your departure; or
- you have been resident in the UK* and you leave to take up full-time employment abroad, and you meet certain conditions (see paragraphs 2.2 –2.3). You are taxed as a resident only up to and including the date of your departure (and from the date when you return to the UK).

*other than resident only as a short term visitor – see paragraph 3.3

1.7 For certain types of income of a non-resident the UK tax charged is limited to any tax deducted before payment (see paragraphs 5.15, 6.3 and 6.11). This only applies, however, to complete years of non-residence. Where the tax year is split, the limitation does not apply to the part of the year for which you are treated as though you were not resident.

Split year treatment does not apply if you come to the UK as a short term visitor, or if you come for only limited periods with no intention to live here permanently or to stay for at least two years. (See paragraph 3.3 for details of the rules that apply in this case.)

CHAPTER 2
LEAVING THE UK

Short absences

2.1 You are resident and ordinarily resident in the UK if you usually live in this country and only go abroad for short periods – for example, on holiday or on business trips.

Working abroad

2.2 If you leave the UK to work full-time abroad under a contract of employment, you are treated as not resident and not ordinarily resident if you meet all the following conditions –

– your absence from the UK and your employment abroad both last for at least a whole tax year;
– during your absence any visits you make to the UK;
    (i)   total less than 183 days in any tax year, and
    (ii) average less than 91 days a tax year. (The average is taken over the period of absence up to a maximum of four years – see paragraph 2.10. Any days spent in the UK because of exceptional circumstances beyond your control, for example the illness of yourself or a member of your immediate family, are not normally counted for this purpose.)

2.3 If you meet all the conditions in paragraph 2.2, you are treated as not resident and not ordinarily resident in the UK from the day after you leave the UK to the day before you return to the UK at the end of your employment abroad. You are treated as coming to the UK permanently on the day you return from your employment abroad and as resident and ordinarily resident from that date.

If there is a break in full-time employment, or some other change in your circumstances during the period you are overseas, we would have to review the position to decide whether you still meet the conditions in paragraph 2.2. If at the end of one employment you returned temporarily to the UK, planning to go abroad again after a very short stay in this country, we may review your residence status in the light of all the circumstances of your employment abroad and your return to the UK.

If you do not meet all the conditions in paragraph 2.2, you remain resident and ordinarily resident unless paragraphs 2.8 – 2.9 apply to you. Special rules apply to employees of the European Community (see paragraph 2.14).

2.4 The treatment in paragraph 2.3 will also apply if you leave the UK to work full-time in a trade, profession or vocation and you meet conditions similar to those in paragraph 2.2.

Meaning of full-time

2.5 There is no precise definition of when employment overseas is 'full-time', and a decision in a particular case will depend on all the facts. Where your employment involves a standard pattern of hours, we will regard it as full time if the hours you work each week clearly compare with those in a typical UK working week. If your job has no formal structure or no fixed number of working days, we will look at the nature of the job, local conditions and practices in the particular occupation to decide if the job is full-time.

If you have several part-time jobs overseas at the same time, we may be able to treat this as full-time employment. That might be so if, for example, you have several appointments with the same employer or group of companies, and perhaps also where you have simultaneous employment and self-employment overseas. But if you have a main employment abroad and some unconnected occupation in the UK at the same time, we will consider whether the extent of the UK activities was consistent with the overseas employment being full-time.

Accompanying spouse

2.6   If you are the husband or wife of someone who leaves the UK within the terms of paragraph 2.2 or 2.4 and you accompany or later join your spouse abroad, you may also by concession (Extra-statutory concession A78) be treated as not resident and not ordinarily resident from the day after your departure to the day before your return, even if you are not yourself in full-time employment abroad. This applies where –

- you are abroad for a complete tax year, and
- during your absence any visits you make to the UK –
    (i)   total less than 183 days in the tax year, or
    (ii)   average less than 91 days a tax year. (The average is taken over the period of absence up to a maximum of four years – see paragraph 2.10. Any days spent in the UK because of exceptional circumstances beyond your control, for example the illness of yourself or a member of your immediate family, are not normally counted for this purpose).

Where the tax years of your departure or return are split in this way, your tax liabilities which are affected by residence status are calculated on the basis of the period you are treated as resident in the UK.

Leaving the UK permanently or indefinitely

2.7   If you go abroad permanently, you will be treated as remaining resident and ordinarily resident if your visits to the UK average 91 days or more a year – see paragraph 2.10. Any days spent in the UK because of exceptional circumstances beyond your control, for example the illness of yourself or your immediate family, are not normally counted for the purposes of averaging your visits.

2.8   If you claim that you are no longer resident and ordinarily resident, we may ask you to give some evidence that you have left the UK permanently, or to live outside the UK for three years or more. This evidence might be, for example, that you have taken steps to acquire accommodation abroad to live in as a permanent home, and if you continue to have property in the UK for your use, the reason is consistent with your stated aim of living abroad permanently or for three years or more. If you have left the UK permanently or for at least three years, you will be treated as not resident and not ordinarily resident from the day after the date of your departure providing –

- your absence from the UK has covered at least a whole tax year, and
- your visits to the UK since leaving
    (i)   have totalled less than 183 days in any tax year; and
    (ii)   have averaged less than 91 days a tax year. (The average is taken over the period of absence up to a maximum of four years – see paragraph 2.10. Any days spent in the UK because of exceptional circumstances beyond your control, for example the illness of yourself or a member of your immediate family, are not normally counted for this purpose.)

2.9 If you do not have this evidence, but you have gone abroad for a settled purpose (this would include a fixed object or intention in which you are going to be engaged for an extended period of time), you will be treated as not resident and not ordinarily resident from the day after the date of your departure providing –

- your absence from the UK has covered at least a whole tax year, and
- your visits to the UK since leaving –
  - (i)   have totalled less than 183 days in any tax year; and
  - (ii) have averaged less than 91 days a tax year.

If you have not gone abroad for a settled purpose, you will be treated as remaining resident and ordinarily resident in the UK, but your status can be reviewed if –

- your absence actually covers three years from your departure, or
- evidence becomes available to show that you have left the UK permanently

providing in either case your visits to the UK since leaving have totalled less than 183 days in any tax year and have averaged less than 91 days a tax year.

Calculating annual average visits

2.10 If it is necessary to calculate your annual average visits to the UK, the method is as follows –

$$\frac{\text{Total visits to the UK (in days)}}{\text{Total period since leaving (in days)}} \times 365 = \text{annual average visits}$$

For this purpose days spent in the UK in the tax year before the date of your original departure are excluded.

Suppose for example you leave the UK on 5 October 1997. The first review of the average of your visits is made after 5 April 1999, and takes account of your visits between those two dates. If you visited the UK for 30 days between 6 October 1997 and 5 April 1998 and for 50 days in 1998–99, the annual average is –

$$\frac{30 + 50}{182 + 365} \times 365 = 53.38 \text{ days}$$

If you continue to remain outside the UK, the annual average is calculated as follows in reviews after 5 April in subsequent years –

- after 5 April 2000 – include visits from 5 October 1997 to 5 April 2000;
- after 5 April 2001 – include visits from 5 October 1997 to 5 April 2001;
- after 5 April 2002 – include visits from 6 April 1998 to 5 April 2002.

After the third review the year of departure is dropped from the calculation. At each subsequent review the oldest year is dropped, so that there is a rolling period of four years being reviewed.

However, if during your absence the pattern of your visits varied substantially year by year, it might be appropriate to look at the absence as being made up of separate periods for the purpose of calculating average visits. This might be necessary if, for example, a shift in the pattern of your visits suggested a change of circumstances, which altered how we viewed your residence status.

Contacting the Inland Revenue

2.11   You should let us know when you leave the UK (other than for short trips as in paragraph 2.1). You will normally be asked to complete form P85, which will help to determine your residence status.

Tax treatment after leaving the UK

2.12   For details of the tax treatment of your earned income (such as earnings from employment) after you have ceased to be resident in the UK, see Chapter 5 and in particular paragraphs 5.1 – 5.3 and the tables at 5.19 – 5.21. For similar details in the case of any investment income you may have (for example, interest arising in the UK), see Chapter 6 and in particular paragraph 6.3

2.13   Some of special provisions applying to those who leave the UK are dealt with as follows –

- earnings of those who come to the UK part way through a tax year: paragraph 5.4
- earnings of those who leave the UK part way through a tax year: paragraph 5.4
- UK Government securities; interest arising in year of departure from UK: paragraph 6.7
- investment income of those leaving the UK part way through a tax year: paragraphs 6.14 – 6.16
- tax allowances: paragraph 7.4
- capital gains: paragraphs 8.3 – 8.6

Special classes of employees

2.14   Special rules apply to some employees working abroad. If one of the classes shown below applies to you, write to the Inland Revenue office shown – the addresses appear in paragraph 9 of the Introduction. Please give your national insurance number and details of your employment abroad. We will advise you of your tax position.

Class	*Write to Inland Revenue*
Crown employees (eg civil servants, diplomats, members of the armed forces, etc)	HM Inspector of Taxes Cardiff 4 (Foreign Section)
European Union (EU) employees	FICO, Bootle
Employees working in oil and gas exploration and extraction industries (where the employer is not resident in the UK)	Foreign Compliance, Compliance Centre 1
Merchant Navy seafarers	HM Inspector of Taxes Cardiff 1

CHAPTER 3
COMING TO THE UK

Coming to the UK permanently or indefinitely

3.1   You are treated as resident and ordinarily resident from the date you arrive if your home has been abroad and you intend –

- to come to the UK to live here permanently, or
- to come and remain here for three years or more.

You 'remain' in the UK if you are here on a continuing basis and any departures are for holidays or short business trips, (the same applies for the other references in this chapter to 'remaining' in the UK.)

Visitors to the UK

3.2 If you come to the UK other than to live here permanently as in paragraph 3.1, the guidelines in the rest of this Chapter will govern your residence and ordinary residence position in the UK.

The Chapter deals in turn with two main groups coming to this country –

- short term visitors – where you visit the UK for only limited periods in one or more tax years without any intention to remain for an extended period;
- longer term visitors – where you come to the UK intending to remain indefinitely or for an extended period, perhaps stretching over several tax years.

At first you may at first fall within one of these categories and later move to the other, depending on your precise circumstances.

Short term visitors – residence

3.3 You will be treated as resident for a tax year if –

- you are in the UK for 183 days or more in the tax year (see paragraph 1.2), or
- you visit the UK regularly and after four tax years your visits during those years average 91 days or more a tax year – see paragraph 3.6. You are treated as resident from the fifth year. However –
    (i)   any days spent in the UK for exceptional circumstances beyond your control, for example the illness of yourself or a member of your immediate family, are not counted for this purpose;
    (ii) you are treated as resident from 6 April of the first year, if it is clear when you first come to the UK that you intend making such visits and you actually carry out your intention; and
    (iii) you are treated as resident from 6 April of the tax year in which you decide that you will make such visits, where this decision is made before the start of the fifth tax year and you actually carry out your decision.

For example –

- You come to the UK with no definite intentions, but your visits during the tax years 1999–2000 to 2002–2003 average at least 91 days a tax year; you are resident from 6 April 2003.
- You first come to the UK during 1999–2000, intending that between then and 5 April 2003 your visits will average at least 91 days a tax year; you are resident from 6 April 1999, provided that your visits in fact reach that level.
- You first come to the UK during 1999–2000 with no definite intentions and you spend, say, 60 days here; you come again during 2000–2001 and decide you will come regularly in future years and your visits will average at least 91 days a tax year; you are resident from 6 April 2000, provided that your visits in fact reach that level.

Short term visitors – ordinary residence

3.4 You will be treated as ordinarily resident if you come to the UK regularly and your visits average 91 days or more a tax year – see paragraph 3.6. Any days spent in the UK for exceptional circumstances beyond your control, for example the illness of yourself or a member of your immediate family, are not normally counted for this purpose.

3.5   The date from which you are treated as ordinarily resident depends upon your intentions and whether you actually carry them out. You will be ordinarily resident –

- from 6 April of the tax year of your first arrival, if it is clear when you first come here that you intend visiting the UK regularly for at least four tax years,
- from 6 April of the fifth tax year after you have visited the UK over four years, if you originally came with no definite plans about the number of years you will visit,
- from 6 April of the tax year in which you decide you will be visiting the UK regularly, if that decision is made before the start of the fifth tax year.

For example –

- You first come to the UK during 1999–2000, you intend visiting regularly until at least 5 April 2003 and your visits will average at least 91 days a tax year. You are ordinarily resident from 6 April 1999.
- You come to the UK with no definite intentions, but you visit regularly during the tax years 1999–2000 to 2002–2003 and your visits average at least 91 days a tax year. You are ordinarily resident from 6 April 2003.
- You first come to the UK during 1999–2000 with no definite intentions; you come again in 2000–2001 and 2001–2002; during 2001–2002 you decide you will come regularly in future years, and your visits will average at least 91 days a tax year. You are ordinarily resident from 6 April 2001.

Calculating annual average visits

3.6   Where it is necessary to calculate your annual average visits, the method is as follows –

$$\frac{\text{Total visits to the UK (in days)}}{\text{Relevant tax years (in days)}} \times 365 = \text{annual average visits}$$

For example, suppose you visited the UK for 80 days in 1995–96, 100 days in 1996–97, 85 days in 1997–98 and 105 days in 1998–99. The annual average is –

$$\frac{80 + 100 + 85 + 105}{366 + 365 + 365 + 365} \times 365 = 92.44 \text{ days}$$

Longer term visitors – residence

3.7   You are treated as resident in the UK from the day you arrive to the day you leave (see paragraphs 1.5 – 1.6) if you come to the UK for a purpose (for example, employment) that will mean you remain here for at least two years. The same treatment will apply if you own or lease accommodation in the UK in the year you arrive here (see paragraph 3.11).

In all other cases you will be treated as resident for the tax year if –

- you spend 183 days or more in the UK in the tax year, or
- you own or lease accommodation in the UK (see paragraph 3.11).

Longer term visitors – ordinary residence

3.8   You will be treated as ordinarily resident in the UK from the date you arrive, whether to work here or not, if it is clear that you intend to stay for at least three years.

If you come to the UK as a student for an extended period of study or education, see paragraph 3.13.

3.9 You will be treated as ordinarily resident from the beginning of the tax year after the third anniversary of your arrival if you come to, and remain in, the UK, but you –

– do not originally intend to stay for at least three years, and
– do not buy accommodation or acquire it on a lease of three years or more.

For example, if you arrive in the UK on 21 November 1999 and are still living in the UK on 6 April 2003, you are ordinarily resident from 6 April 2003.

3.10 If, after you have come to the UK, you decide to stay for at least three years from the date of your original arrival, you will be treated as ordinarily resident from –

– the day you arrive if your decision is made in the year of arrival, or
– the beginning of the tax year in which you make your decision when this is after the year of arrival.

For example –

– you arrive in the UK on 4 January 2000 and decide on 16 May 2000 to stay permanently. You are ordinarily resident from 6 April 2000;
– you come to the UK to work on 14 July 1999 on a 2 year contract of employment, but in December 2001 your assignment is changed and your contract is extended until after July 2002*. You are ordinarily resident from 6 April 2001.

* If there is a change in the circumstances of your assignment, but no formal change to the terms of a contract, whether you are treated as ordinarily resident and from what date will depend on the precise facts.

3.11 If you come to, and remain in the UK, you will be treated as ordinarily resident –

– from the day you arrive, if –
  (i) you already own accommodation here,
  (ii) you buy accommodation during the tax year of arrival, or
  (iii) you have or acquire accommodation on a lease of three years or more during the tax year of arrival, or
– from 6 April of the tax year in which such accommodation becomes available, when this occurs after the year of arrival.

3.12 If you are treated as ordinarily resident solely because you have accommodation here (paragraph 3.11) and you dispose of the accommodation and leave the UK within three years of your arrival, you may be treated as not ordinarily resident for the duration of your stay if this is to your advantage.

3.13 If you are a student who comes to the UK for a period of study or education and you will be here for less than four years, you will be treated as not ordinarily resident, providing –

– you do not own or buy accommodation here, or acquire it on a lease of three years or more, and
– on leaving the UK you will not be returning regularly for visits which average 91 days or more a tax year.

Contacting the Inland Revenue

3.14 You should let us know when you come to the UK. You will normally be asked to complete form P86, which will help to determine your residence status.

Tax treatment after arrival in the UK

3.15   For details of the tax treatment of your earned income both in the UK and abroad (such as earnings from employments) after you have become resident in the UK, see Chapter 5 and in particular paragraphs 5.1 – 5.3, 5.9 – 5.12 and the tables at 5.19 – 5.21. For details of the treatment of any investment income you may have, see Chapter 6 and in particular paragraph 6.2.

3.16   Some special provisions applying to those coming to the UK are dealt with as follows –

- earnings of those who come to the UK part way through a tax year: paragraph 5.4
- lump sums from overseas pension schemes and provident funds: paragraph 5.16
- UK Government securities: interest arising in year of arrival in UK: paragraph 6.7
- investment income of those coming to the UK part way through a tax year: paragraph 6.17
- tax allowances: paragraph 7.4
- capital gains: see paragraph 8.3–8.6

CHAPTER 4
DOMICILE

4.1   Domicile is a general law concept. It is not possible to list all the factors that affect your domicile, but some of the main points are explained in this chapter.

4.2   Broadly speaking, you are domiciled in the country where you have your permanent home. Domicile is distinct from nationality or residence. You can only have one domicile at any given time.

Domicile of origin

4.3   You normally acquire a domicile of origin from your father when you are born. It need not be the country in which you are born. For example, if you are born in France while your father is working there, but his permanent home is in the UK, your domicile of origin is in the UK.

Domicile of dependency

4.4   Until you have the legal capacity to change it – see paragraph 4.5 – your domicile will follow that of the person on whom you are legally dependent. If the domicile of that person changes, you automatically acquire the same domicile (a domicile of dependency), in place of your domicile of origin.

Domicile of choice

4.5   You have the legal capacity to acquire a new domicile (a domicile of choice) when you reach age 16. To do so, you must broadly leave your current country of domicile and settle in another country. You need to provide strong evidence that you intend to live there permanently or indefinitely. Living in another country for a long time, although an important factor, is not enough in itself to prove you have acquired a new domicile.

Married women

4.6   Before 1974, when you married you automatically acquired your husband's domicile. After marriage this domicile would change at the same time as your husband's domicile changed. If your marriage ended, you kept your husband's domicile until such time as you legally acquired a new domicile.

This rule is modified by the terms of the double taxation agreement between the UK and the

USA. A marriage before 1974 between a woman who is a US national and a man domiciled within the UK is deemed to have taken place on 1 January 1974 for the purpose of determining her domicile on or after 6 April 1976 for UK tax purposes.

4.7   From 1 January 1974 your domicile is not necessarily the same as your husband's domicile. It is decided by the same factors as for any other individual who is able to have an independent domicile. If, however, you were married before 1974 and had acquired your husband's domicile (see paragraph 4.6), you retain this after 1 January 1974 until such time as you legally acquire a new domicile.

Overseas electors

4.8   From 6 April 1996 registering and voting as an overseas elector is not normally taken into account as one of the factors for determining whether you are domiciled in the UK, for the purpose of establishing your tax liability here.

Tax treatment of those not domiciled in the UK

4.9   Those who are resident in the UK but not domiciled here receive special tax treatment in respect of income and gains arising outside the UK. For details, see paragraphs 5.12 and 6.2 (income tax) and 8.8 (capital gains tax). We will consider the question of your domicile only where this will affect your current tax liability.

For inheritance tax purposes, see booklet IHT 18 'Inheritance tax. Foreign aspects'.

PART II
LIABILITY TO UK TAX

CHAPTER 5
EARNED INCOME

Basis of liability

5.1   If you are resident in the UK under the rules in Part I of this booklet, you will normally pay UK tax on all your earned income, wherever it arises. As well as earnings for employment, earned income includes items such as pensions and income from a trade, profession or vocation. You may, however, be entitled to a reduction in the UK tax you have to pay if you receive overseas earnings and spend long periods abroad (see paragraphs 5.9–5.10) or if you receive an overseas pension (see paragraph 5.11). In certain cases where you are resident but not ordinarily resident in the UK, or resident but not domiciled here, we will deal with your overseas income on the 'remittance basis' (see paragraphs 5.9, 5.11–5.12).

5.2   If you are not resident in the UK, we will generally tax you on any UK pensions or on earnings from employment the duties of which are carried on in this country. Where your duties are carried on partly in the UK and partly abroad, an allocation, based on days worked in the UK and days worked abroad, will normally be made to ascertain the earnings for duties carried on in this country which are liable for UK tax. We will not tax you on earnings from an employment which is carried on wholly abroad (see paragraph 5.5). See paragraph 5.4 for the position if you become resident in the UK part way through a tax year and 5.9 regarding overseas earnings taxable on the remittance basis. In some cases you may make a claim under a double taxation agreement for exemption from UK tax on your UK pension, or on earnings arising in this country (see Chapter 9 and in particular paragraphs 9.3, 9.4 and 9.6).

We will tax you on the profits of a trade, profession or vocation which is not carried on wholly outside the UK.

5.3 The tables at the end of this Chapter show in more detail how your pensions, earnings from any office or employment or profits from a trade, profession or vocation will be taxed, depending on your residence status and the place where your duties are performed. You should ask your tax office if you need further information or advice about your own tax position (paragraph 7 of the Introduction).

Special rules apply in the case of Crown employees – see paragraph 2.14.

Earnings of those who come to, or leave, the UK part way through a tax year

5.4 If you come to the UK during a tax year and are treated as resident here from the date of your arrival, by concession (Extra-statutory concession A11) you will not pay tax on earnings for the part of the year before you arrive here, where these are from an employment carried on wholly abroad.

A similar concession applies if you leave the UK during a tax year and are treated as resident here up to and including the date of your departure. You will not pay tax on earnings for the part of the year after you leave the UK, where these are from an employment carried on wholly abroad.

In the case of earned income other than earnings from employment, the rules are the same as those for unearned income – see paragraphs 6.14 – 6.24.

If you are paid for a period of leave spent in the UK following work abroad, we treat this 'terminal leave pay' as arising during the period to which it relates even if your entitlement to it was built up over a period of overseas employment. Leave pay is normally taxable in the UK where an individual is resident here. It may, however, be covered by the 'foreign earnings deduction' if the leave immediately follows a period abroad which is a 'qualifying period' (see paragraphs 5.9 – 5.10, and footnote 2 to the table at 5.19, on the foreign earnings deduction).

Where your duties are performed

5.5 The table at 5.19 shows that the place where your duties are performed is a key factor in deciding the tax treatment of your earnings. If your work is usually done abroad but some duties are performed in the UK, we will treat these as though they had been performed abroad as long as they are merely incidental to your overseas duties (see paragraphs 5.7 and 5.8).

5.6 Where you are a seafarer or a member of an aircraft crew, we normally treat your duties as performed in the UK if –

- the voyage or flight does not extend to a place outside the UK, or
- you are resident in the UK and the voyage or flight begins or ends in the UK, or
- you are resident in the UK and embarked on part of a voyage or flight which begins or ends in the UK.

A different rule applies for the purposes of the foreign earnings deduction (see paragraphs 5.9 – 5.10 and footnote 2 to the table at 5.19).

Incidental duties

5.7 Whether duties you perform in the UK are 'incidental' to your overseas duties (paragraph 5.5) depends on all the circumstances. If the work you do in the UK is of the same kind as, or of similar importance to, the work that you do abroad, it will not be merely incidental unless it can be shown to be ancillary or subordinate to that work. It is normally the nature of the duties performed in the UK rather than the amount of time spent on them that is important, but if the total time you spend working in the UK is more than 91 days in a year, the work will not be treated as incidental. Examples of duties which we do not normally regard as incidental are –

– attendance at directors' meetings in the UK by a director of the company who normally works abroad,
– visits to the UK as a member of the crew of a ship or aircraft,
– visits to the UK in the course of work by a courier.

5.8　If the work you do in the UK has no importance in itself, but simply enables you to do your normal work abroad, it may be treated as incidental. We will decide after looking at all the circumstances in your case. Examples of duties which we regard as incidental are –
– visits to the UK by an overseas representative of a UK employer to report to the employer or to receive fresh instructions, or
– training in the UK by an overseas employee as long as –
　(i)　the total time spent in the UK for training is not more than 91 days in a year, and
　(ii)　no productive work is done in the UK in that time.

Earned income arising outside the UK

5.9　In the case of earnings from employment, the table at 5.19 sets out the tax position. If you are resident in the UK, we will normally tax you on all earnings you receive from sources abroad. In certain circumstances, however, you may be entitled to a deduction of 100 per cent on certain earnings from an employment performed wholly or partly overseas, if you are resident (and ordinarily resident) in the UK but spend a sufficient number of days abroad (see paragraph 5.10).

We tax you on the earnings from your overseas employment on the remittance basis (see paragraph 5.12) if you are –

– resident but not ordinarily resident in the UK, or
– resident and ordinarily resident but not domiciled in the UK – but only in the case of 'foreign emoluments' where the duties of the employment are performed wholly outside the UK (see footnote 1 to the table at 5.19).

5.10　The foreign earnings deduction in certain circumstances provides a deduction of 100 per cent from the amount of earnings chargeable where the following conditions are met –

– the duties of your employment are performed wholly or partly overseas;
– you remain resident and ordinarily resident in the UK while working abroad;
– the earnings are for a period which is part of a qualifying absence lasting 365 days or more.

Up to 16 March 1998 the Foreign Earnings Deduction could be claimed by all employees, but after that date it is only available to seafarers. 'Seafarers' are individuals who perform the duties of their employment on a ship. A 'ship' would not include offshore installations such as mobile offshore drilling rigs.

For further details of the current rules –

– seafarers may contact HM Inspector of Taxes Cardiff 1 (see paragraph 9 of the Introduction);
– workers in the oil and gas industry may obtain further information from Foreign Compliance, Compliance Centre 1 (see paragraph 9 of the Introduction and paragraph 5.17).

5.11　In the case of other types of earned income, such as overseas pensions and income from an overseas trade, profession or vocation, the tables at 5.20 and 5.21 set out the position. We will normally tax you on all the income you receive from overseas sources if you are resident in the UK. You may, however, be entitled to a 10 per cent deduction from the amount chargeable in the case of overseas pensions.

We tax you on your other earned income from overseas sources on the remittance basis (see paragraph 5.12) if you are –

- – resident but not domiciled in the UK, or
- – resident but not ordinarily resident in the UK, and either a Commonwealth citizen (which includes a British citizen) or a citizen of the Republic of Ireland.

The remittance basis does not apply to other types of earned income arising in the Republic of Ireland.

5.12 Where the remittance basis applies, you are liable to UK tax on the amount of your overseas income that is remitted to the UK. Income is remitted if it is paid here or transmitted or brought to the UK in any way. In working out your tax liability, we include all income remitted to the UK.

Where you are taxed on the remittance basis, you will not be able to claim either the 100 per cent deduction for foreign earnings (see paragraphs 5.9 – 5.10) or the deduction for overseas pensions (see paragraph 5.11).

The remittance basis may also apply to any overseas investment income you receive (see paragraph 6.2) and to capital gains arising overseas (see paragraph 8.8).

Change of location of a trade, profession or vocation

From 6 April 1997 (or from 6 April 1995 for businesses which started on or after 6 April 1994)

5.13 If you have been carrying on a business wholly or partly outside the UK and you either become resident in the UK or cease to be resident in the UK, we will treat you at that point as having discontinued one business and started a new one. This means that the special cessation provisions will apply up to the date of 'deemed' cessation and the special commencement provisions from the date of deemed commencement. These provisions are described in booklet CWL1 'Starting your own business?'.

Cessation and commencement of residence (and therefore deemed cessation and commencement of trade) usually take place at the start of the tax year in which your change of residence occurs. However, if you satisfy the conditions set out in paragraphs 1.5 – 1.6, the deemed cessation and commencement will take place on your actual date of arrival or departure.

Despite the deemed cessation and commencement, any losses incurred before the change of residence can be carried forward and set against profits of the business, as long as it would have been the same business under the rules in paragraph 5.14.

Before 6 April 1997 (or, where appropriate, 6 April 1995)

5.14 Whether a change of residence triggers the discontinuance of one business and the commencement of another is a question of fact. It depends on where the business is carried on rather than where the proprietor resides. Most trades and professions are carried on in a particular location (for example a shop, office or factory), so that a significant change of business location (such as from one country to another) will normally mean that the new business is a different one from the old business. This means that the cessation provisions will apply to your old business and the commencement provisions to the new one. It also means that losses from your old business cannot be carried forward and set against profits of the new business.

A few businesses, mainly of professional people, are not localised in this way, but are carried on wherever in the world the person happens to be. Examples are international actors, musicians, authors and sportsmen/women. If you are carrying on this kind of profession and continue to carry it on in the same way after a change of residence, it will be the same profession, and neither the cessation nor the commencement provisions will apply. However, for the year of change of residence, we will only assess you on a proportion of your profits for the full year, reflecting the profits made in the period from the date of your arrival in the UK to the following 5 April (or in the period from the preceding 6 April to the date of departure from the UK).

UK social security benefits

5.15   Various UK social security benefits including, for example, National Insurance Retirement Pension and widow's payments, are liable to UK tax. However, some relief from UK tax may be due under the terms of a double taxation agreement if you are not resident in the UK (see also paragraph 9.3).

From the year 1996–97, if you are not resident in the UK for the whole of a tax year and do not claim relief under the terms of a double taxation agreement, your liability on taxable UK social security benefits is limited to the tax, if any, deducted before payment.

Lump sums from overseas pension schemes and provident funds

5.16   By concession (Extra-statutory concession A10), we will not charge income tax (or we will charge it only on a reduced amount) if you receive lump sum retirement benefits, relating to an employment overseas, under an overseas pension scheme or provident fund.

The level of relief will depend on the extent of your overseas service. You qualify for full exemption where in that employment –

- at least 75 per cent of your total service was overseas, or
- your total service exceeds 10 years and the whole of the last 10 years of service have been overseas, or
- your total service exceeds 20 years and not less than 50 per cent of total service, including any 10 of the last 20 years, was overseas.

If you do not meet the conditions for full exemption, we will charge income tax only on that percentage of the lump sum equivalent to your non-overseas service in that employment.

Offshore oil and gas workers

5.17   If you work offshore in connection with the exploration or exploitation of UK oil or gas, the rules set out in the first part of this Chapter still normally apply to you. In this context 'offshore' means –

- the territorial sea of the UK (see paragraph 6 of the Introduction), and
- the UK continental shelf outside the territorial sea.

If, however, you are a resident of a country with which the UK has a double taxation agreement, the normal rules may be affected by that agreement (see Chapter 9 on agreements generally). Some of these include provisions specific to offshore oil and gas activities. You should put any queries about your tax liabilities to your tax office, if your employer is resident in the UK; or to Foreign Compliance, Compliance Centre 1, if your employer is not resident in the UK.

Partnerships

5.18 If you carry on a trade or profession in a partnership, the table at 5.21 sets out the position. In those circumstances, the remittance basis (see paragraph 5.12) may apply to your overseas profit, where the trade is carried on wholly abroad, or is carried on partly abroad and the partnership is managed and controlled abroad, and in either case you are a UK resident partner and are –

- not domiciled in the UK, or
- not ordinarily resident in the UK, and a Commonwealth citizen or a citizen of the Irish Republic.

Scope of liability to income tax of earnings (Table 1)

5.19

		Duties of employment performed wholly or partly in the UK		Duties of employment performed wholly outside the UK
		In the UK	Outside the UK	
Foreign emoluments[1]	Employee resident and ordinarily resident in the UK	Liable – less possible deduction[2]	Liable – less possible deduction[2]	Liable if received in the UK[3]
	Resident but not ordinarily resident	Liable	Liable if received in the UK[3]	Liable if received in the UK[3]
	Not resident	Liable	Not liable	Not liable
Other earnings	Resident and ordinarily resident	Liable – less possible deduction[2]	Liable – less possible deduction[2]	Liable – less possible deduction[2]
	Resident but not ordinarily resident	Liable	Liable if received in the UK[3]	Liable if received in the UK[3]
	Not resident	Liable	Not liable	Not liable

NOTES TO TABLE

[1] 'Foreign emoluments' is the term used in the Taxes Acts to mean the earnings of someone who is not domiciled in the UK and whose employer is resident outside, and not resident in, the UK (nor in the Republic of Ireland).

[2] There may be a foreign earnings deduction of 100 per cent in these cases from the amount chargeable, if the earnings are for a period which is part of a qualifying absence lasting 365 days or more – this means that such earnings for that period will be free from UK tax. See paragraphs 5.9–5.10 for further details, and a summary of the changes that were introduced from 17 March 1998.

[3] See paragraph 5.12 for details of the remittance basis which applies in these cases.

Scope of liability to income tax on individuals receiving pensions (Table 2)
5.20

| | Paid by or on behalf of a person | |
	In the UK	Outside the UK *(overseas pension)*
Residence status and domicile		
Resident and ordinarily resident, and domiciled	Liable	Liable[1]
Resident and ordinarily resident, not domiciled	Liable	Liable if received in the UK (para 5.12)[2]
Resident but not ordinarily resident, domiciled	Liable	Liable[1,3]
Resident but not ordinarily resident, not domiciled	Liable	Liable if received in the UK (para 5.12)[2]
Not resident	Liable[4,5]	Not liable

NOTES TO TABLE

[1] Less 10 per cent deduction.
[2] You are taxable on the whole of a pension arising in the Republic of Ireland, less 10 per cent deduction; but if the pension is from the Irish Government, you are taxable only if you are a UK national without also being an Irish national.
[3] If you are a Commonwealth (this includes a British) citizen or an Irish citizen, the remittance basis applies and the 10 per cent deduction is not due, unless the pension arises in the Irish Republic, in which case note 2 applies.
[4] See Chapter 9 about possible relief under a double taxation agreement.
[5] See paragraph 5.15 in the case of UK social security benefits such as National Insurance Retirement Pension.

Scope of liability to income tax on profits of individuals carrying on a trade or profession (Table 3)

5.21

Residence status and domicile	Trade or profession carried on wholly or partly in the UK	Trade or profession carried on wholly outside the UK
Resident and ordinarily resident, and domiciled	Liable	Liable[1]
Resident and ordinarily resident, not domiciled	Liable	Liable if received in the UK (paragraph 5.12)[1]
Resident but not ordinarily resident, domiciled	Liable	Liable[2]
Resident but not ordinarily resident, not domiciled	Liable	Liable if received in the UK (paragraph 5.12)[1]
Not resident	Liable[3]	Not liable

NOTES TO TABLE

[1] You are taxable on the whole of the income from a trade or profession carried on wholly in the Republic of Ireland.

[2] If you are a Commonwealth (this includes a British) citizen or an Irish citizen, the remittance basis applies, unless the trade or profession is carried on wholly in the Irish Republic, in which case note 1 applies.

[3] You are liable on the profits of the part of the trade or profession carried on in the UK.

CHAPTER 6
INVESTMENT INCOME

General

6.1 Broadly, investment income means any income which is not a pension and is not earned by you as an employee, or from carrying on your profession or from running your own business. Among the more common types are –

- interest from bank and building society accounts;
- dividends on shares (see also paragraphs 9.11 – 9.13);
- interest on stocks; and
- rental income (unless your business amounts to a trade).

6.2 If you are resident in the UK, you will normally pay UK tax on all your investment income, wherever it arises. The remittance basis will apply to overseas investment income (other than investment income arising in the Republic of Ireland) if you are –

- resident but not domiciled in the UK, or
- resident but not ordinarily resident in the UK, and either a Commonwealth citizen (this includes a British citizen) or a citizen of the Republic of Ireland.

Where the remittance basis applies, you are liable to UK tax on the amount of your overseas investment income that is remitted to the UK. Income is remitted if it is paid here or transmitted or brought to the UK in any way. In working out your tax liability, we include all income remitted to the UK.

6.3 If you are not resident in the UK, we will only charge UK tax on investment income arising in the UK. Except in the case of UK rental income, if you are not carrying on a trade, profession or vocation through a UK branch or agency, your liability on investment income from 1996–97 will be limited to the tax, if any, deducted at source. However, if you have other UK income which is fully taxable, any personal allowances will be set against your investment income first.

If you are a resident of a country with which the UK has a double taxation agreement (see Chapter 9), you may in some cases be able to claim exemption or partial relief from UK tax on investment income (other than rental income from property in the UK).

Investment income arising in the UK

Income from property in the UK

6.4 Any profits you make from letting property situated in the UK are taxable in the UK, even if you cease to be resident in the UK. New rules apply to the taxation of UK rental income from 6 April 1996.

Before 6 April 1996

6.5 If you were not resident in the UK (or if your usual place of abode was outside the UK) –

- where you received rental income direct from the tenant, the tenant first deducted tax at the basic rate and paid it to the Inland Revenue. If the tax deducted exceeded your tax liability you could claim a repayment of tax overpaid;
- where a letting agent collected the property income for you, the Inland Revenue assessed the letting agent, who was responsible for paying the tax. The letting agent was entitled to recover the tax out of the rental income collected on your behalf.

Your tax office or an Inland Revenue Enquiry Centre will be able to give you more information.

From 6 April 1996

6.6 If your usual place of abode is outside the UK –

- where you receive rental income direct from the tenant, the tenant must first deduct tax at the basic rate and pay it to the Inland Revenue;
- where a letting agent collects the rental income for you, the letting agent must deduct tax at the basic rate from the income received less the allowable expenses paid on your behalf.

In either case you can set off the tax against your UK income tax liability when you complete your tax return.

You can, however, apply to FICO at Bootle (see paragraph 9 of the Introduction) for approval for your property income to be paid without tax being deducted providing –

- your UK tax affairs are up to date, or
- you have never had any UK tax obligations, or
- you do not expect to be liable to UK income tax

and in all cases you undertake to comply with all your UK tax obligations.

More information can be found in leaflet IR140 'Non-resident landlords, their agents and tenants'. You can obtain a copy from FICO at Bootle (see paragraph 9 of the Introduction) or from any tax office or Inland Revenue Enquiry Centre.

UK Government securities

6.7 UK tax is not chargeable on interest arising on UK Government FOTRA securities, if you are not ordinarily resident in the UK. FOTRA stands for 'Free of Tax to Residents Abroad'. Where we treat you as becoming, or ceasing to be, ordinarily resident in the UK part way through the tax year, no tax will normally be charged on interest payable while you are not ordinarily resident – that is, before the date you arrive here or after the date you leave.

Before 6 April 1998 FOTRA status only applied to certain UK Government securities. Please write to FICO at Nottingham (see paragraph 9 of the Introduction) if you want a list of the securities that had FOTRA status before 6 April 1998, or a form to claim repayment of tax.

6.8 UK tax is, however, charged if the interest forms part of the profits of a trade or business carried on in the UK. It is also charged in cases where laws to prevent tax avoidance provide that the income is to be treated as belonging to another person.

6.9 If you hold securities with a nominal value of more than £5,000 during a tax year in which you are resident in the UK at any time, special tax provisions (known as the 'accrued income scheme') normally apply when the securities are transferred. You are charged income tax on the interest that has built up over the period you owned the securities following the last interest payment, even if you were not resident in the UK for part of that period. Leaflet IR68 'Accrued income scheme – Taxing securities on transfer' gives further details.

Interest from building societies and banks

6.10 Building societies, banks and other deposit takers in the UK normally deduct UK tax from interest paid or credited to your account. But if you are not ordinarily resident in the UK, you may be able to have the interest paid or credited without tax deducted. You can arrange this – assuming it is an option under the terms and conditions of your account – by completing a 'not ordinarily resident' declaration.

Any interest you receive without tax deducted is still liable to UK tax, but see paragraph 6.11 if you are not resident in the UK for a whole tax year.

If your account includes the facility to make a 'not ordinarily resident' declaration and you want to arrange for your interest to be paid or credited without deduction of tax –

- ask the building society, bank or deposit taker for a declaration form R105,
- if your account is a joint account, you can complete the declaration only if all the people who are beneficially entitled to the interest are not ordinarily resident in the UK,
- give the completed declaration form to your building society, bank or deposit taker,
- the declaration will have effect from the date on which your building society, bank or deposit taker receives it. It cannot be backdated to cover earlier interest payments,
- if you later become ordinarily resident in the UK (or, in the case of a joint account, if any of the people who are beneficially entitled to the interest becomes ordinarily resident in the UK), you must notify your building society, bank or deposit taker without delay.

6.11 For years up to and including 1995–96, by concession (Extra-statutory concession B13, obsolete for later tax years), no UK tax would be charged if, for the whole of any tax year, you were not resident in the UK and you received interest from a UK source without tax being deducted. This concession would not, however, apply if –

- the tax due could be recovered by setting it off against any tax relief in respect of your other UK income (unless the relief arose because the other UK income is exempt under the Taxes Acts or is relieved under a double taxation agreement, in which case the concession would still apply), or
- an agent or branch in the UK had management or control of the interest (in which case the agent or branch would be charged).

From the year 1996–97, where you are not resident for the whole tax year, your liability on interest from a UK bank or building society is limited to the tax, if any, deducted before payment, unless you carry on a trade, profession or vocation through a UK branch or agency.

Investment income arising outside the UK

6.12 Special rules apply where foreign dividends and interest are paid to you through a paying agent in the UK, or are received by a collecting agent in the UK, for example a bank acting on your behalf. The paying or collecting agent will normally deduct tax before paying the income to you. If you are not resident in the UK, you can claim repayment of the tax deducted, or in some circumstances arrange for the paying or collecting agent to pay the income to you without deducting tax (see also paragraphs 6.14 and 6.17).

6.13 Some income from overseas sources may not have UK tax deducted before it is paid to you. If you are resident in the UK, you will have to pay the tax due. From 6 April 1997 the tax due will be calculated on the whole amount arising or, if the remittance basis applies (see paragraph 6.2), the amount received in the UK in the year concerned. For years before 6 April 1997 different rules may apply; for further advice, contact your tax office.

Investment income of those who leave, or come to, the UK part way through a tax year

Leaving the UK

6.14 If you leave the UK during a tax year and cease to be resident here from the day after the date of your departure, we will only charge you tax on overseas income you receive through a paying or collecting agent (see paragraph 6.12) up to and including the date of your departure.

However, if you wish to receive overseas income without deduction of tax from a paying or collecting agent after you have ceased to be resident here, you will need to complete a declaration and give it to the paying or collecting agent. You should make the declaration on form PA1 (in the case of a paying agent) or form CA1 (in the case of a collecting agent). The forms are available from paying and collecting agents.

6.15 For all other overseas investment income where you are not taxed on the remittance basis, you will pay tax on the smaller of –

- the actual overseas investment income arising for the period from 6 April to the date of your departure, and
- the same fraction of your total overseas income for the year of departure (or, for years before 6 April 1997, for the previous year, if that is the proper basis of assessment) as the fraction of the full tax year for which you are resident in this country. For example, if you are resident in the UK from 6 April until 6 October in the same tax year, i.e. 6 months, the fraction is $^6/_{12}$.

6.16 For overseas investment income where you are taxed on the remittance basis (see paragraph 6.2), you will pay tax on the smaller of –

– the actual overseas investment income remitted to the UK in the period from 6 April to the date of your departure, and
– the same fraction of the total overseas income you remit to the UK in the year of departure (or, for years before 6 April 1997, in the previous year, if that is the proper basis of assessment) as the fraction of the full tax year for which you are resident in this country.

Coming to the UK

6.17 If you come to the UK during a tax year and become resident here from the date of your arrival, we will only charge tax on overseas income you receive through a paying or collecting agent in the UK (see paragraph 6.12) from the date of your arrival.

6.18 Paragraphs 6.19 and 6.20 apply for years before 6 April 1996 and after 5 April 1997. There are special rules for the tax year 1996–97 which are explained at paragraphs 6.21–6.24.

Years before 6 April 1996 and after 5 April 1997

6.19 For the tax year of your arrival, where you receive overseas investment income from which tax has not been deducted and you are not taxed on the remittance basis, the following rules apply –

– You will not have to pay tax on income from a source which ceases before the date of your arrival.
– Where the source continues after your arrival, but ceases in the same tax year, you will only pay tax on the income arising from the date of your arrival to the date the source ceased.
– Where the source ceases in the tax year following the year of your arrival, you may be charged to tax for both years –
  (i) for the year of arrival, you will pay tax on the greater of –
  (a) the same fraction of your overseas investment income for the year of arrival as the fraction of the full tax year for which you are resident in this country, and
  (b) for years before 6 April 1996 the same fraction as in (a) of your overseas income for the year preceding the year of arrival if the source was in existence at 5 April 1994, and
  (ii) for the year following the year of arrival, you will pay tax on the overseas income arising from 6 April in that year to the date when the source ceased.
– Where the source continues to the end of the tax year of your arrival and beyond, and income first arose –
  (i) in the tax year of your arrival but before you became resident here, or
  (ii) for years up to and including 1995–96, in the previous tax year if the source was in existence at 5 April 1994,

you will only pay tax on the same fraction of your total overseas income for the year of arrival as the fraction of the full tax year for which you are resident in this country

EXAMPLE

You come to the UK on 6 August 1993, and are resident for the rest of the tax year of your arrival (ending 5 April 1994). Your investment income continues beyond 5 April 1994, and first arose at some time between 6 April 1992 and 5 August 1993 (that is, in the tax year 1992–93 or the first part of the year of your arrival). You are resident for 8 months during 1993–94, and are therefore taxed on $^8/_{12}$ of the whole of your investment income for that year.

- For years up to and including 1995–96 where the source continued as in the previous example, but income first arose earlier than the tax year before the year of your arrival, the fraction of income on which tax was chargeable was worked out in the same way as in the previous example, but the income in question was that of the year before the year of your arrival if the source was in existence at 5 April 1994.

EXAMPLE

As in the previous example, but your investment income first arose before 6 April 1992. You are taxed in the year of your arrival, 1993–94, on $^8/12$ of your investment income for the tax year 1992–93.

6.20 For the tax year of arrival, where you receive overseas investment income from which tax has not been deducted and you are taxed on the remittance basis (see paragraph 6.2), the following rules apply –

- You will not have to pay tax on overseas investment income you remit from a source which ceased before the date of your arrival (for example, a bank account which you have closed).
- Where the source continues after your arrival but ceases in the same tax year, you will pay tax on the lesser of –
  (i) the total overseas investment income that you remit to the UK in the year, and
  (ii) the overseas income arising from the date of your arrival to the date the source ceased.
- Where the source ceases in the tax year following the year of your arrival, you may be charged to tax for both years –
  (i) for the year of arrival, you will pay tax on the lesser of –
   (a) the overseas investment income you remit to the UK in that year (if the source was already in existence at 5 April 1994, the income remitted to the UK in the previous year if this is greater), and
   (b) the same fraction of your total overseas income for the year of arrival (if the source was already in existence at 5 April 1994, the income remitted to the UK in the previous year if this is greater) as the fraction of the full tax year for which you are resident in this country, and
  (ii) for the year following the year of your arrival, you will pay tax on the overseas income you remit to the UK in that year, but reduced if necessary so that the sum taxed for the two years does not exceed the total of –
   (a) an amount worked out on the lines of (b) above for the year of your arrival, and
   (b) the amount of income arising from 6 April in the following year up to the date the source ceased.

Coming to the UK during the tax year ended 5 April 1997

6.21 You will not have to pay tax on income from a source which ceases before the date of your arrival.

6.22 If the source of income ceases during the year ended 5 April 1997 but after the date of your arrival in this country, you will pay tax on income as follows –

- if you are not taxed on the remittance basis, on the income arising from the date of your arrival to the date the source ceased;
- if you are taxed on the remittance basis, on the lesser of –
  (i) the total overseas income you remit to the UK during the year ended 5 April 1997, and
  (ii) the overseas income arising from the date of your arrival to the date the source ceased.

6.23 If the source of income ceases during the year ended 5 April 1998, you will pay tax on income as follows for the year ended 5 April 1997 –

– if you are not taxed on the remittance basis, on the same fraction of your total overseas income for the year ended 5 April 1997 as the fraction of the full tax year for which you are resident in this country;

– if you are taxed on the remittance basis, on the lesser of –

(i)   the total overseas income you remit to the UK during the year ended 5 April 1997, and

(ii)   the same fraction of your total overseas income for the year ended 5 April 1997 as the fraction of the full tax year for which you are resident in this country.

6.24   If the source of income continues beyond 5 April 1998, you will pay tax on income as follows for the year ended 5 April 1997 –

(a) If you are not taxed on the remittance basis, on the proportion on a time basis, from the date of your arrival to 5 April 1997, of the sum of 50 per cent of the income arising in each of the years ended 5 April 1996 and 5 April 1997. However, where income from the source first arose after 5 April 1994, you will pay tax on the proportion on a time basis, from the date of your arrival to 5 April 1997, on the full amount of the income arising in the year ended 5 April 1997.

(b) If you are taxed on the remittance basis, on the sum of 50 per cent of the amounts you remit to the UK in the years ended 5 April 1996 and 5 April 1997. However, where income from the source was first received in the UK after 5 April 1994, you will pay tax on the whole of the income you remit to the UK in the year ended 5 April 1997 or, if less, on the amount worked out on the lines of (a) above.

Scope of liability to income tax on individuals receiving investment income

6.25

	Investment income		UK Government 'FOTRA' securities (see para 6.7)
Residence status and domicile	*Arising in the UK*	*Arising outside the UK*	
Resident and ordinarily resident, and domiciled	Liable	Liable	Liable
Resident and ordinarily resident, not domiciled	Liable	Liable if received in the UK[1]	Liable
Resident but not ordinarily resident, domiciled	Liable	Liable[2]	Not liable
Resident but not ordinarily resident, not domiciled	Liable	Liable if received in the UK[1]	Not liable[2]
Not resident but ordinarily resident, domiciled	Liable	Not liable	Liable
Not resident but ordinarily resident, not domiciled	Liable[3,4]	Not liable	Liable
Not resident and not ordinarily resident, not domiciled	Liable[3,4]	Not liable	Not liable
Not resident and not ordinarily resident, not domiciled	Liable[3,4]	Not liable	Not liable

NOTES TO TABLE

[1] You are taxable on the whole of the income arising in the Republic of Ireland.
[2] If you are a Commonwealth (this includes a British) citizen or an Irish citizen, the remittance basis applies, unless the income arises in the Irish Republic, in which case note 1 applies.
[3] See Chapter 9 about possible relief under a double taxation agreement.
[4] The charge to tax may be limited – see para6.11.

CHAPTER 7
TAX ALLOWANCES AND RELIEFS

Allowances for UK residents

7.1   If you are resident in the UK, you are entitled to certain allowances and reliefs, based on your personal circumstances, which reduce the amount of tax charged on your income. Leaflet IR90 'Tax allowances and reliefs' explains in more detail.

7.2   UK residents who are employees have tax deducted at source from their wages or salaries under the Pay As You Earn (PAYE) system. The employer deducts tax on the basis of code numbers issued for each employee by the Inland Revenue. These codes take account of the tax allowances and reliefs to which each individual is entitled. For more details, ask your Tax Office for leaflet IR34 'PAYE. Pay As You Earn'.

Allowances for non-UK residents

7.3   If you are not resident in the UK, you may claim tax allowances if you are any one of the following –

  – a Commonwealth citizen (this includes a British citizen),
  – a citizen of a state within the European Economic Area (EEA), that is Austria, Belgium, Denmark, Finland, France, Germany, Greece, Iceland, Italy, Liechtenstein, Luxembourg, Netherlands, Norway, Portugal, Republic of Ireland, Spain, Sweden and the United Kingdom,
  – a present or former employee of the British Crown (including a civil servant, member of the armed forces, etc.),
  – a UK missionary society employee,
  – a civil servant in a territory under the protection of the British Crown,
  – a resident of the Isle of Man or the Channel Islands,
  – a former resident of the UK and you live abroad for the sake of your own health or the health of a member of your family who lives with you,
  – a widow or widower of an employee of the British Crown,
  – a national and/or resident of a country with which the UK has a double taxation agreement which allows such a claim.

Allowances for those coming to, or leaving, the UK part way through a tax year

7.4   If you either become, or cease to be, resident in the UK during a tax year, you will be able to claim full allowances and reliefs for the year of arrival or departure.

Mortgage interest relief

7.5   Tax relief for mortgage interest on a loan to buy your home in the UK is available for interest paid up to 5 April 2000. Relief is commonly given under the Mortgage Interest Relief At Source (MIRAS) scheme. If you have to move away from your home temporarily because of your employment, tax relief may continue, by concession (Extra-statutory concession A27), provided that you expect to be away for no more than four years and you expect to live in your home again on your return. There is no relief for mortgage interest paid after 5 April 2000.

How to claim tax allowances

7.6 If you wish to make a claim for tax allowances, you must do so –

– for years before 1996–97, within six years from the end of the tax year to which the claim relates. For example, if you wish to claim for the tax year 1995–96 (6 April 1995 to 5 April 1996), you have until 5 April 2002 to make your claim;
– from the year 1996–97, within 5 years 10 months from the end of the tax year to which the claim relates. For example, if you wish to claim for the tax year 1996–97 (6 April 1996 to 5 April 1997), you have until 31 January 2003.

7.7 UK residents may be sent a tax return. If you get one, you can use it to claim your allowances and reliefs. If you do not get a tax return, you can write to your tax office to claim allowances and reliefs.

7.8 If you are not resident in the UK, you should contact FICO at Bootle, unless you are an employee of the British Crown or receive a pension for Crown service, when you should contact HM Inspector of Taxes Cardiff 4 (Foreign Section). The addresses are in paragraph 9 of the Introduction

CHAPTER 8
CAPITAL GAINS TAX

Basis of liability

8.1 If you are either resident or ordinarily resident in the UK, you may be liable to capital gains tax on gains arising when you dispose of assets situated anywhere in the world. Disposing of an asset means selling, exchanging or transferring it, or giving it away, or realising a capital sum from it. Usually you will not pay capital gains tax –

– on the transfer of an asset to your spouse,
– on disposing of private motor vehicles,
– on disposing of household goods and personal effects up to a value of £6,000 per item,
– on disposing of a private home which has been treated as your only or main residence throughout the time you have owned it,
– on gains arising from certain other assets – for example Save-As-You-Earn (SAYE) terminal bonuses, National Savings Certificates, Premium Bonds and investments held within an Individual Savings Account or Personal Equity Plan. Leaflet CGT1 'Capital gains tax – An introduction' contains a fuller list.

If you have two or more residences, you can nominate one of them as your main residence for capital gains purposes by notifying your tax office. The residence you nominate need not be the same one as your main residence for mortgage interest tax relief purposes.

No tax is charged on the gains (after reliefs) you receive in any one year up to a certain amount. The 'annual exempt amount' is set at £7,100 for the tax year 1999–2000. Husbands and wives are both entitled to their own annual exempt amount.

8.2 If you dispose of an asset you acquired before 31 March 1982, only the change in value since that date will generally be taken into account for determining the gain or loss. You may be able to make an election for this to apply in every case. An allowance is made for the effects of inflation up to April 1998 when computing gains. Taper relief, which reduces the amount of a gain which is chargeable to tax by reference to whole years of ownership, may be due for disposals on or after 6 April 1998. Leaflet CGT1 'Capital gains tax – An introduction' gives more details.

Gains by those who leave, or come to, the UK part way through a tax year

8.3 If you leave the UK during a tax year and cease to be resident or ordinarily resident in the UK, you may, by concession (Extra-statutory concession D2), not be liable to capital gains tax on gains arising to you from disposals made after the date of your departure. However, if you leave the UK on or after 17 March 1998, you can qualify for this concession only if you were neither resident nor ordinarily resident in the UK for the whole of at least four of the seven tax years immediately preceding the tax year in which you leave the UK.

If you become resident in the UK during a tax year, having been neither resident nor ordinarily resident in the UK at any time during the five tax years immediately preceding that year, you are, by concession (Extra-statutory concession D2), liable to capital gains tax only on gains arising from disposals made after the date of your arrival. If you arrived in the UK before 6 April 1998, the concession applied if you were neither resident nor ordinarily resident throughout the whole of the 36 months before the date of your arrival.

There is normally no charge to capital gains tax on your assets when you leave the UK if you do not actually make a disposal, nor is there any revaluation of assets when you come to the UK. However, in some cases, gains on which a charge has been held over or deferred, or which have been subject to a claim to reinvestment relief, may be brought back into charge if you become neither resident nor ordinarily resident in the UK. This charge will not apply if the reason you become neither resident nor ordinarily resident in the UK is that you are working abroad, provided that you become resident or ordinarily resident in the UK again within three years.

Temporary non-residence

8.4 If you have left the UK and dispose of assets while you are temporarily non-resident, special rules may apply for gains that would have been chargeable, and losses that would have been allowable, if you had been resident or ordinarily resident in the UK for the tax years in question. You are 'temporarily' non-resident if you have been neither resident nor ordinarily resident in the UK for fewer than five complete tax years.

The special rules have the effect of treating these gains and losses as though they arise in the tax year in which you return to the UK.

The special rules do not apply for gains and losses arising from disposals of any assets you acquired while you were temporarily non-resident, provided that the assets were not derived in some part from assets you held while you were resident or ordinarily resident in the UK.

8.5 The special rules apply only if all the following conditions are met –

– there is a tax year (the 'year of return') for which you satisfy the residence requirements,*
– you did not satisfy the residence requirements* for one or more tax years immediately preceding the year of return,
– no more than four tax years fell between the most recent tax year for which you satisfied the residence requirements* (the 'year of departure') and the year of return,
– you satisfied the residence requirements* for at least four of the seven tax years immediately preceding the year of departure.

* You satisfy the 'residence requirements' for a tax year if you are ordinarily resident in the UK during that year or if you are resident in the UK for any part of it.

If any of these conditions is not met, there is no charge to capital gains tax on gains arising on the disposal of assets during your temporary non-residence. Similarly, losses arising in these circumstances will not be allowable losses for capital gains tax purposes.

8.6 Where the special rules apply, you may be able to claim relief from tax in the year in which you resume residence in the UK, if at the time you disposed of the assets you were a resident of a country with which the UK has a double taxation agreement. Any such relief (which may take the form of credit for the overseas tax or, in some cases, exemption from UK tax) will depend on the terms of the relevant agreement. In certain circumstances you may also be able to claim credit for overseas tax against UK tax where there is no double taxation agreement.

Non-residents with a UK branch or agency

8.7   If you are neither resident nor ordinarily resident in the UK and carry on a trade, profession or vocation through a branch or agency in the UK, you will be liable to capital gains tax on any gains on the disposal of assets in the UK which were used in the trade, profession or vocation, or by the branch or agency. You may also be liable to capital gains tax if the activity ceases or you transfer the assets outside the UK.

Overseas assets

8.8   An overseas asset is one situated outside the UK under the capital gains tax rules. For assets such as land and most types of movable property the asset is situated where it is located. For other assets (for example shares and securities) the rules are more complex. Your tax office will be able to advise you further.

If you are resident or ordinarily resident in the UK, and dispose of overseas assets, you will normally be liable to capital gains tax on any gains arising. But if you are not domiciled in the UK, you are taxed on such gains only to the extent that they are received in or remitted to the UK in a tax year for which you are resident or ordinarily resident in the UK. There is no capital gains tax charge on gains remitted to the UK before you become resident in the UK. (See also paragraph 5.12 on the remittance basis.) Where the proceeds of a disposal are remitted, an appropriate proportion of the proceeds is treated as a remittance of the gain.

Gains in a foreign currency

8.9   Where prices are expressed in a currency other than sterling, we calculate gains on the basis of sterling equivalents of the considerations for acquisition and disposal, converted at the date of purchase or sale as appropriate. Except where it is for personal expenditure outside the UK, foreign currency is a chargeable asset for capital gains tax purposes. Its disposal in return for any other asset will normally give rise to a chargeable gain or allowable loss.

Exempt assets

8.10   Gains on the disposal of gilt-edged securities and qualifying corporate bonds are exempt from capital gains tax.

Further information

8.11   In the space available in this Chapter it is only possible to offer general guidance on some of the more important topics. For more detailed information about capital gains tax you can obtain leaflet CGT1 'Capital gains tax – An introduction' from any tax office.

Scope of liability to capital gains tax

	Gains on disposal of	
	UK assets[1]	Overseas assets
Residence status and domicile		
Resident and ordinarily resident, domiciled	Liable	Liable
Resident and ordinarily resident, not domiciled	Liable	Liable if received in the UK
Resident but not ordinarily resident, domiciled	Liable	Liable
Resident but not ordinarily resident, not domiciled	Liable	Liable if received in the UK
Not resident but ordinarily resident, domiciled	Liable[2]	Liable
Not resident but ordinarily resident, not domiciled	Liable[2]	Liable if received in the UK[2]
Not resident and not ordinarily resident, domiciled	Not liable[3,4]	Not liable[4]
Not resident and not ordinarily resident, not domiciled	Not liable[3,4]	Not liable[4]

NOTES TO TABLE

[1] There is no liability if the disposal is of certain UK Government securities..
[2] See Chapter 9 about possible relief under a double taxation agreement.
[3] Liability will arise if the assets were used or held for the purposes of a trade, profession or vocation carried on in the UK through a branch or agency or by the branch or agency.
[4] Gains arising during a period of temporary non-residence may be chargeable (see paragraphs 8.4–8.6).

CHAPTER 9
DOUBLE TAXATION RELIEF

9.1 If you have income or gains from a source in one country and are resident in another, you may be liable to pay tax in both countries under their tax laws. To avoid 'double taxation' in this situation, the UK has negotiated double taxation agreements with a large number of countries. A list of these is given at paragraph 9.16.

Non-residents, and residents of more than one country

9.2 If you are a resident of a country with which the UK has a double taxation agreement, you may be able to claim exemption or partial relief from UK tax on certain types of income from UK sources. You may also be able to claim exemption from capital gains tax on the disposal of assets. The precise conditions of exemption or relief can be found in the relevant agreement. It is not possible to give full details here as they vary from agreement to agreement. If you are resident both in the UK and a country with which the UK has a double taxation agreement, there may be special provisions in the agreement for treating you as a resident of only one of the countries for the purposes of the agreement.

9.3   Normally, you will receive some relief from UK tax on the following sources of income under an agreement –

- pensions and some annuities (other than UK Government pensions),
- royalties,
- dividends (paid before 6 April 1999), and
- interest.

Some agreements state that you must be subject to tax in the other country on the income in question before you get relief from UK tax.

9.4   If you receive a pension paid by the UK for service to the UK Government or to a local authority in the UK, you will usually be taxed only by the UK.

9.5   If you are carrying on a trade or running a business through a permanent establishment in the UK, you may not qualify for any relief from UK tax on royalties, interest or dividends connected with the permanent establishment. A 'permanent establishment' includes, for example, a place of management, a branch or an office.

Earnings from employment and professional services

9.6   Under many double taxation agreements you may be able to claim exemption from UK tax on –

- earnings from an employment, and
- profits or earnings for independent, personal or professional services

carried on in the UK, if you are a resident of the overseas country for the purposes of the agreement (see paragraph 9.2). The usual conditions to be met are –

- in the case of employments –
  (a) you must not be in the UK for more than 183 days in the period (often, twelve months) specified in the agreement, and
  (b) your remuneration must be paid by (or on behalf of) an employer who is not resident in the UK, and it must not be borne by a UK branch of your employer
- in the case of independent, personal or professional services, you must not operate from a fixed base in the UK (or, in the case of some agreements, spend more than a specified number of days in the UK).

Teachers and researchers

9.7   Under some agreements, if you are a teacher or professor who comes to the UK to teach in a school, college, university or other educational establishment for a period of two years or less, you are exempt from UK tax on your earnings from the teaching post. Temporary absences from the UK during this period normally count as part of the two years.

Some agreements cover persons who engage in research. Where this is so, the rules are normally the same as for teachers.

9.8   If you stay for more than two years you cannot claim exemption and you will be liable to tax on the whole of your earnings from the date you arrived. Some agreements only allow exemptions to be given if the earnings are liable to tax in your home country. If you have already received exemption for a visit (or visits) of up to two years, some agreements will not allow you to claim the exemption again if you make a further visit at a later date.

Students and apprentices

9.9 Under most agreements, if you are an overseas student or apprentice visiting the UK solely for full-time education or training, you will not pay tax on payments from sources outside the UK for your maintenance, education or training.

A number of agreements also provide that students or apprentices visiting this country will be exempt from UK tax on certain earnings from employment here. Individual agreements impose various restrictions on this relief, including, for example, monetary limits and conditions as to the type of employment.

Entertainers and sportsmen/women

9.10 Under most agreements, if you are not resident in the UK and you come here as an entertainer or sportsman/woman, any payments you receive will be liable to UK tax. The exemption described in paragraph 9.6 will not apply. You should contact the Foreign Entertainers Unit (see paragraph 9 of the Introduction) for advice on how your income as an entertainer or sportsman/woman will be treated for tax purposes.

This includes, for example, actors and musicians performing on stage or screen and those participating in all kinds of sports.

Dividends

9.11 If you are resident in the UK, you are entitled to a tax credit when you receive a dividend from a company resident in the UK. We charge income tax on the total of the dividend and the tax credit. The tax credit is available to reduce your tax liability. The rate of the tax credit was reduced from 20 per cent to 10 per cent from 6 April 1999, reflecting the reduction in the rate of tax on dividend income from that date.

For dividends paid up to 5 April 1999, if all or any part of your dividend income is not taxable (for example, because you are a non-taxpayer), you may make a claim for the tax credit to be paid to you. However, payment of tax credits cannot be claimed in respect of dividends paid after 5 April 1999. (Tax credits will continue to be paid on dividends within an individual savings account or personal equity plan, up to 5 April 2004.)

Prior to 6 April 1999 companies with dividends paid wholly out of foreign source income could opt to have them treated as 'foreign income dividends' (FIDs). FIDs do not carry any tax credit, and are treated as paid to shareholders with notional income tax already deducted. This notional tax cannot be repaid to you.

9.12 If you are not resident in the UK, the normal rule is that you are not entitled to a tax credit when you receive a dividend from a UK company. From 6 April 1996 you do not pay UK tax (and before that date you would have paid UK tax, if at all, only at the higher rate) on any dividends.

You may, however, be entitled to a tax credit if you are a resident of a country with which the UK has a double taxation agreement, and the agreement provides for payment of the same tax credit as a UK resident would be entitled to receive. In that case, you are liable to income tax on the total of the dividend and tax credit, at the rate of tax laid down in the agreement. For periods up to 5 April 1999, you may claim payment of the tax credit in excess of the amount which the UK is entitled to retain.

From 6 April 1999, all double taxation agreements that provide for payment of a tax credit on dividends paid by UK companies continue to give that right. However, because the rate of tax credit has been reduced (see paragraph 9.11), the amount which the UK is entitled to retain under those agreements will in practice cover the whole of the tax credit. So if you make a claim under an agreement where a dividend has been paid on or after 6 April 1999, there will be no balance of tax credit left for us to pay to you.

9.13   You may also have the right to a tax credit if you receive UK tax allowances and reliefs through a claim in accordance with paragraph 7.3. But if you can only claim these allowances because of the terms of a double taxation agreement (the final category in paragraph 7.3), whether you are entitled to the tax credit will depend on the terms of the agreement.

Capital gains

9.14   Under many agreements, if you are a resident of another country for the purposes of the agreement, you will often be liable to tax only in the other country on any gains you make from disposing of assets. In that case, you will be exempt from capital gains tax in the UK even if you are ordinarily resident here. If, however, you are carrying on a trade or running a business through a permanent establishment in the UK, any gains you make from disposing of assets connected with the permanent establishment will continue to be chargeable to capital gains tax in the UK.

UK residents

9.15   If you are resident in the UK and have overseas income or gains which are taxable in both the UK and the country of origin, you may qualify for relief against UK tax for all or part of the overseas tax you have paid. Even if there is no double taxation agreement between the UK and the other country concerned, you may still be entitled to relief under special provisions in the UK's tax legislation.

List of the UK's double taxation agreements

9.16   Countries with which the UK has double taxation agreements in force covering taxes on income and/or capital gains (other than limited agreements concerned solely with air transport and shipping) at October 1999 were as follows –

CHAPTER 10
APPEALS

10.1   If you have any dispute with the Inland Revenue about your residence, ordinary residence or domicile, or about any claim for relief from UK tax, and agreement cannot be reached, you have the right to have your case considered by an independent tribunal.

10.2   If the Inland Revenue write to you giving a formal decision, they will explain to you how you may appeal and how long you have for this purpose. You may choose to have an appeal heard by either the General Commissioners or the Special Commissioners in connection with your residence status and claims for relief. All appeals in connection with your ordinary residence status and domicile are heard by the Special Commissioners.

10.3   Both the General Commissioners and the Special Commissioners are independent of the Inland Revenue. Their decisions on questions of fact are final, but you can appeal against their decisions on questions of law to the High Court. Leaflet IR37 'Appeals against tax, national insurance contributions, Statutory Sick Pay and Statutory Maternity Pay' explains the procedures in full. It can be obtained from any tax office or Inland Revenue Enquiry Centre.

PART III
PAYMENT OF UK NATIONAL INSURANCE CONTRIBUTIONS

CHAPTER 11
NATIONAL INSURANCE CONTRIBUTIONS

General

11.1 This chapter deals briefly with the rules for payment of national insurance contributions (NICs) for individuals leaving or coming to the UK. The position broadly depends on whether you are going to or arriving from an EEA country, a country with which the UK has a bilateral Social Security Agreement covering NICs, or some other country.

The EEA countries are Austria, Belgium, Denmark, Finland, France, Germany, Greece, Iceland, Italy, Liechtenstein, Luxembourg, Netherlands, Norway, Portugal, Ireland (Republic of), Spain and Sweden.

The countries with which the UK has a bilateral Social Security Agreement in force covering NICs at October 1999 were as follows –

Barbados	Jersey
Bermuda	Macedonia [2]
Bosnia Herzegovina [2]	Malta
Canada (excluding Quebec)	Mauritius
Croatia [2]	Philippines
Cyprus	Slovenia [2]
Guernsey	Switzerland
Isle of Man	Turkey
Israel	USA
Jamaica	Yugoslavia (Federal Republic) [2]

[1] Some agreements include the Isle of Man, Guernsey and Jersey as part of the UK; where that is the case the benefits and obligations of the agreement apply also to those countries.

[2] The UK's agreement with Yugoslavia is to be regarded as in force between the UK and the former Yugoslav states marked.

11.2 The terms 'resident' and 'ordinarily resident' in relation to NICs do not have the same meaning as they do for tax purposes. The tax rules set out in the first part of this booklet are not therefore relevant. Leaflet NI38 'Social Security abroad' gives guidance on the rules that apply for NI purposes.

11.3 If you want further information about paying UK NICs, or copies of leaflets mentioned in this Chapter, you should contact the Inland Revenue's National Insurance Contributions Office, International Services (see paragraph 9 of the Introduction), or your local National Insurance Contributions Office.

Going abroad

EEA countries

11.4 If you are going to another EEA country, the European Community Social Security Regulations apply. The general rule is that you will be subject to the social security legislation of the country in which you work; but there are some exceptions, as explained in the following paragraphs. Leaflet SA29 'Your social security insurance, benefits and health care rights in the European Community, and in Iceland, Liechtenstein and Norway' gives further details.

11.5 If your UK employer sends you to work in another EEA country for not more than

12 months at the outset, you and your UK employer will usually continue paying UK NICs as if you were still in the UK. Your employer will need to apply on your behalf to the National Insurance Contributions Office, International Services, for form E101. This confirms that you will continue to pay UK NICs while working in the other country and will ensure that you are not required to contribute to the other country's social security scheme.

Form E128 (which will be issued with form E101) provides healthcare cover abroad for you and any family members who accompany you for the period of your employment in the other country. This form will cover the same period as form E101.

11.6 If your job in the other EEA country lasts longer than 12 months – even though you did not expect it to – you and your UK employer may continue paying UK NICs, for not more than another 12 months. However, the social security authorities in the other country must first agree to this. Your UK employer must, before the end of the first 12 months, apply on forms E102 to the social security authorities in the other country. These forms can be obtained from the National Insurance Contributions Office, International Services. If the social security authorities in the other country agree to the request, another form E128 will be issued to provide cover for healthcare.

There are also special arrangements that allow you to continue paying UK NICs for longer periods, but usually for no more than five years. The social security authorities in the other country must agree to this.

11.7 Similar rules apply if you are self-employed. You must obtain forms E101/E102/E128 from the National Insurance Contributions Office, International Services.

11.8 Different rules apply if you belong to one of the following groups –

- those who work in more than one country,
- mariners,
- transport workers,
- civil servants,
- members of the staff of diplomatic or consular posts,
- those who work for a member of the staff of a diplomatic or consular post,
- members of the staff of the European Communities,
- members of Her Majesty's forces,
- civilians who work for Her Majesty's forces in Germany, or for an organisation like NAAFI which serves Her Majesty's forces.

In many of these cases, you will continue to pay UK NICs.

11.9 If you work in another EEA country in any other circumstances (for example, for a foreign employer) or you intend to remain abroad indefinitely, you will probably have to pay social security contributions to the other country's scheme. If so, you will not be required to pay UK NICs. However, it may be possible for you to pay UK voluntary NICs to protect your UK basic pension rights. There are more details in leaflet NI38, which contains an application form to pay UK voluntary NICs.

Agreement countries

11.10 If you are going to a country with which the UK has a bilateral Social Security Agreement covering NICs, the position will depend on the terms of the particular agreement. The general rule is that you will be subject to the social security legislation of the country in which you work; but there are some exceptions to this rule, as explained in the following paragraphs. There are information leaflets for each country (see paragraph 11.3 on how to obtain copies).

11.11   If your UK employer sends you to work in a country with which the UK has an agreement, you may be required to continue paying UK NICs as if you were still in the UK. How long you continue to pay UK NICs depends on the particular agreement. Your employer will need to apply on your behalf to the National Insurance Contributions Office, International Services for a certificate confirming that UK NICs continue to be paid while you are working in the other country. This will ensure that you are not required to contribute to the other country's social security scheme.

Unlike the EEA, there is no general provision for healthcare arrangements in most of the bilateral agreements.

Some agreements include provisions which may allow you to continue paying UK NICs for longer than the normal period under the agreement.

11.12   Not all agreements cover the self-employed. In the case of those that do, similar rules apply as for those in employment.

Certain agreements contain special rules for particular groups, such as civil servants, mariners or transport workers.

11.13   If you work in a country with which the UK has an agreement in any other circumstances, for example, for a foreign employer, or you intend to remain abroad indefinitely, you will probably have to pay social security contributions to the other's country scheme. If so, you will not be required to pay UK NICs. However, it may be possible for you to pay UK voluntary NICs to protect your UK basic pension rights. There are more details in leaflet NI38, which contains an application form to pay UK voluntary NICs.

Other countries

11.14   If you are going to any other country, the position will depend on the domestic rules there. Leaflets NI38 and NI132 'National insurance for employers of people working abroad' give information.

11.15   If your UK employer sends you to work in a country outside the EEA and not covered by a bilateral agreement, you will be required to continue paying UK NICs for the first 52 weeks of employment in the other country where all the following conditions apply –

- your employer has a place of business in the UK,
- you are ordinarily resident in the UK,
- you were resident in the UK immediately before starting the work abroad.

11.16   No certificate is required to confirm that you continue to pay UK NICs. Some countries will require you, in addition to your UK NICs, to contribute to their social security scheme. After 52 weeks you are not required to continue paying UK NICs, but you may pay voluntary NICs to protect your UK basic pension rights. There are more details in leaflet NI38, which contains an application form to pay UK voluntary NICs.

Should you decide not to pay voluntary UK NICs, your UK national insurance record will still be protected for certain social security benefits (but not retirement pension or widow's benefit) on your return to the UK.

Arriving from abroad

11.17   If you arrive here from abroad and take up employment with a UK employer, or take up self-employment, you will generally be required to pay UK NICs; but there are some exceptions to this rule, as explained in the following paragraphs.

EEA countries

11.18 If an employer in another EEA country sends you to work in the UK for up to 12 months (longer in special cases), you may be able to continue paying foreign social security contributions. If form E101 is issued by the foreign social security institution, confirming that you continue to contribute to the foreign scheme, you will not have to pay UK NICs. Similar provisions apply to self-employed people who are working temporarily in the UK. Leaflet SA29 gives further information.

Agreement countries

11.19 If you are sent to work temporarily in the UK by an employer in a country with which the UK has a bilateral Social Security Agreement covering NICs, you may be able to continue paying foreign social security contributions. If a certificate is issued by the foreign social security institution, confirming that you continue to contribute to the foreign scheme, you will not have to pay UK NICs.

The information leaflet for each country (see paragraph 11.10) gives further details, and also explains if there are provisions for the self-employed in a particular agreement.

Other countries

11.20 If you are sent to work temporarily in the UK by an employer in a country which is outside the EEA and not covered by a bilateral Social Security Agreement, the general rule is that neither you nor your employer has to pay UK NICs for the first 52 weeks of your employment in the UK. NICs are payable from the 53rd week. If the foreign employer does not have a place of business in the UK, NICs are due from the UK 'host' employer (if the posting began on or after 6 April 1994).

INDEX

Introduction. The index covers Chapters 1 to 10 and the appendix. Index entries are to paragraph numbers, those referring to items in the notes being followed by 'n', and those referring to the appendix being preceded by 'App'. Alphabetical arrangement is word-by-word, where a group of letters followed by a space is filed before the same group of letters followed by a letter, eg 'Tax returns' will appear before 'Taxation'.

Tolley's
Tax Annuals
2002-03

Tolley
LexisNexis™

Tolley's Tax Annuals 2002-03 are the 'must have' reference works for all taxation professionals who want to make the tax advice they provide on behalf of clients more effective. They have served accounting professionals and taxation practitioners for decades and are the most reliable, authoritative, comprehensive and user-friendly tax guides ever published. The latest developments to **Tolley's Tax Annuals 2002-03** include:

- Full expert coverage of FA 2002
- Updated case studies
- Fully updated computational examples

Available with or without Budget supplements for as little as £59.95.

Title	Pub.date	Price	Code	ISBN
Tolley's Income Tax 2002-03				
With post Budget supplement	May/Sept	£74.95	IT2	0 7545 1726 8
Without supplement	Sept	£59.95	IT2AO	0 7545 1710 1
Tolley's Corporation Tax 2002-03				
With post Budget supplement	May/Sept	£74.95	CT2	0 7545 1728 4
Without supplement	Sept	£59.95	CT2AO	0 7545 1711 X
Tolley's Capital Gains Tax 2002-03				
With post Budget supplement	May/Sept	£74.95	CGT2	0 7545 1727 6
Without supplement	Sept	£59.95	CGT2AO	0 7545 1709 8
Tolley's NI Contributions 2002-03				
With post 'Green' Budget supplement	Dec	£74.95	NIC2	0 7545 1858 2
Without supplement	July	£59.95	NIC2AO	0 7545 1708 X
Tolley's Value Added Tax 2002-03	March/Sept	£99.00*	VAT2	0 7545 1705 5

* Price includes two complete volumes. The first edition will be dispatched with an invoice and the second edition will be sent out without charge in September 2002

Tolley's Inheritance Tax 2002-03	Sept	£59.95	IHT2	0 7545 1712 8

How To Order

To order, please contact LexisNexis Butterworths Tolley
Customer Service Dept: **LexisNexis Butterworths Tolley,**
FREEPOST SEA 4177, Croydon, Surrey CR9 5WZ
Telephone: **020 8662 2000** Fax: **020 8662 2012**

Tolley
LexisNexis™
Butterworths Tolley, 35 Chancery Lane, London WC2A 1EL
A division of Reed Elsevier (UK) Ltd
Registered office 25 Victoria Street London SW1H OEX
Registered in England number 2746621
VAT Registered No. GB 730 8595 20

Tax Direct is the ultimate on-line service that provides you with instant access to the most authoritative tax information ... all via the internet.
For more information on all of our products, please visit our website at www.butterworths.com

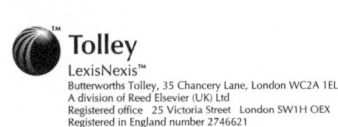